THE ORIGINAL
1955 GM MOTORAMA
265 CID CHEVY V-8
CUTAWAY ENGINE

Chevy SMALL-BLOCK V-8

50 YEARS of HIGH PERFORMANCE

Mike Mueller • Foreword By Dave McLellan

MOTORBOOKS

First published in 2005 by Motorbooks, an imprint of MBI Publishing Company, Galtier Plaza, Suite 200, 380 Jackson Street, St. Paul, MN 55101-3885 USA

The information in this book is true and complete to the best of our knowledge. All recommendations are made without any guarantee on the part of the author or Publisher, who also disclaim any liability incurred in connection with the use of this data or specific details.

This publication has not been prepared, approved, or licensed by General Motors. We recognize, further, that some words, model names, and designations mentioned herein are the property of the trademark holder. We use them for identification purposes only. This is not an official publication.

Motorbooks titles are also available at discounts in bulk quantity for industrial or sales-promotional use. For details write to Special Sales Manager at MBI Publishing Company, Inc., Galtier Plaza, Suite 200, 380 Jackson Street, St. Paul, MN 55101-3885 USA.

ISBN 0-7603-2103-5

On the title page: 1967 Z/28 V-8
On the back cover: Two early Chevys in a drag race. *Getty Images*

Editorial: Lindsay Hitch
Design: Rochelle Schultz

Printed in China

Contents

Foreword

CHEVROLET'S SMALL-BLOCK V-8 ISN'T SO "SMALL" ANYMORE, OTHER THAN IN SIZE AND WEIGHT. Technology and computer-aided engineering have transformed it in ways that its original designers couldn't have imagined. First installed in the Chevrolet passenger car and the Corvette in 1955 and rated at 195 horsepower, the small block today, in Corvette Z06 form, is producing 500 horsepower. Turbocharged and intercooled, the small block is capable of delivering 1,000 transient horsepower in street car applications!

The small block was the centerpiece of the all new 1955 Chevrolet program led by Chevrolet's chief engineer, Ed Cole. Chevrolet would re-emerge in 1955 with an entirely new car powered by Chevrolet's first V-8 engine. The introduction of the Corvette sports car actually lead this resurrection by about a year and was intended to signal the rebirth of Chevrolet. Unfortunately, the V-8 was not available for the first Corvettes, which were built with a modified version of the, by then, antiquated "Stovebolt" I-6. These first Corvettes were a marketplace failure. With the introduction of the V-8, the Corvette began its transformation into a rapacious performer and went on to become an automotive icon.

The Chevrolet small block was the beneficiary of the learning that had produced the high specific output, liquid-cooled, aero engines of World War II, the wedge combustion chamber developments of GM Research Labs and its modern predecessor V-8s at Cadillac and Oldsmobile. In order to be cost competitive in the low-priced field Chevrolet was competing in, the small-block V-8 was a functionally lean design. As example, the stamped valvetrain rockers operated on floating pivots and the cam valley cover was integrated with the intake manifold. Yet, as history has proven, it was also a robust design capable of considerable performance expansion. This is testament to its combustion chamber design, cooling efficiency, and bearing capacity.

In its first three decades, the small block reached a performance peak, going from 195 horsepower to 370 horsepower (gross rating). However, this horsepower came with a price—a thirst for high octane leaded fuel, spark plug fouling, and accessory/water pump belt failures at high rpm. Ultimately, the performance of the small block was not sustainable as emission controls and fuel economy regulations choked its performance.

Looking back, the simple analog controls that managed the engine had become totally inadequate for the complex demands of the engine as a system. Digital electronic controls have changed the paradigm. The engine that started life at 195 horsepower (gross) with a four-barrel carburetor is now producing 500 horsepower (net) in emission-controlled applications and achieving an installed fuel economy of over 24 miles per gallon.

A digression... Until 1971, GM used the SAE gross horsepower rating for its engines. The gross rating was without accessory loads or intake and exhaust restrictions. Starting in 1971, the lower and much more realistic SAE net rating, essentially the engine in the car with all accessory loads and intake and exhaust restrictions, was used. The effect of this rating change was a paper loss of 60 to 90 horsepower.

Anil Kulkarni, who led the team that produced the Gen II small block and laid the foundation for the Gen III, argues that unlike racing engines where engine displacement is limited and the designer uses complexity of valve gear to maximize performance, a road car engine is not so regulated. It should be thought of as a "black box" that produces shaft power and waste heat with inputs of fuel and air. In these terms, the seeming lack of complexity (some would argue sophistication) of the small block makes sense. It was this size and mass efficiency that led Corvette to cancel the four-valve, four-cam LT5 engine in favor of the smaller and lighter aluminum small block for the C5. Because of its performance and efficiency, the small block is now becoming the performance engine of choice in Pontiac and Cadillac cars, and SUVs and light trucks from all GM brands.

The small block survived GM's stillborn attempt at a Wankel engine, the emasculation of emission controls, and it must face off with smaller hybrid powerplants and ultimately the hydrogen fuel cell. If the small block is still with us 50 years from now it will be as a result of continuous technological infusion and the sophistication of its digital control system giving greater and greater efficiency and performance.

By the way, 1,000 horsepower will launch a Corvette to 60 miles per hour in 3 seconds and cover the 1/4 mile in 10, finishing at 170 miles per hour. Not bad for an engine that has passed its 50th birthday. Read on.

Dave McLellan
Corvette Chief Engineer, 1975–1992

Dave McLellan at the Detroit Auto Show, January 2005. FRANK KIDD

Acknowledgments

AS MUCH AS I HATE TO ADMIT IT, I'D NEVER BE ABLE TO MISS SO MANY DEADLINES IF NOT FOR THE HELP OF SO MANY LITTLE PEOPLE. And they don't come much smaller than my beloved brother-in-law, Frank Young, of Savoy, Illinois. Little did I know when my sister Kathy married Frank so many eons ago that I'd get so much free assistance—or free lodging—later on down the road. Both the fabulous Young home and the Youngs themselves proved indispensable during the production of this epic. How I'll ever pay Frank and Kathy back is anyone's guess, as is when.

The same goes for my able-bodied brothers, Dave and Jim Mueller, both of the Champaign-Urbana area in central Illinois. These two great guys did everything for me save for snapping the shutter on my Hasselbad while I was capturing many of the images you'll see soon enough on the following pages. Is a free copy of this book payment enough? I think not, though it will have to do.

Special thanks also go to a host of helpful souls back in my hometown of Champaign. Tom Sellers and his better half Kelly literally bent over backward to make my work easier, as did Steve Mechling, Elmer Lash, Bob and Linda Ogle, Jerry Weeks, and David Clark. Greg Stallmeyer of GS Customs in Seymour, Illinois, and Joe Kern of Custom Fab (also in Seymour) not only run the best little tag-team rod shop in the Midwest, they also aren't afraid to jump through hoops on really short notice. Stallmeyer's trusted staff—made up of paint man Derek Fatheree and fabricator Jeff Dunnam—also lent itself well to my every demand. My appreciation is as immeasurable as your remuneration is unaccountable.

Deserving of equal rewards is my good friend and noted Corvette collector Bill Tower of Plant City, Florida. Shooting Bill's racing machines is always a treat, as is dinner for life. That offer also remains open to the guys at Floyd Garrett's Muscle Car Museum in Sevierville, Tennessee, that is if Floyd ever stops grabbing the tab first. Floyd's sidekick, Bob Hancock, probably doesn't care either way—he'll remain well fed regardless of who pays. Last but not least, I must thank Don and Pat Garlits for allowing me to ransack their museum in Ocala, Florida. Garlits' veteran crew chief T. C. Lemons, Tommie Kennedy, Dennis Youngs, and Peggy Hunnewell also were of immense help during various photo shoots staged at the Garlits Museum of Drag Racing.

Further special mention goes to the many great folk who supplied me with research material and historical photos. Legendary hot rodder Pat Ganahl in Glendale, California, supplied both, while literature dealer Walter Miller (Syracuse, New York), Chevrolet memorabilia expert Dave Newell (Orinda, California), and Dan Reid of GM Racing Communications loaded me down with facts and figures. Additional archival images came from racing historian Spencer Riggs, Michael Lamm, Susan Elliott at the Pikes Peak Auto Hill Climb Museum in Colorado, Jerry Conrad and Claudia Jew at The Mariners Museum in Newport News, Virginia, and Greg Sharp at the NHRA Motorsports Museum in Pomona, California.

Let me not forget the work of supermodels Erin Anderson of Mahomet, Illinois, and Justin Larocque of nearby Urbana. Jim Turner of O'Brien Auto Park in Urbana, Illinois, allowed me to drive off with a gorgeous low-mileage 1984 Corvette, which appears in Chapter 5. And Mike Kirby at Kirby's Tire and Service center in Champaign, Illinois, deserves kudos for a little tire/wheel swapping on my brother Jim's 1981 Corvette, which also shows up in Chapter 5.

Then there are all the people who allowed me to photograph their vehicles for these pages. In general order of appearance, they are:

1955, 1956, and 1957 Bel Airs, Larry Young, Port Charlotte, Florida; 1967 SS-350 Camaro convertible, Steve Conti, Brooksville, Florida; 1997 Corvette, Tom and Kelly Sellers, Champaign, Illinois; 1961 Corvette, Elmer Lash, Champaign, Illinois; 1974 Manta kit car, Jerry Weeks, Champaign, Illinois; 2000 Boss Hoss V-8 motorcycle, Rich McKinney, St. Joseph, Illinois; 1955 Bel Air

hardtop, 1957 fuel-injected Bel Air convertible, and 1957 fuel-injected Nomad, Bill and Barbara Jacobsen, Silver Dollar Classic Cars, Odessa, Florida; 1955 Bel Air convertible (red), Dennis and Mary Schrader, Tarpon Springs, Florida; 1955 Nomad, Erol Tuzcu, Del Ray Beach, Florida; 1955 Corvette, Elmer Puckett, Elgin, Illinois; 1955 Chevrolet pickup (red), Rich New, Adairsville, Georgia; 1955 Cameo pickup and 1955 3100-series pickup, Ken Craig, Lakeland, Florida; 1956 Bel Air coupe (bronze and cream), Fred Gaugh, Terry Sheafer, and Jerome Cain, Lakeland, Florida; 1957 "Airbox" Corvette, Milton Robson, Gainesville, Georgia; 1959 fuel-injected Impala convertible, Dick Hubbard, Monticello, Indiana; 1964 L76 Chevelle SS, Scott Gaulter, Waukee, Iowa; 1965 fuel-injected Corvette, Gary and Carol Licko, Miami, Florida; 1965 Chevelle SS convertible, Charlie Stinson, Mt. Dora, Florida; 1965 El Camino, Bill Worthington, Apopka, Florida; 1966 L79 Nova SS, Roger Quin, Washington, Illinois; 1967 L79 Nova SS, Dave Metz, Lakeland, Florida; 1970 LT-1 Corvette, Phil Vitale, Port St. Lucie, Florida; 1970-1/2 Z/28 Camaro, Kevin Emberton, Edmonton, Kentucky; 1972 LT-1 Corvette, Steve and Nora Gussack, Winter Springs, Florida; 1957 "Black Widow" Chevrolet racer, Floyd Garrett, Sevierville, Tennessee; 1956 Betty Skelton beach racer Corvette, 1956 SR-2 Corvette, 1963 Grand Sport Corvette, and 1986

NASCAR Monte Carlo Aero Coupe, Bill Tower, Plant City, Florida; 1967 Z/28 Camaros (pair), Paul McGuire, Melbourne, Florida; 1950 Studebaker pickup street rod (bare-chassis shown), Jeff Wingo; 1948 Chevrolet street rod, Judi and Lyn Barrows, White Heath, Illinois; 1934 Chevy street rod, Aaron Grote, Cisco, Illinois; 1923 Model T street rod, Randy and Tanya Green, Champaign, Illinois; 1932 Ford "Milner Coupe," Rick Figari, San Francisco, California; 1946 Studebaker pickup street rod, David and Joy Clark, Urbana, Illinois; 1957 Bel Air street machine, Bill and Joyce Frye, Paxton, Illinois; 1940 Ford street rod (with LS1 V-8), Elmer Lash, Champaign, Illinois; 1940 Ford (with 350 V-8), Bob and Linda Ogle, Champaign, Illinois; 1981 Corvette, Jim Mueller Jr., Urbana, Illinois; 1982 Collectors Edition Corvette, Dan Holton, Gainesville, Florida; 1985 IROC-Z Camaro, Terry Flick, Rantoul, Illinois; 1989 Corvette, Frank and Kathy Young, Savoy, Illinois.

Thank you, all.

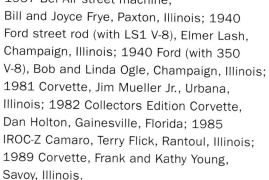

Cheap help is good to find, and they don't come any cheaper than the author's brother-in-law, Frank Young (left). Pausing with Young after a hard day photographing his gorgeous 1989 Corvette are the author's brothers, Jim (center) and Dave Mueller.

BORN TO RUN:
50 Years of
Small-Block Power

Chevrolet's small block displaced 265 cubic inches when born in 1955. Fifty years later, it's still running strong.

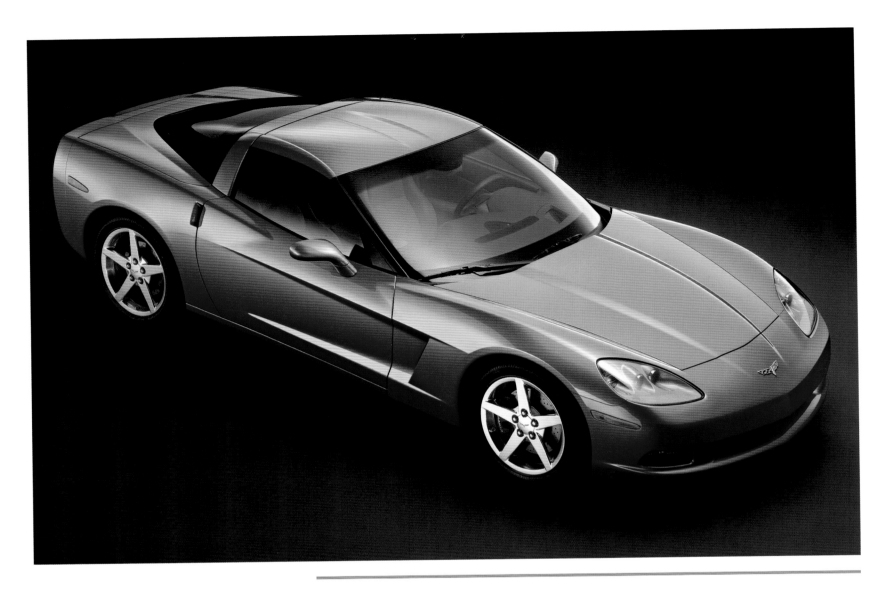

T HE JURY REMAINS OUT AS CHEVROLET'S RESTYLED, REVAMPED C6 CORVETTE MAKES ITS WAY AROUND AMERICA LATE IN 2004. Most armchair judges approve of the way the best 'Vette yet was recontoured and truncated into a dynamic new shape that cheats the wind even better than its predecessor—and the C5 certainly was no slouch as far as cutting-edge aerodynamics were concerned. But, being true to their name, ever-present purists aren't happy at all about the deletion of hideaway headlights, a Corvette trademark dating all the way back to 1963. Many in turn don't like the way those exposed lamps up front now allegedly help make the 2005 model look more like a Dodge Viper than a Corvette—guess you can't make everyone happy.

Then again, you'd have to listen really hard to hear any complaints whatsoever about the 2005 Corvette's equally new power source. Beneath that sleek beak is a whopping 400 horses' worth of what division engineers like to call their Gen IV V-8, named

A revamped sixth-generation Corvette appeared just in time to help mark the small block's 50th anniversary. Powering the 2005 C6 Corvette is the 6.0-liter LS2 V-8 rated at 400 horsepower.

New for 2005 is the LH6 5.3-liter Vortec V-8
featuring fuel-saving Displacement on
Demand (DOD) technology. The DOD V-8 is
an option for the 2005 Trailblazer EXT.

David Kimble

appropriately for its status as the latest, greatest generation in Chevrolet's legendary, long-running small-block V-8 family, now in its 50th year. This all-aluminum, electronically injected 6.0-liter wonder is not only the Corvette's most powerful standard engine ever, it is also nicely fuel efficient, even more so than the 2004 C5's base 350-horse 5.7-liter V-8. Hmmm . . . more displacement, 50 more ponies, *and* more miles per gallon—is this heaven?

No, it's Chevrolet. And it's also nothing necessarily new. Performance breakthroughs like this have been par for the course throughout much of the small block's sensationally successful career, beginning with the

Gen IV's cast-iron, carbureted ancestor in 1955. Back then it was case closed as soon as Chevy's first modern postwar V-8 started running: This was *the* greatest thing since sliced bread.

And it's still slick as melted butter in 2005. As you might've guessed, three generations of small blocks have come before this one, with the retroactively named Gen I V-8 kicking things off in 1955. The markedly upgraded 5.7-liter Gen II followed in 1992, and then was superseded by the radically redesigned Gen III in 1997. Horsepower hounds know the Gen II and Gen III V-8s better by their now-revered regular production option (RPO) codes: LT1 and LS1, respectively.

The 2005 SSR pickup is fitted with the Corvette's LS2 small block. Advertised output for the SSR's 6.0-liter V-8 is 390 horsepower.

When was a small block not a small block? Despite sharing various dimensions (including its 4.40-inch bore centers and 5.7-liter displacement) with its corporate cousins, the ZR-1 Corvette's LT5 V-8 is not considered a member of the small-block family. Its all-aluminum construction, dual overhead cams, and four valves per cylinder set it apart big-time, as do the facts that it was designed by Lotus and built by Mercury Marine. The LT5 ZR-1 was offered from 1990 to 1995.

Whether mild or wild, the classic '57 Chevy
remains a popular hot rodder's choice to
this day. This 350-powered Bel Air
convertible is lightly modified with modern
Rally wheels.

Find someone who doesn't recognize a Chevrolet built (left to right) in 1955, 1956, or 1957 and you've done something. Optional small-block V-8s combined with good looks in a low-priced package each year to help produce three modern classics.

ABOVE LEFT: Some things old can be new again. In 1970, the Corvette's LT-1 V-8 (top) was one of the hottest things going. Much the same could be said about the second-generation LT1 small block, introduced in 1992. Shown at the bottom is the 1996 rendition of the LT1.

ABOVE RIGHT: Chevrolet wowed the automotive world again in 1957 with its Ramjet fuel injection system, offered for both passenger cars and the Corvette. "Fuelie" small blocks remained on the scene up through 1965.

A top-shelf version of the Gen II, the LT4, appeared for 1996 only, and the supreme Gen III, the LS6, debuted in 2001.

It should be pointed out that both generations also fostered various offshoots for applications other than Chevrolet's two performance packages, Corvette and Camaro. In 1994, the full-sized Caprice was treated to a 4.3-liter version of the Gen II, RPO L99. Five years later, Silverado pickup (and GMC Sierra) buyers were presented with three new optional Vortec V-8s based on the Gen III design: the 4.8-liter LR4, 5.3-liter LM7, and 6.0-liter LQ4. Basically a new-and-improved, bored-out LS1, the C6 Corvette's Gen IV small block has been given the LS2 tag, and

a 390-horse LS2 is now the heart of the 2005 SSR pickup, too. At the same time, another Gen IV variation—the 5.3-liter LH6— also carries over into the truck line's Vortec ranks and is being offered as an option for the 2005 Trailblazer EXT and GMC's Envoy XL and Envoy XUV.

Initially estimated at 290 to 295 horsepower (an official rating was still in the works as this epic went to press), the Trailblazer's Vortec 5300 V-8 features cost-conscious "Displacement on Demand" (DOD) operation. In Chevrolet's own words, "DOD has the capability to disable the combustion process in half the LH6's cylinders in certain driving conditions, enabling fuel savings of 6 to

Chevrolet Chief Engineer Ed Cole (left) was the main man behind the small block's creation, and he continued keeping an eye on his baby even as he progressed up the GM corporate ladder. He became Chevrolet general manager in 1956.

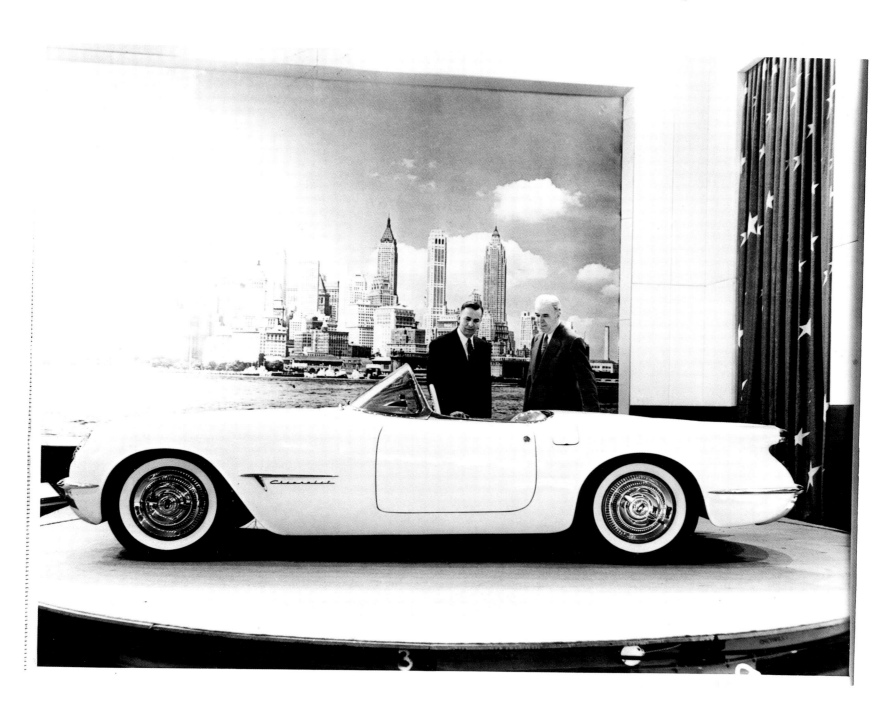

Chevy's big-block V-8 legacy began in 1958 with the 348-cubic-inch "W-head" engine, nicknamed for its zigzag valve layout. Shown here is a triple-carb 348 installed in a 1958 Impala convertible.

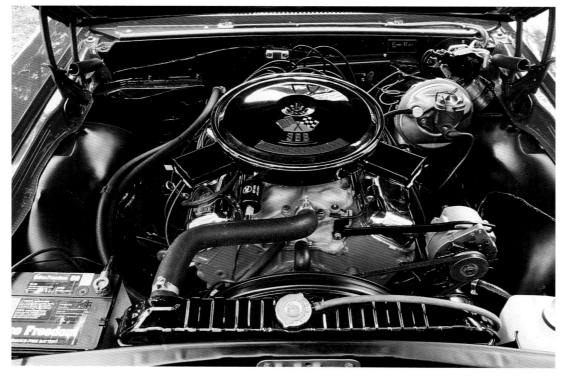

A thoroughly modern big block debuted in the spring of 1965. Displacing 396 cubic inches, the Mk. IV V-8 was offered in the Corvette, the full-sized line, and the Chevelle. Shown here is the latter installation, the first of Chevy's famed SS 396 Chevelles.

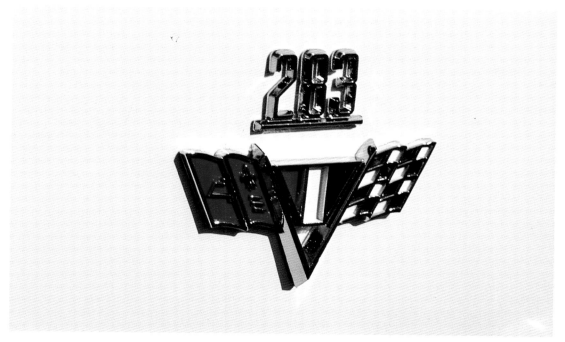

8 percent." Chevy people are also quick to point out that "the process is instantaneous and virtually imperceptible, and the engine delivers horsepower and torque bands comparable to previous non-DOD small-block engines." According to Engineering Chief Sam Winegarden, "Technology such as Displacement on Demand demonstrates the small block's adaptability in the face of evolving marketplace expectations." The LS2 does not incorporate DOD.

But wait just a sec; who said that the small block's adaptable nature needed demonstrating? Isn't a half-century in continuous operation proof enough of this mechanical marvel's unparalleled flexibility? Sure, many Detroit-watchers had given up on Chevy's little V-8 back in the technologically troubled late 1970s, with some critics in the early 1980s suggesting that 25 years was long enough for any engine to survive. Yet this one amazingly continued rolling on, and another 25 years later it's still wowing curbside kibitzers with its seemingly endless stamina.

"The Gen IV is the best example yet of the continuous refinement in performance and

efficiency that has been part of the small block's legacy since day one," added Winegarden in October 2003, well ahead of the LS2's public unveiling. "This long history is one of the reasons the new generation of engines is so powerful and efficient. GM has almost 50 years of experience with its valve-in-head design, and that has provided immeasurable detail for keeping the small block a viable, relevant engine for today and the future."

Fifty years old in 2005, and the small block is still as frisky as ever. Who'da thunk it? Certainly not Ed Cole, the engine's recognized "father." Even as much of a forward-thinker as he was, Papa Cole could not have imagined such a historic run, nor did he expect it. A dozen years or so probably would've suited him fine. But nothing could stop his baby. And today no other engine family presently resting in Detroit's hallowed archives comes anywhere close to matching this one in either longevity or production count. Chevrolet officials estimate that, by the end of the 2005 model year, more than 90 million small-block V-8s will have hit the streets. That's a really big pile in anyone's book.

ABOVE LEFT: Small-block displacement went from 265 cubic inches to 283 in 1957. And in 1962, the 283 was joined by the 327.

ABOVE RIGHT: In 1967 the 327 was bored out to 350 cubic inches, which remained a small-block standard for many years to come.

Chevy's FIRST V-8

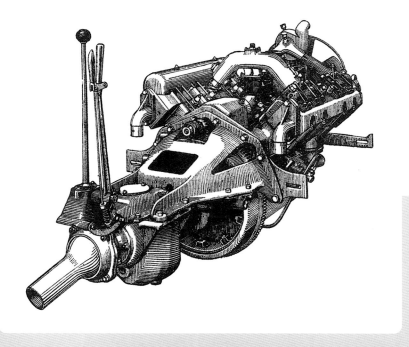

Chevrolet's first V-8 didn't arrive in 1955; it actually showed up in 1917, six years after William Durant founded the firm. Perhaps the greatest wheel-dealer in Detroit history, Durant fathered General Motors in 1908, only to find himself booted out on his tail two years later by concerned bankers alarmed by his aggressive expansionism. No biggie—he simply picked himself up and opened the Chevrolet Motor Company in November 1911. His goal was to amass another fortune and buy his way back into GM via stockholder channels.

The plan worked perfectly. Chevrolet carved out its own entry-level niche almost overnight with nary a hitch. Company coffers were already filling up nicely when Chevy's prototype Model 490 appeared in January 1915. Its name came from its affordable price tag, $490, the same as ol' Henry's Model T. And like the Tin Lizzie, the 490 Chevy sold like hot cakes, giving Durant the dough he needed. After gaining control of 54.5 percent of GM stock, he retook the young corporation's reins in September 1915. Then on May 2, 1918, he brought Chevrolet into the General Motors fold.

The rest is history, as was Durant just a few short years down the road. His aggressiveness once more got him into trouble, this time with a lot of help from an economic recession. After GM stock nose-dived in 1920, angry stockholders forced a corporate reorganization resulting in Durant being shown the door a second time. He never made it back into the GM realm, but the momentum he had created at Chevrolet carried on. By the end of the decade, GM's low-priced leader had done the unthinkable: It had unseated Ford as the industry's sales leader.

Not all at Chevrolet had come up roses, however, during its relatively quick rise to prominence. Such was the case with the ill-fated Series D, introduced late in 1917 in two forms, two-door roadster and four-door touring car. Rolling on an uncharacteristically regal (for Chevrolet) 120-inch wheelbase—1 1/2 feet longer than the successful 490's hub-to-hub stretch—the massive Model D was priced at about $1,500, more than twice as much as a garden-variety four-cylinder Chevy.

Why the uncharacteristically sky-high price? To help haul all that mass around, the upscale D was powered by a cutting-edge 90-degree V-8, featuring pushrod-actuated overhead valves in cross-flow cylinder heads. Bore and stroke measured 3 3/8 and 4 inches, respectively, equaling 288 cubic inches. Output reportedly was 55 horsepower, 50 percent more than Chevrolet's meat-and-potatoes four-cylinder produced.

According to Chevrolet records published in 1995, only 2,781 V-8-powered Series D models were built before the big car was scuttled in 1918. Leftovers apparently were sold in 1919, but this short story did end once those supplies were exhausted. Explaining the sudden demise was simple: the car-buying masses in those days simply couldn't afford a V-8, and customers who could simply preferred more prestige than a V-8 Chevy could offer. The D clearly ran contrary to the practical ideals originally laid down at Chevrolet by Durant, and some say the car was perhaps created at least partially "behind his back" while he was busy reestablishing his GM empire.

Whatever the case, both Billy Durant and Chevrolet's first V-8 were in the archives by 1920. Durant did make another go of it, but he never regained such lofty heights. As for Chevy's little four, it soldiered on alone until superseded by the "Cast-Iron Wonder," a milestone six-cylinder mill eventually nicknamed "Stovebolt" for its unmatched durability. The reliable Stovebolt six, introduced in 1929, carried on into the 1950s, when it finally was upstaged by Chevrolet's second V-8.

Fifty years later that V-8 is still purring like a kitten.

Chevrolet's first V-8 was this 288-ci overhead-valve engine, unveiled in 1917. It was cancelled a year or so later.

Independent manufacturers also have turned to the small block over the years. Built by various firms following Studebaker's demise in the 1960s, the classic Avanti has reappeared more than once with a Chevrolet engine beneath its hood. This 1985 Avanti GT is powered by a 350 Chevy V-8.

Was there a better home for the small block than GM's F-body pony car platform?

Introduced in 1967, the Camaro remained a popular choice for both performance purists and budget-minded buyers until its cancellation in 2002. Shown here is a 1967 SS 350 (back) and a 1994 Z28, the latter powered by a 275-horsepower LT1.

Within that stack are many different varieties beyond the four generations already mentioned. Thirteen different displacements have been tried—14 if you note that the 5.7-liter LS1 actually translated into roughly 345 cubic inches, as opposed to the 350 cubes encapsulated within Chevy V-8s previously seen wearing the "5.7L" label. The smallest small block displaced 262 cubic inches, the largest 400. Ten different bores and seven different strokes have mixed and matched their ways into those varying cubic counts. Advertised outputs have ranged from a nibbling net rating of only 110 horses all the way up to the LS6's 405, and none of us have enough fingers and toes to help keep count of the different power levels listed between those two extremes over the years. Throw in various engineering changes made here and there—two-bolt main bearing caps versus four-bolt, carburetors versus injectors, small crankshaft journals versus medium versus large—and the heap truly grows large.

Funny that, when introduced, the original small block, at 265 cubic inches, wasn't considered small at all, especially from the perspective of a Chevy owner who was fondly familiar with the division's tried-and-true 235-cubic-inch six-cylinder. Detroit's heftiest V-8 in those days, Lincoln's, measured 341 cubes, and cutting-edge counterparts from Cadillac and Chrysler both displaced 331. Though industry-leading displacements would soar soon enough, a 265-ci engine was still considered a big one in 1955, and similar opinions remained in some minds concerning the 327 small block when it debuted in 1962. So what's in a name?

Originally helping put the "small" in small block were the engine's overall external dimensions, far more compact than most other V-8s seen to that point. It also was predictably lighter than existing V-8s—it even weighed less than the old, reliable "Stovebolt" six, which Chevrolet had been offering proudly since 1929. Nestled nice-and-tidy-like way down there between '55 Bel Air fenders, Chevy's 265 V-8 might've even reminded some imaginative cuss of a little mouse in his hole, thus supplying early inspiration for a streetwise nickname that later came into vogue.

From a more formal perspective, the name-calling became official after Chevrolet introduced its definitely large 348-ci "W-head" engine family in 1958. The famed 409 V-8's forerunner, the 348, was also the first of Chevrolet's so-called "big blocks." And when the redesigned Mk. IV big-block family debuted in 1965 (first at 396 cubic inches, followed by 427 in 1966, then 454 in 1970), the nickname game evolved fully. In slang terms, the small block became known as the "mouse motor," the Mk. IV big block a "rat." Get it?

Small blocks have been big winners on race tracks of all types, but they've made the most noise on the NASCAR stock car circuit. Here, Jeff Gordon's Monte Carlo cruises around Atlanta Motor Speedway in 1997 on the way to the first of back-to-back Winston Cup championships.

Small-Block BIKE

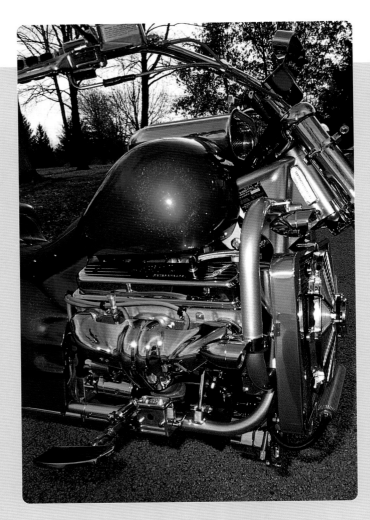

Bikers by nature are a bold breed.
They brave the elements, and the bugs, to feel the ultimate freedom of the road, and they do so on a wide array of motorcycles that range from outrageous crotch-rockets to lavish hogs. Then there's the easy

rider who knows the best of both worlds: prestigious power combined with all the comfort of a full-dress cruiser. His (or her) bike of choice is the Boss Hoss, a V-8-powered dream machine built in Dyersburg, Tennessee.

Boss Hoss Cycles, Inc. was founded in 1990 by Monte Warne, a commercial pilot and aircraft technician who obviously knew more than a bit about power and precision before beginning this venture. Along with his expertise, Warne was also a little lucky. He wanted to market a V-8 motorcycle, and Chevrolet had done him a favor the year before by introducing its first 350 High-Output (HO) crate motor, recognized immediately by its manufacturing code prefix, "ZZZ." Its strength (345 horsepower), easy availability, and inherent compactness made the ZZZ small block the perfect choice 15 years ago—so perfect that its successors have remained a Boss Hoss staple ever since. An

upgraded HO, the ZZ1, debuted in 1991, followed by the ZZ2 in 1992, ZZ3 in 1993, and ZZ4 in 1996. Adding LT4 Corvette heads and boosting compression from 9.8:1 to 10.0:1 helped the ZZ4 produce 10 more horsepower than its forerunners. The 355-horsepower ZZ4 is still the standard Boss Hoss engine today.

Early Boss Hoss bikes used a single-speed, right-angle-drive transmission that allowed the Chevy small block to be mounted inline in the frame. This one-speed gearbox was later traded for a two-speed automatic with reverse to help make the certainly heavy Boss Hoss easier to handle in everyday operation. As for the frame, it's welded up with care from 1.5-inch chrome-moly tubing at the company's 22,000-square-foot shop in Tennessee.

According to Boss Hoss' website, "Every assembly that we weld is placed in a custom jig fixture designed and built at this facility. This allows us to maintain a high level of control over the quality and integrity of our in-house fabricated components." Boss Hoss people are especially proud of their V-8 bike's trusted ruggedness, and they're also quick to point out that this isn't "a monster on two wheels."

Owned by Rick McKinney of St. Joseph, Illinois, this 2000 Boss Hoss motorcycle is powered by a ZZ4 Chevrolet crate engine rated at 355 horsepower. The transmission is a proprietary two-speed automatic with reverse.

A V-8 in a motorcycle might sound intimidating, but the Boss Hoss bike is painstakingly designed to safely handle all that extra power. And its purposeful proportions look really good, too, with or without rider Erin Anderson. The dummy bug-catcher air scoop is an owner-installed customization.

Boss Hoss Cycles, Inc. of Dyersburg, Tennessee, has been building Chevy-powered V-8 motorcycles since 1990. Boss Hoss also offers a big-block bike along with this small-block model. A Boss Hoss trike is available, too.

"Every Boss Hoss is engineered for total performance, not just speed," explains a company brochure. "Anyone into performance knows that all the power in the world is useless if it's unwieldy, unmanageable, and unsafe. A control-designed low center of gravity makes the Boss Hoss easy to handle. And its race-bike-inspired weight distribution formula makes every ounce of the Boss Hoss work together for smoother, more controlled tracking of curves and city streets compared to many bikes half its size."

Owners themselves can attest to this V-8 bike's user-friendly ways. According to Rick McKinney, who rides a metallic-blue 2000 Boss Hoss, once you get acclimated to the extra torque you're in like Flynn—he jaunts about on his with no extra effort at all.

But if you're into real challenges, you might try out the big-block Boss Hoss with its 502-horsepower 502-ci V-8. Bold isn't a big enough word for this one.

Interestingly enough, that pioneering powerplant, though a failure, featured advanced overhead valves, as opposed to the less-complicated valve-in-block L-head layout used by so many prewar engine builders. As car buyers discovered soon enough after World War II, the advantages of the overhead valve (OHV) design over the L-head were many, including improved breathing and a serious increase in volumetric efficiency. L-heads, by nature, were notoriously bad breathers, since the fuel/air charge and spent gases had to follow such inhibited, circuitous routes into and out of the combustion chamber/cylinder arena, which, as you again may have guessed, was shaped like an inverted L from a longitudinal perspective. Overhead valves, however, allowed much smoother passages into and out of a combustion chamber that was located fully atop the cylinder—no sideways extension areas were present to complicate efficient flame propagation and limit compression increases, as was the case within an L-head.

The clunky-yet-easy-to-engineer L-head design, however, remained the norm throughout the 1930s, and that was the layout Henry Ford's engineers turned to in 1932 when they began mass-producing the world's first affordable V-8. Aptly nicknamed "flathead," Ford's own milestone motor would set the standard for the Chevy small block to chase 20-some years later. Along with being reasonably powerful, the "flattie" was simple, cheap, and plentiful; about 12 million were put into the hands of Average Joes across America until Ford finally replaced the flathead with a modern overhead-valve V-8 for 1954.

Big or small, trailing a tail or not, an eight-cylinder engine configured in the shape of a "V" was certainly nothing new when Chevrolet officials introduced the milestone machine they called "The Hot One" in 1955. The "V" layout itself can be traced back as far as a two-cylinder Daimler engine developed in 1889. Reportedly the first automotive V-8 was created by aviation pioneer Clement Ader in 1903, and this was followed by the world's first series-production V-8 from France's de Dion seven years later. Cadillac is credited with pioneering V-8 installations in America late in 1914, inspiring the rapid development of more than 20 rivals. A Detroit newcomer named after race driver Louis Chevrolet even tried rolling out a trendy V-8 in 1917, only to cancel it the following year.

When introduced in 2001, the Z06 Corvette's LS6 V-8 produced 385 horsepower. The LS6 was then upgraded to 405 horsepower in 2002, making it the most powerful regular-production small block ever built.

By then, OHV V-8s had become all the rage around Detroit. General Motors kicked off the postwar craze in 1949, first from Cadillac, then Oldsmobile immediately thereafter. Chrysler joined the club with its truly hot Firepower V-8 in 1951, and this innovative "hemi-head" design was then passed down to De Soto in 1952 and Dodge in 1953. Studebaker became the first independent to offer a modern OHV V-8 in 1951, and Lincoln's came the following year, followed by Buick's in 1953 and Mercury's in 1954. So what was the big deal about Chevrolet introducing an OHV V-8 in 1955? Archrival Ford, after all, had already beaten the Bowtie boys out of the blocks.

While both competing firms' underhood advances represented a breath of fresh air in the low-priced field, it was Chevy's new small

block that ran away with the attentions of Joe and friends, due to its truly hot nature. "Perhaps the continued popularity of Chevrolet lies in the fact that it is an 'average' car for an 'average' buyer," explained technical editor Racer Brown in *Hot Rod* magazine's January 1955 issue. "But the average American driver is becoming more performance minded. He expects things to happen when he punches the throttle."

Things certainly happened when Mr. (or Mrs.) Average put a '55 V-8 Chevy's pedal to the metal, and they happened fast. The new small block's notably short stroke, a mere 3.00 inches, working in concert with an innovative lightweight valvetrain, made this hair-raising rodent a high-winding howler, easily the highest revving V-8 yet to come down the pike. At 162 horsepower, its

ABOVE LEFT: Dropping a modern small block into a vintage Chevrolet has long been a hot rodder's tradition. A Chevy man through and through, noted collector Floyd Garrett commemorates this tradition with a familiar shop scene in his Muscle Car Museum in Sevierville, Tennessee.

ABOVE RIGHT: The largest small block was the 400 V-8, introduced for family cars and trucks in 1970.

output rating was the same as Ford's 1955 "Y-block" V-8, yet it still stirred the soul to far greater degrees. And once all that high-rpm excitement was wrapped up in a bodacious, beautiful body and planted atop a seriously upgraded chassis, the deal was done—Chevrolet had itself a really big winner and a modestly priced one to boot.

That Ed Cole had been chosen to shepherd in the age of the small block was no coincidence. Before becoming Chevrolet chief engineer in April 1952 he had been at Cadillac, where he played a major role in the development of GM's first modern OHV V-8. Though many great minds worked under him during the small block's development—including Harry Barr, Maurice "Rosey" Rosenberger, Russ Sanders, Al Kolbe, and Don McPherson, to name just a few—Cole was still the boss; he made all the big decisions, and thus garnered the lion's share of the credit.

"I guarantee that Cole always had the final word," recalled Wes Yocum Jr., during the celebration of the small block's 40th birthday in 1995. Then Chevrolet Raceshop's assistant motor sports marketing manager, Yocum had joined Cole's staff as an 18-year-old errand boy in November 1953, and he watched as the chief engineer

Now known as the Nextel Cup Series, NASCAR's annual race for the championship presently serves as the test track for Chevrolet's awesome SB2 competition engine, a 358-ci small block that makes more than 700 horsepower.

The same merits on dry land—so much power from so little mass—made the Chevy small block a prime choice for marine applications. Various Chris-Craft boats relied on this 185-horsepower 283 V-8 during the early 1960s. Chris-Craft also used "marinized" 327 small blocks. THE MARINERS MUSEUM COLLECTION

Chris-Craft technicians prepare a Model 283 V-8 marine engine for installation in a 1961 Cavalier cruiser. THE MARINERS MUSEUM COLLECTION

himself made things happen. "If he wanted the valves just so, that's how they were going to be," added Yocum. "Looking back, I think you'd have to say he did a pretty good job. Every Saturday morning, he would come in through the back door of the building. He walked around the room and talked with each one of the draftsmen at their boards. If a designer had a problem, he and Cole would come up with a solution. That was how the small block was designed."

Yocum also marveled at how much drawing boards themselves have changed since those good ol' happy days of the early 1950s. "The draftsmen designed the small-block V-8 with lead pencils and slide rules," he continued. "Today, my son, Steve, designs blocks and cylinder heads for GM Motorsports on a computer. He hits one key and the computer draws a perfect ellipse—it used to take us hours to do what he can do in seconds."

So much progress, so many small blocks—and so many satisfied customers.

RIGHT: Over the years hot rodders have managed to squeeze small blocks into every imaginable space, however tight. Shown here is a Chevy-powered Porsche.

Along with typical Chevy buyers, your average American hot rodder too has long been particularly fond of the mouse motor, dating almost all the way back to 1955. Up until 1960 or so, Ford's old flathead V-8 had been the staple on the hop-up scene, due primarily to its affordability, availability (junkyards had been full of them for decades), and its easy-to-tinker-with nature. Once the Chevy V-8 began filling up scrap yards, it became the new favorite of the rodding set. Born to run and equally easy on the wallet, it too was easy to tweak, and it offered far more power potential than the antiquated flattie.

That potential quickly became the focus of countless speed shops, which had supplied flathead fans with all kinds of go-fast goodies during the 1950s. Legendary speed merchants like Dean Moon, Vic Edelbrock, and Harvey Crane Jr., wasted little time flooding the market with hot parts for the Bowtie V-8 as the 1950s became the 1960s. And almost overnight a Chevy engine swapped into an old Ford rod became the norm. Today this combo remains the street rodder's top choice.

Like their "civilian" counterparts, professional racers have also embraced the little mouse, both with and without factory support from Chevrolet. Either way, the small block has powered more race-winning machines than any other manufacturer's product, and has done so over a wide range of venues. Bowtie power has been especially dominating over the years around sprint car dirt tracks and up the dusty gravel road to the top of Pikes Peak in Colorado. Small blocks have taken on The Brickyard in Indianapolis and countless quarter-mile drag strips across the country. They've won titles in, among others, the SCCA Trans-Am and NASCAR leagues. On the latter's tracks, no make has won more races than Chevrolet, and since 1957 the small block has taken 21 different drivers to NASCAR championships, also the most recorded by any Detroit firm. Chevrolet itself has garnered 22 manufacturers' titles on the nation's leading stock car circuit, yet another record.

Beyond that, small blocks have also found their way into everything from motorboats to motorcycles during the last 50 years. But most importantly, they have powered the Chevrolet cars and pickups that continue to keep the human race running on. And on. And on. How much longer the small-block legacy will remain alive and well is anyone's guess. As long as Americans keep buying 'em, Chevy probably will keep building 'em—and building them better to boot.

Backing up the Manta's mid-mounted 350 small block was a Corvair transaxle mounted on a Kelmakr Engineering adapter. The Corvair box had to be modified to operate in the opposite direction it normally did.

Chevy small blocks long have been popular among the build-it-yourself kit car crowd.

But this sleek machine, created by Manta Cars of Costa Mesa, California, back in the 1970s, was more than a kit car. Designed by Brad LoVette, it was modeled after a Can-Am racer and featured a high-tech tubular space frame and a midships-mounted 350 Chevy V-8.

Chapter 1

WINDING UP:
The Hot One Arrives in 1955

Chevrolet called its 1955 V-8 model "The Hot One" for good reason. Never before had so much power and style been offered to Average Joe.

Looking somewhat frumpy in comparison was the car the '55 Chevy replaced. Nonetheless, the 1954 Chevrolets were still America's best-selling automobiles.

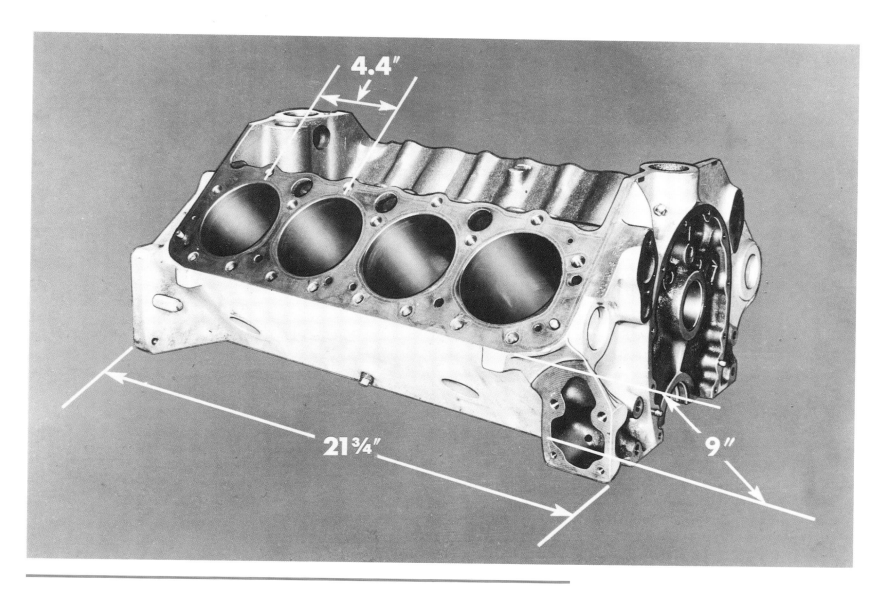

4.4"

21¾"

9"

H OT, NEW CARS WERE
EVERYWHERE YOU
LOOKED IN 1955,
A YEAR THAT STILL
RANKS AS THE GREATEST
IN DETROIT HISTORY FOR ITS
HEADLINE-MAKING UPDATES
AND ADVANCEMENTS. From an image
perspective, it was Chrysler Corporation that
made the most news, after spending a small
fortune on a sensationally sexy restyle for its
entire lineup, with low-priced Plymouth especially benefiting from a dose of award-winning
good looks. Complementing that fashion
statement was a totally redesigned chassis
and Plymouth's own fresh-out-of-the-box V-8.

Packard people, too, introduced a modern
V-8 in 1955, and they also dressed it up in
some seriously reshaped sheet metal.
Packard's new V-8 was used by fellow inde-
pendents Hudson and Nash, which had
merged in 1954 and reappeared a year later
sharing yet another radically revised body.
Indiana-based Studebaker, having joined
forces with Packard in 1954, could afford to
make no real changes for 1955. But, back in

The same basic 4.40-inch bore-center
layout has remained constant throughout
the small-block V-8's 50-year history.

the Big Three mainstream, Ford, Mercury, Buick, and Pontiac were all treated to major makeovers, with Pontiac also rolling out its first V-8. Capping things off for the year in grand fashion were two new models: Chrysler's C-300, arguably Detroit's first true muscle car, and Ford's two-seat Thunderbird, a modern classic that car lovers still adore.

Then there was Chevrolet—good ol' reliable Chevy. As the most affordable rung on General Motors' divisional ladder, the "Bowtie" company's role had long been to put as many practical everyday transports into public hands as possible, which it had done year in, year out. As 1954 wound down, advertisements proclaimed proudly that "for the 19th straight year, more people bought Chevrolets than any other car!" On June 9, the division rolled out its 29 millionth vehicle, and the 30 millionth would follow by year's end. If it ain't broke, don't fix it, right?

Yes and no. Even though Chevrolet continued leading the industry sales race into the mid-1950s, by 1953 archrival Ford was showing serious signs of finally catching the long-time leader. And by some accounts Dearborn actually did take over the sales lead in 1954—creative number crunching and fast talking allowed Chevrolet's propaganda masters to run that "19th straight year" ad with little worry of being called liars. As it was, nearly 1.5 million Chevys hit the streets in 1954; with that kind of volume, what did it matter which company was *numero uno* on paper?

A dumb question indeed—General Motors' execs had long been fiends for being first, and in all facets. Along with dominating sales scores, GM had been Detroit's widely recognized styling leader dating back to

Chevrolet's yeoman "Stovebolt" six-cylinder engine dates back to 1929. When equipped with Chevy's Powerglide automatic (as shown here) in 1954, the 235-cubic-inch "Blue Flame Six" produced 125 horsepower. With the standard three-speed, that figure dropped to 115 horsepower.

1955 Turbo-Fire V-8

CONSTRUCTION:
**cast-iron block
w/cast-iron cylinder heads**

DISPLACEMENT (CUBIC INCHES):
265

BORE & STROKE (INCHES):
3.75 x 3.00

LIFTERS:
hydraulic

COMPRESSION:
8:1

INDUCTION:
**single two-barrel
carburetor**

HORSEPOWER:
162 at 4,400 rpm

TORQUE:
257 at 2,200 rpm

1927, when Harley Earl opened the American automotive industry's first in-house design studio. Engineering excellence was a given, both before and after World War II, and was reiterated in 1949, the year Cadillac and Oldsmobile engineers unveiled their trend-setting overhead-valve V-8s. With such a reputation for supreme success cemented away, and with Ford running up hard and fast, it was only a matter of time before GM decision-makers would opt to treat their low-priced leader to its own modernization or face the disgrace of second place.

Mechanicals became the main focus as the decision to "turn Chevrolet around" was made during a GM Engineering Policy Committee meeting in December 1951. Cadillac man Ed Cole was made chief engineer five months later, and he quickly enlisted another Cadillac engineer, Harry Barr, to become his assistant. Barr was put in charge of chassis and drivetrain development, while veteran engineer Al Kolbe was assigned to directly oversee the design of the division's first modern V-8. On Kolbe's team

was Don McPherson, who later became director of engineering at Chevrolet in 1972 and retired in 1985 as GM vice president.

McPherson spoke reverently of his deceased comrade during Chevrolet's celebration of the small block's 40th anniversary in 1995. "Kolbe was a meticulous man of German descent," he recalled. "Every drafting tool had its place on the drafting table, and every detail of the design had to be carefully handled. Al was a very neat dresser, and I can remember him getting very upset one day when the white stitching on his brown shoes became tarnished. It ruined his day. It was this attention to detail on Al's part that made the engine a success."

Though Cole had the final say, Kolbe was responsible for the bulk of the small block's hands-on design work. He and his team of draftsmen toiled away in a building that had previously been a bank, across the street from GM headquarters. Kolbe was there every day, however long, to make sure everything was drawn up correctly and on time. "There were 14 draftsmen working 60 hours

David Kimble

a week on the new small-block V-8," remembered Wes Yocum in 1995, "and they were
under the gun to get it finished."

All told, Cole's group was allotted a mere
15 weeks to bring the design together.
Chevrolet's former head engineer, Edward
Kelley, already had plans for the company's
new V-8 in place before Cole took over. But
the new chief liked nothing about Kelley's
little 231-cubic-inch proposal and found
himself starting over from scratch. Kelley,
then a manufacturing manager, even helped
his replacement with the new design after his

own had been shot down—apparently egos
were less complicated then, too.

Much the same could be said for GM's
corporate pecking order back in the 1950s.
That Cole and crew met that deadline was
impressive enough on its own. That they did
so with a milestone mill that's still running
strong 50 years later represents the stuff
legends are made of. Then again, Chevrolet's
movers and shakers a half-century back
weren't shackled by the corporate red tape
wound all around Detroit nowadays. Chevy
engineers may not have had superfast

Precise casting techniques allowed
Chevrolet engineers to build a
truly compact, lightweight V-8 for 1955.
Valvetrain weight was also kept low
thanks to those individual stamped-steel
rocker arms.

computer-aided design tools during the 1950s, but they also didn't have to seek approval at countless levels every time they felt a sneeze coming on. The engineers only had to answer to Ed Cole, and he was a prime mover who wasted no time whatsoever shaking things up.

Cole's immediate goal after killing off Kelley's idea was to establish more suitable parameters, which Chief Chassis Engineer Russell Sanders detailed in a paper he presented at the Society of Automotive Engineers (SAE) Golden Anniversary meeting, held in Detroit on January 12, 1955. "In our research over a period of years we have investigated many types of V-8 engines," wrote Sanders in his epic essay, titled "The New Chevrolet V-8 Engine." "During the early stages, we developed an engine with 231 cubic inches of displacement, but with changing conditions a greater displacement was considered desirable. We began thinking about a 245-cubic-inch engine, but when we got further into this study we found we could

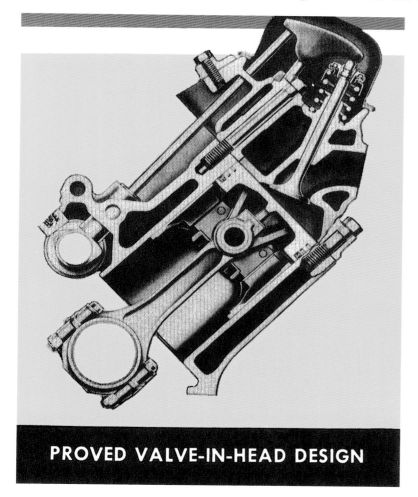

PROVED VALVE-IN-HEAD DESIGN

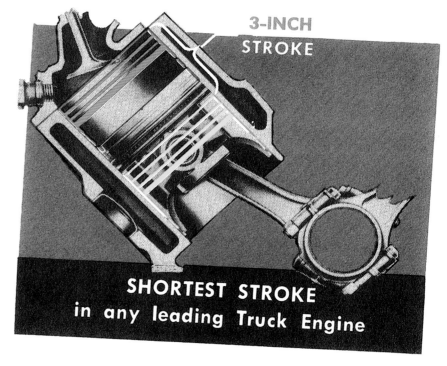

3-INCH STROKE

SHORTEST STROKE in any leading Truck Engine

Unlike Ford, which had long relied on its archaic valve-in-block flathead V-8, Chevrolet had used overhead-valve engines from its humble beginning in 1911.

Lightweight valve gear combined with a really short stroke to help make Chevrolet's small-block V-8 a high-winding screamer.

A Man WITH A PLAN

Ed Cole knew a thing or two about building V-8s when he moved over from Cadillac to Chevrolet in 1952, and one of the main lessons he had learned involved durability. "An engine must be made to hang together under any circumstances," he later said. That the small-block Chevy has hung on strong now for 50 years certainly stands as an undeniable testament to his expertise.

Born in Marne, Michigan, in 1909, Cole was demonstrating mechanical proficiencies at an early age. By his teens he was tinkering with radios, and then cars—his first personal ride was a four-cylinder Saxon that he hot rodded into a rubber-burning road rocket. Although Cole initially enrolled at Grand Rapids Junior College with intentions of earning a law degree, he soon transferred to the General Motors Institute for engineering training. After joining a work/study program at Cadillac, he was hired on by GM's flagship division as a full-time engineer in 1933.

Among early feathers in Cole's cap were various military design projects, including a new engine for the U.S. Army's M-3 light tank. Then came the assignment that made his career:

Cadillac's lightweight, high-compression, overhead-valve V-8, introduced in 1949. Within a few years Cole was managing Cadillac's Cleveland plant. He was then transferred to Chevrolet, which GM execs had decided was in need of some new blood. Cole immediately obliged his bosses by expanding the division's engineering staff from 850 members to 2,900—such was the pressing need to revitalize Chevrolet from the ground up.

After doing just that, and in short order to boot, Cole was rewarded in July 1956 with a promotion up the corporate ladder to Chevrolet general manager and GM vice president, then on to president of General Motors in 1967. He retired in 1974.

All along, though, he remained a true "car guy," a plain fact that the Corvette clan could attest to. It was Cole's steadfast support, along with that of GM Styling Chief Harley Earl, that kept America's Sports Car alive during its darkest days just prior to the installation of Chevy's hot new small-block V-8 in 1955. Yet perhaps Cole's greatest contribution to the Corvette legacy was his decision to hire Zora Arkus-Duntov in May 1953, after Duntov had been refused an engineering position at Chevrolet the

year before. It was Zora, of course, who then put his heart and soul into the car that was soon considered his "baby," even though he wasn't even present at conception.

Duntov's first boss, on the other hand, had been there from the very beginning, though few casual witnesses today seem to remember. If any one man with a plan does deserve credit for getting Chevrolet really rolling during the 1950s, it is Ed Cole. Had Cole not been tragically killed in a private plane crash in 1977, he probably would have joined Duntov during the latter's many celebrations of the Corvette's long heritage before Duntov's own death in 1996. Together, the two could've told some tale.

Ed Cole got his first job at General Motors in 1933. He was killed in a plane crash three years after retiring from GM in 1974.

just as well go to about 260 or 265 with no penalty of extra weight, knowing that ample displacement is fundamentally the most economical way to ensure high torque and resultant good performance economy."

Initial discussions resulted in a 3.75-inch bore, which required a 2.93-inch stroke to equal 260 cubic inches. Engineers decided to round the stroke up to an even 3.00 inches, resulting in a slight boost to 265 cubes, and that was that. After the bore centers were set 4.40 inches apart, the crankshaft length was figured and engine block dimensions were laid down. The block's length came to a tidy 21.75 inches, its height (from oil pan rail to deck) only 9 inches.

Every effort was made to keep the new small block small, and not just to allow an easy fit between Chevrolet fenders. "Anything we could slice off the top or bottom of the block, or from the bores, would mean less heavy iron and less water required to cool it," added Sanders. "This was one of our prime objectives—to make that basic block just as compact as possible."

Compactness translated into minimized weight, another important objective. The new V-8's block weighed 147 pounds compared to 163 for the six-cylinder Stovebolt's inline block. The V-8's crankshaft tipped the scales at 47 pounds, 32 less than the six's lengthy counterpart, while the V-8's two cylinder

Shown bolted into a truck chassis, this early V-8 casting was created in May 1953. Eagle eyes might notice the "DUMMY" stamping on the left cylinder head—these heads contained no internal passages.

    MICHAEL LAMM, LAMM-MORADA PUBLISHING

Workers prepare Chevrolet V-8 castings at
GM's Saginaw foundry in December 1954.

Compared to the 22 casting cores (left) required to create a Cadillac V-8,
the Chevrolet small block needed only nine major and three minor cores.
For some reason four cores were not included on the Chevy side in this layout.
MICHAEL LAMM, LAMM-MORADA PUBLISHING

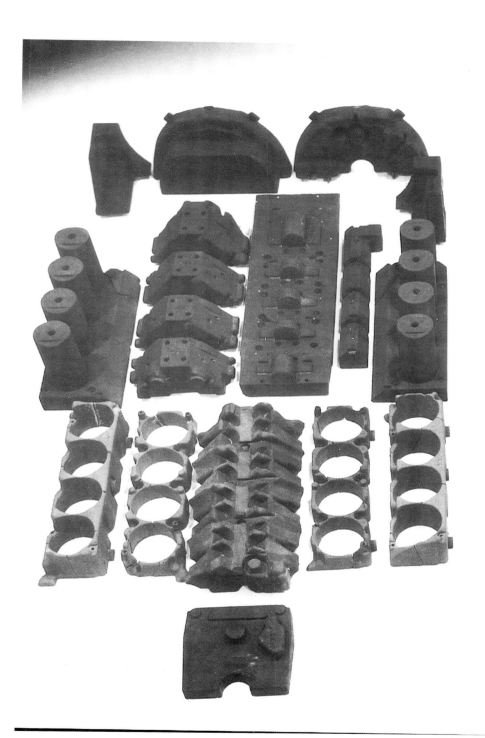

heads—at 77 pounds total—weighed only 5 pounds more than the inline-engine's single head. Overall weights were 531 pounds for the 265-ci V-8, 572 for the 235-cube Stovebolt. As for power, maximum advertised ratings were 136 horses for the six, 162 for the eight. Smaller size, fewer pounds, yet more displacement, increased output—was this magic? Not at all—it was simply GM engineering supremacy at its best.

That expertise was demonstrated further in the new V-8's manufacturing process. Keeping construction simple was yet another goal, and a vital one, considering the need to keep costs down per Chevrolet tradition. A projected high price was the prime reason Cole cancelled Edward Kelley's 231-ci engine, which was little more than a scaled-down version of Cadillac's V-8. Its bottom line reportedly would have doubled that of Chevy's existing Stovebolt, and that simply was unacceptable.

Cole managed to cut the cost of his V-8 by relying on a new casting technique that required fewer sand cores and allowed the engine block to be cast upside down. Compared to Cadillac's V-8, which needed 22 cores to create a block, the Chevrolet V-8 block was cast using only nine major and three minor cores. "Fewer cores mean that our section thicknesses can be controlled much more accurately, and we have less sand to handle," explained Russ Sanders. "The end result is a precision casting which is lighter as well as lower in cost."

According to Cole, laying out the casting upside down allowed for more overall dimensional precision, because the plate that held the bore cores could be located to tighter specs. The enhanced accuracy meant that

Once a few early teething problems were worked out, the sum of these parts would go on to equal Detroit's most durable engine.

MICHAEL LAMM, LAMM-MORADA PUBLISHING

This odd "mule" was used to test the
Chevrolet V-8 in the summer of 1954.
It was a 1953 model with 1955 grille and
fenders grafted on.

MICHAEL LAMM, LAMM-MORADA PUBLISHING

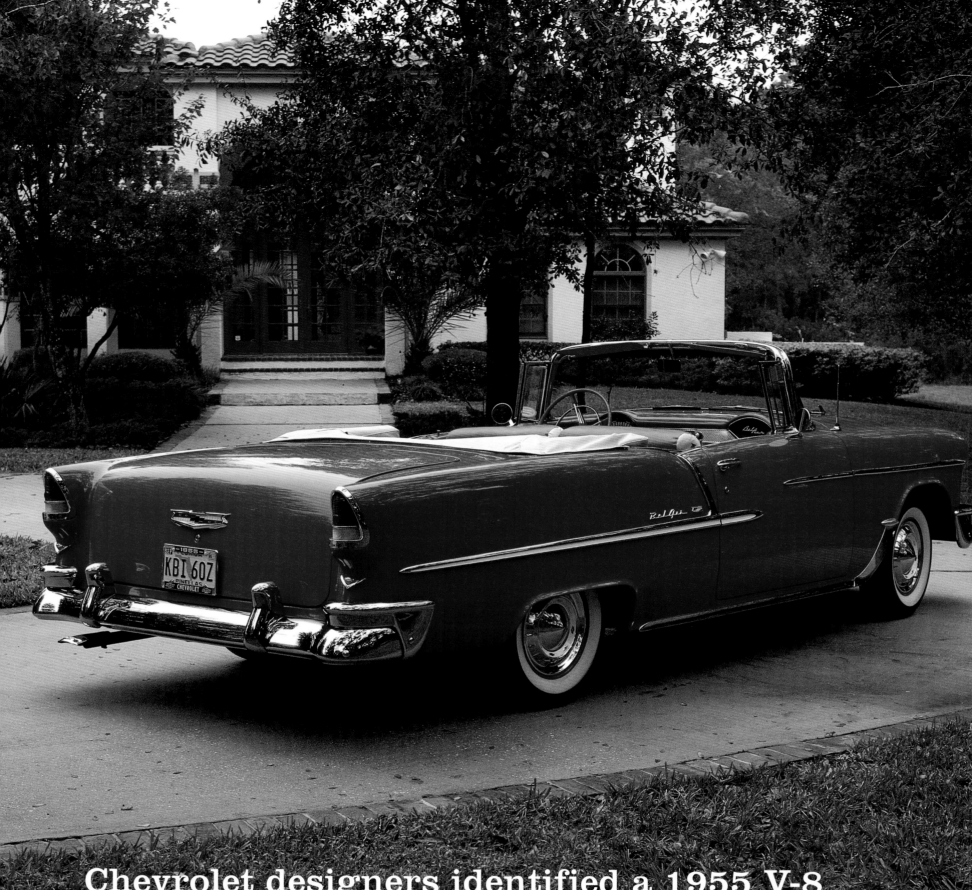

Chevrolet designers identified a 1955 V-8 model with special "V" badges added below each taillight. Also notice the single exhaust, signaling the presence of the Turbo-Fire 265 small block.

crankcase walls could be confidently cast as thin as 5/32 inch at a time when GM foundry people sternly specified nothing thinner than 5/16. And a key to that upside-down technique was the use of "green sand" instead of conventional dry-sand cores, a new practice credited to GM Engineering Staff member John Dolza.

As Dolza explained to *Special Interest Autos* magazine's Michael Lamm in 1975, "Green sand is when you put the pattern into a foundry flask and just blow upon the damp sand and tamp it down to get an impression of the shape of the pattern. A dry core is when you blow the sand, which has a different binder, into a box, then either cure it slowly on a core mold or make it hard like a brick. The (dry-sand) core is baked. The green sand is not. It's just like a sandcastle on the beach."

Cost-consciousness also dictated the design of the cross-flow cylinder heads, which Cole expected to be equally compact and in need of minimal machining to finish them off after casting. "I sketched until I came up with the current head configuration," said Don McPherson in 1995. "Upon seeing the sketches, Ed said, 'That's it!' I was not at all convinced that my sketches would make a workable cylinder head, but, fortunately, they did."

McPherson's design was conventional as far as its inline valves and combustion chamber shape were concerned. "We settled on

continued on page 51

With a single exhaust and a two-barrel carburetor, the Turbo-Fire 265 V-8 was rated at 162 horsepower in 1955.

RIGHT: This external oil filter appeared for 1955 only; in 1956, the filter was mounted in conventional fashion directly to the cylinder block's lower left rear corner.

FAR RIGHT: Adding optional power steering in 1955 meant mounting the pump directly behind the generator.

1955 Corvette V-8

CONSTRUCTION:
cast-iron block w/cast-iron cylinder heads

DISPLACEMENT (CUBIC INCHES):
265

BORE & STROKE (INCHES):
3.75 x 3.00

LIFTERS:
hydraulic

COMPRESSION:
8:1

INDUCTION:
single four-barrel carburetor

HORSEPOWER:
195 at 5,000 rpm

TORQUE:
260 at 2,800 rpm

Good Looks AND IT COULD COOK

Chevrolet's totally redesigned 1955 models represented a full-court press of sorts; potential buyers simply had no defense against this tantalizing new player in the low-priced field.

While Ed Cole's engineers addressed the nuts and bolts, Clare MacKichan's creative staff handled style, and their "Futuramic" makeover was every bit as historic as Cole's newborn small-block V-8. Looks alone probably would have made the 1955 Chevy a big seller—affordability had never before looked so fabulous.

Promotional people didn't call it "The Hot One" for nothing. These pretty babies jumped out of dealers' hands like oven-fresh potatoes and proceeded to warm drivers' blood quicker than cars costing much more. Thanks to Chevrolet, after 1955 Detroit's bottom shelf no longer would be such a bland place to shop for everyday transportation.

Keys to the new attraction were many of GM styling mogul Harley Earl's pet

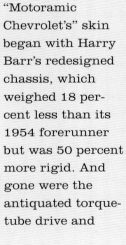

cues, including the car's low, sweeping roofline and equally low belt-line with its trademark notch directly ahead of each rear quarter panel. Another was the "Sweep-Sight" wraparound windshield up front. Earl was also credited with adding the Ferrari-inspired egg crate grille, a design then slightly ahead of its time. While most today feel that grille looks every bit as hot as the car itself, many critics in 1955 didn't like it at all. This led MacKichan's men to try again in 1956, with a different layout featuring a little less crate and a bit more chrome.

Beauty beneath the so-called "Motoramic Chevrolet's" skin began with Harry Barr's redesigned chassis, which weighed 18 percent less than its 1954 forerunner but was 50 percent more rigid. And gone were the antiquated torque-tube drive and

kingpin-type front suspension used in 1954; in their place were modern Hotchkiss drive and ball joints. Front suspension geometry was also reworked considerably for excellent anti-dive characteristics, while the lengthened leaf springs in back were relocated outside the frame rails in "outrigger" fashion to increase roll stiffness.

Any way you looked at it—on top, underneath, inside, beneath the hood—the '55 Chevy was a thoroughly modern remake of proportions previously unheard of at the affordable end of Detroit's spectrum. "It was a brand-new engine and a brand-new body, too," explained Cole to *Special Interest Autos* magazine's Michael Lamm in 1974. "Today, if you wanted to take the same sort of risk at Chevrolet, you'd promptly be fired."

Clare MacKichan's stylists unabashedly borrowed the '55 Chevrolet's "egg-crate" grille from Ferrari. Critics bashed it, inspiring MacKichan to try again in 1956.

The two bright dress-up exhaust tips below this 1955 Bel Air coupe's rear bumper announce the presence of the Super Turbo-Fire 265 V-8.

continued from page 47

the high-turbulence, wedge-type design for combustion control and combustion smoothness, because it controls the rate of pressure rise in the chamber," continued Sanders' SAE report. "We feel that the type of chamber which exposes a high volume of the fuel/air charge early in the burn cycle and then goes out into a quench area gives low octane requirement and smoothness of operation."

The heads' interchangeability and the valvetrain gear perched atop them, on the other hand, were not at all typical. A single symmetrical casting worked for both right and left sides—yet another concession to plain old simplicity. And instead of using rocker arms all mounted together on a central shaft,

Chevrolet's 265 V-8 featured individual stamped-steel rockers, each mounted on a ball-pivot stud. This not only meant that deflection wouldn't be passed on from one arm to the others via that shaft, it also translated into a tidy weight loss—fewer parts meant less weight. Along with being lighter, the ball-stud rocker arm layout was simply easier to manufacture and thus cheaper than conventional shaft-mounted arrangements. And, working in concert with that oh-so-short 3.00-inch stroke, those lightweight stamped-steel rockers helped the Chevy small block wind up like no other V-8 then on the market.

Although commonly credited to Chevrolet today, the ball-stud rocker actually came from Pontiac Motor Division, which had been

Fed by a four-barrel carburetor and fitted with more efficient dual exhausts, the Super Turbo-Fire 265 small block produced 180 horsepower in 1955.

New for 1955 as well was Chevrolet's super-cool Nomad station wagon.

Not only is this Nomad fitted with the Turbo-Fire V-8, it also features

optional air conditioning, a rarity in 1955.

developing its own OHV V-8 since 1946. PMD engineer Clayton Leach came up with the idea in 1948, and his rockers were implemented in the design project intended to make Pontiac more competitive in the rapidly changing 1950s marketplace. Pontiac's first V-8 appeared ready for a 1953 introduction, but development problems and budget factors helped delay that debut by two years. By then Ed Cole had "borrowed" Pontiac's rocker design and applied it to his project.

Nearly all else about the first small block was of genuine Chevrolet design. Additional innovations included hollow pushrods that fed all-important lubricants to the engine's top end, doing away with the need for troublesome external lines or extra oil

passages within the block. Up top, an intake manifold also served as a cover for the valley formed between cylinder banks in the "V" configuration. Separate valley covers and intakes—the latter items with individual runners (to each intake port) set apart by open spaces—were common in V-8s of the day. Now serving double duty, the Chevy intake was cast "solid" with webs filling the open spaces to completely seal off the top of the engine. This manifold not only eliminated the traditional valley cover, it also required less machining than typically "spacey" intakes, due to the absence of all the excess iron flash created by the many parting lines inherent to complicated castings.

continued on page 59

The engine compartment of a 1955 Chevrolet became a crowded place when air conditioning was ordered. The compressor and handler unit can be seen at the upper left.

Chevrolet people were especially proud of their new air conditioning option in 1955.

Special upholstery with waffle-type inserts was standard for the 1955 Nomad wagon. Notice the air conditioning ducts at each end of the dashboard.

Looks like hills weren't the only things "flattened" in 1955. Advertising artists back then loved to accentuate automotive dimensions; in this case making the 1955 Chevrolet appear lower than low was the goal.

Chevrolet's *red-hot* hill-flatteners!
162 H.P. V8 - 180 H.P. V8

See that fine fat mountain yonder?

You can iron it out, flat as a flounder . . . and easy as whistling!

Just point one of Chevrolet's special hill-flatteners at it (either the 162-h.p. "Turbo-Fire V8," or the 180-h.p. "Super Turbo-Fire"*) . . . and pull the trigger!

Barr-r-r-r-o-o-O-O-OOM!

Mister, you got you a flat mountain!

. . . At least it *feels* flat. Because these silk-and-dynamite V8's gobble up the toughest grades you can ladle out. And holler for more. They love to climb, because that's just about the only time the throttle ever comes near the floorboard.

And that's a pity. For here are engines that sing as sweetly as a dynamo . . . built to pour out a torrent of pure, vibrationless power. Big-bore V8's with the shortest stroke in the industry, designed to gulp huge breaths of fresh air and transmute it into blazing acceleration.

So most of the time they loaf. Even at the speed limit they just dream along, light and easy as a zephyr, purring out an effortless fraction of their strength.

You don't have to be an engineer to know that these are the sweetest-running V8's you ever piloted. Just drop in at your Chevrolet dealer's, point the nose at the nearest hill, and feather the throttle open. *These* V8's can do their own talking . . . and nobody argues with them!

SEE YOUR CHEVROLET DEALER
*Optional at extra cost.

motoramic *Stealing the thunder from the high-priced cars with the most modern V8 on the road!*

Eight MADE IT GREAT

Considering its slow start, it's a wonder the Corvette survived five years, let alone a half-century.
Initial sales of the Polo White roadsters in 1953 were weak, with only about 180 of the 300 built finding homes by the end of the year. Then, after projecting production of 10,000 Corvettes for 1954, Chevrolet officials cut off the next year's run at 3,640, of which nearly a third were still sitting unsold on January 1, 1955. Future prospects at that time looked bleak to say the least, helping explain why only 700 '55 Corvettes rolled off the St. Louis line.

Apparently American buyers weren't exactly fond of the car's relatively crude nature. They didn't like that leaky folding top with its clumsy side curtains, nor were they used to a car devoid of exterior door handles. Last but not least were the early Corvette's 150-horsepower Blue Flame six-cylinder and Chevy's Powerglide automatic transmission. A sports car simply didn't come without a stick, and a six, no matter how hot, was still just a six, a plain reality that became especially painful after Ford began showing models of its upcoming Thunderbird early in 1954. Along with conventional roll-up windows, convenient door handles and a removable hardtop, the planned two-seat T-bird also would feature nothing less than a V-8. Ed Cole and crew had no choice but to respond accordingly.

A prototype V-8 Corvette was undergoing testing as early as May 1954 under the direction of performance consultant and three-time Indy 500 winner Mauri Rose. Cole hired Rose in August 1952 to oversee the division's performance parts development projects, and among Rose's first challenges was the development of the Blue Flame six's triple-carb setup. He then found that trading out six cylinders for eight beneath that forward-hinged fiberglass hood was basically no sweat, with the Corvette's X-member frame requiring only a minor modification to allow clearance for the 265's fuel pump.

"Installation of the compact V-8 in the Corvette is very neat," wrote *Motor Life's* Ken Fermoyle. "The engine fits so nicely, in fact, that one suspects that the possibility of using a V-8 was considered when the Corvette was designed." The only other noticeable change involved the addition of a bigger radiator with a fan shroud.

Only 700 1955 Corvettes were built, most of them fitted with a V-8 backed by Chevrolet's Powerglide automatic transmission. Some early cars left the St. Louis line with six-cylinder engines and some late models featured three-speed manual gearboxes.

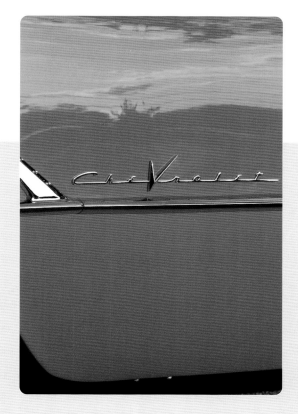

A large gold "V" added to the "Chevrolet" fender script announced the presence of a V-8 Corvette in 1955.

While as few as 10 very early 1955 Corvettes were equipped with the Blue Flame six, the rest featured the 195-horsepower 265 V-8. An equally coveted three-speed manual gearbox was also introduced that year, apparently behind only the small block. Estimates put three-speed Corvette production for 1955 at about 75.

As for more important numbers, according to *Road & Track,* the new V-8 Corvette could run from rest to 60 miles per hour in a reasonably scant 8.7 sec-

onds. The far end of the quarter-mile showed up only 7.8 ticks later. Comparable *R&T* test numbers for a '54 Corvette were 11 seconds for the time-honored 0–60 run and a lukewarm 18 clicks for the quarter-mile. The V-8 Corvette's top end was a tad short of 120 miles per hour, up from the 107-mile-per-hour limit recorded in 1954. All told, these numbers added up to a bright future for America's Sports Car.

"Whether the addition of the V-8 engine will hypo Corvette sales remains to be seen," wrote Fermoyle. "The blazing performance the Corvette now offers should attract more buyers."

The attraction then grew even greater in 1956, when a reshaped, stunningly sexy body appeared with roll-up windows and an optional lift-off hardtop. Newfound beauty beneath the skin also included chassis upgrades, courtesy of quick-thinking Zora Arkus-Duntov, who kept making the Corvette better each year thereafter. Sales responded accordingly: 3,476 in 1956; 6,339 in 1957; beyond 10,000 by 1960. Once back from the brink in 1955, the Corvette couldn't be stopped, all thanks to the little V-8 engine that could.

Offered only in Polo White for 1953, Chevrolet's two-seat sports car was treated to optional colors in 1954. Gypsy Red is the color of this 1955 model.

Zora Duntov himself road tests a
high-flying prototype V-8 Corvette in 1954.

MICHAEL LAMM, LAMM-MORADA PUBLISHING

continued from page 53

Mounted atop the intake in base form, the two-barrel carburetor, along with 8:1 compression, helped the 265 V-8 produce those 162 horses. Buyers who wanted even more power could shell out extra bucks for the power pack option, which added a four-barrel carburetor and dual exhausts, additions that bumped the output ante up to 180 horsepower. Throw in the optional overdrive for the three-speed manual transmission and 4.11:1 gears in the rear and there was no stopping you. All this hot hardware, wrapped up in a Bel Air coupe, cost about $2,300 in 1955, and that too represented really big news.

A triple-digit top end had never before come that cheap, nor had cutting-edge passenger-car acceleration, reasonable road-handling characteristics, and dashing good looks. GM had earmarked $300 million for Chevy's 1955 rebirth, and it certainly showed. "New" simply wasn't a big enough word for the totally redesigned car that Chevrolet officials preferred to call "The Hot One."

In the words of *Mechanix Illustrated* magazine's Tom McCahill, the new V-8 model on the block was "the most glamorous-looking and hottest-performing Chevrolet to come down the pike." *Popular Mechanics'* Floyd Clymer called it the "best-handling Chevrolet I have ever driven." *Motor Trend* went even further, proclaiming that the all-new '55 Chevy (along with the '55 Mercury) was Detroit's best road car, period. Additional publicity came when a V-8-powered Bel Air convertible was chosen as the prestigious pace car for the 1955 Indianapolis 500.

On the street, the hottest Chevy for 1955 was virtually unbeatable. As *Road & Track* explained, "It certainly appears that a

Chevrolet V-8 with the optional 180-horsepower engine and 4.11 axle will out-accelerate any American car on the market today!" *R&T's* road test results were startling, to say the least: 0–60 in 9.7 seconds, 17.2 ticks for the quarter-mile. Any American car running under 10 seconds from rest to 60 miles per hour was news enough in those days. That this machine was a Chevrolet—just a year departed from its mundane Stovebolt existence—certainly represented grounds to write home to mother.

And even more exciting news awaited the fortunate few able see the U.S.A. from behind the wheel of a two-seat Chevrolet in 1955. Then in its third year, the Corvette was also treated to V-8 power, and the switch from the previously used Blue Flame six proved to be just the ticket to get that little baby rolling after it was very nearly tossed out with the bath water in 1954. If not for the heavyweight support of Harley Earl and Ed Cole, "America's Sports Car" probably would've died off due to disappointing sales just as redemption waited around the corner.

A work order dated October 26, 1953, first instructed Cole's engineers "to install a

Billboards like these were a common sight across the USA in 1955.

Sharing many styling cues with its car-line sibling, Chevrolet's all-new "Task Force" trucks debuted in the spring of 1955. They too could've been fitted with a small-block V-8—as the fender badge on this 3100-series half-ton attests.

V-8 engine in a 1953 Corvette for mock-up purposes in order to facilitate determining design problems encountered in a 1955 production Corvette." The second Corvette, built in June 1953, later designated EX-122, became the mule for the installation, and the initial swap involved a nonrunning V-8 substitute—complete with a dummy air cleaner made of wood—to check clearances.

In actual application, the 1955 Corvette's 265 V-8 was topped by a low-restriction chrome air cleaner. Additional chrome dress-up was applied to the valve covers and the distributor's suppressive shielding, the latter required to prevent ignition voltage from interfering with radio reception, a gremlin inherent in the car's fiberglass body construction. Standard steel body panels supplied the shielding on conventional cars.

As for more important details, a Carter four-barrel carburetor (with automatic choke) and a lumpier, more aggressive cam worked together to boost the Corvette V-8's output to a formidable 195 horsepower. Compression, meanwhile, remained at 8:1. Completing the deal, a large gold "V" was tacked on to the "Corvette" script located on each front fender—in this case, "V" stood for "va-va-voom."

"Loaded for bear," was *R&T's* description for the 195-horse Corvette. According to Ken Fermoyle at *Motor Life*, "The V-8 engine makes this a far more interesting automobile and has upped performance to a point at least as good as anything in its price class." Along with that, Walt Woron and staff at *Motor Trend* were impressed that the bigger, badder V-8 apparently also improved perform-

ance in the turns. "Whether or not this slight weight differential (between the 6 and V-8) would make any handling difference is hard to determine," concluded an August 1955 *MT* report. "But it at least *seemed* like the V-8 stuck in corners a bit longer before the rear end broke loose."

And to think this was just the beginning—for both the Corvette and the small-block V-8 that would make it famous soon enough.

Chevrolet's light-duty pickup engines were painted gray during the 1950s and 1960s. The 265 small block was renamed "Taskmaster" in truck ranks.

The Cameo's main attraction was its fiberglass-sided cargo box, which featured car-like taillights—quite a change compared to Chevrolet's standard 3100-series (right) 1955. Notice the plain (no "V" badge) fender on the green pickup. It features the Stovebolt six, not the small block.

Like the new Nomad wagon, the Cameo
Carrier introduced some serious
style and flair to the utility market in 1955.

The Cameo came with either a six or a small block that year—notice the

V-8 fender badge.

Chapter 2

FANNING THE FLAMES:
From 265 to 400

It wasn't broke, but Chevrolet fixed it. A mild restyle and even more small-block power
made the 1956 Chevy an even greater attraction.

Chevrolet proved best in Pikes Peak Secret Test!

Time — 17:24 minutes from Start to Finish

A CHAMPION IN THE MAKING

1956 CHEVROLET

PIKES PEAK RECORD BREAKER

Chevrolet has won many honors in the more than 40 years of its leadership history, but none is more meaningful to motorists than the new, official* Pikes Peak record set by the preproduction model of the 1956 Chevrolet "Super Turbo-Fire V8" in a secret test on September 9, 1955. For, in so doing, it not only proved itself the champion in performance, but also the champion in safe motoring.

Officiated by National Association for Stock Car Auto Racing.

MOUNTAINS OF STAMINA! Chevrolet's rugged valve-in-head engine; safe, sure Jumbo Brakes; rigid all-steel Body by Fisher and sturdy box-girder frame, are among the many features that helped flatten Pikes Peak in record time. Proving that the '56 Chevrolet can take it under the most extreme driving conditions.

TRIGGER-QUICK TAKE-OFF! The 1956 Chevrolet's lightning acceleration, a vital factor in the success at Pikes Peak, is an important safety feature on any road—providing a husky passing reserve ready to whip into action on any occasion.

HANDLING EASE! Hitting high speeds over 12 miles of twisting Pikes Peak roads put Chevrolet's Ball-Race steering to the supreme test—and proved it unequaled! Likewise, safe highway and city driving demand Chevrolet's precision control.

VICTORY! A new Pikes Peak record by a full two minutes—indeed a prideful victory for the 1956 Chevrolet and a still bigger one for every '56 Chevrolet buyer. For here's another big reason why there's so much pride of ownership attached to owning a new 1956 Chevrolet.

COMMAND POWER! The need will seldom arise to use all the power it took to break the Pikes Peak record. But it's there to lend a hand in any emergency as well as to make Chevrolet driving always more pleasurable.

SURE-FOOTED ROADABILITY! Chevrolet for '56 couldn't have set a new Pikes Peak record without the rock-solid stability and superior cornering qualities of its Glide Ride Front Suspension and Outrigger Rear Springs. Chevrolet's true balance means greater car safety.

The hot one's even HOTTER! —1956 CHEVROLET!

THE DATE WAS SEPTEMBER 9, 1955; THE PLACE, PIKES PEAK. The car was a 1956 Chevy disguised with striped paint and dummy covers over the headlamps and taillights. Why the costume? Chevrolet officials didn't want any unauthorized eyes catching a sneak peek of their restyled model before its official introduction, still about a month away. So what were they doing with this one on the side of a mountain in Colorado? It took Zora Arkus-Duntov about a quarter-hour to explain.

An engineer who knew a little (make that a lot) about generating serious speed, Duntov took the wheel of the camouflaged sedan and, at 7:17 a.m., mashed the foot feed to the floor. In front of him were 12.42 miles of treacherous gravel and 170 twisting turns, many of the hair-rising hairpin variety, running some 9,400 feet up to the summit. Not a problem—Duntov's Chevy reached the top in a mere 17 minutes and 24.05 seconds, an amazing 2 minutes and 1.65 seconds faster than the previous best run made by an American stock sedan at the

Zora Duntov's dash up Pikes Peak in September 1955 helped Chevrolet announce that it was heating things up for 1956.

Is this the first small block built for 1957?

Casting dates for the block and heads were July 27 and July 23 (1956), respectively, and the assembly date was August 21. At the time Chevrolet was still building 1956 engines, yet this 265 two-barrel V-8 was clearly tagged for 1957 production. Today it belongs to Brad Smith of Brad's Classics in Hindsboro, Illinois.

As in 1955, dual exhaust tips beneath a Chevrolet's bumper in 1956 signified the presence of extra horses beneath the hood.

In this Bel Air's case, those dual exhausts lead to the Super Turbo-Fire V-8.

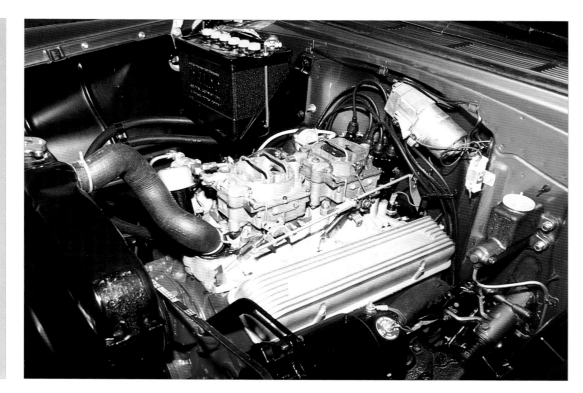

1956 Turbo-Fire V-8

CONSTRUCTION:
**cast-iron block
w/cast-iron cylinder heads**

DISPLACEMENT (CUBIC INCHES):
265

BORE & STROKE (INCHES):
3.75 x 3.00

LIFTERS:
solid

COMPRESSION:
9.25:1

INDUCTION:
**dual four-barrel
carburetors**

HORSEPOWER:
225 at 5,200 rpm

TORQUE:
270 at 3,600 rpm

king of all hillclimbs. Though the car itself may have been cloaked in secrecy, the numbers it scored that September morn were soon being shown off to all of America. Promotional people wasted little time spreading the word: thermometers wouldn't stand a chance in 1956; Chevrolet was turning up the heat.

As if The Hot One hadn't been warm enough in 1955, Ed Cole's engineers kept pushing for even more performance, resulting in the smokin' small block Duntov relied on during his jaunt up Pikes Peak. Chevy buyers who thought that 1955's optional Super Turbo-Fire 265 V-8, rated at 180 horsepower, was a sizzling sensation had another thing coming. Powering Zora's hillclimber was a new four-barrel-fed Super Turbo-Fire—this one pumping out 205 horses—that would help inspire another mercury-tainted ad pitch. Introduced in late October 1955, Chevrolet's second-edition V-8 models rolled out to trumpets of "The Hot One's Even Hotter," and this represented one occasion when the corporate promo guys couldn't be knocked for blowing their own horns.

Every bit as enthusiastic about those rising temperatures was legendary *Mechanix Illustrated* scribe Tom McCahill, who called the 205-horsepower 1956 Chevy the "best performance buy in the world." Succinctly reported in "McCahill-ese," this factory hot rod "would whiz by a Duesenberg like Halley's Comet," and "the vacuum as it went by would suck the stork off a Hispano-Suiza." According to a more-to-the-point *Road & Track* road test, the Super Turbo-Fire Chevrolet could zip from 0 to 60 miles per hour in 9.0 seconds and tour the quarter-mile in 16.6 seconds—both startling performance figures for 1956.

And this was just the beginning.

Duntov's baby, the Corvette, not only was treated to a beautiful new body and tweaked chassis in 1956, it also was fitted with a 210-horsepower version of the single-carb Super Turbo-Fire V-8. Far more popular, though, was the strongest small block yet, the 225-horsepower solid-lifter 265 topped with twin four barrels, each flowing about 375 cfm. Again according to *Road & Track*,

Chevrolet's new, hotter powertrain parts for 1956 were shown off during that year's National Sales Convention.

Chevrolet's dual-four V-8 could haul the revitalized Corvette through the quarter-mile in only 15.8 seconds, while the 0–60 clocking read a scant 7.3 ticks. Tooting horns was one thing; blowing the tops off those thermometers was more like it in the 1956 Corvette's case. As *Sports Car Illustrated* magazine's Roger Huntington saw it, the 225-horsepower V-8 surely represented "one of the hottest production engines in the world—regardless of piston displacement."

Chevrolet fanned the flames even further that year by also offering the Corvette's twin-carb 265 as an option for its passenger cars, kicking off a crowd-pleasing practice that would continue off and on throughout the small block's 50-year run—witness, among others, the Camaro receiving Corvette power in the forms of the LT1 in 1993 and the LS1 five years later. In 1956, installing those 225 healthy horses into, say, a Bel Air sport coupe resulted in what Tom McCahill called "a poor man's answer to a hot Ferrari."

Well-known for his flowery prose, McCahill was especially impressed by the way this mechanical-tappet motor revved like no other

Father FIGURE

Zora Arkus-Duntov officially retired on January 1, 1975, after 21 years and seven months with General Motors. Two decades earlier, he boldly wrote Ed Cole about a job after seeing the Corvette prototype on stage at GM's Motorama auto show in New York. "Now there's potential," he remembered thinking in a 1967 *Hot Rod* interview. "I thought it wasn't a good car yet, but if you're going to do something, this looks good." Duntov's letter led to a job as an assistant staff engineer at Chevrolet beginning May 1, 1953. "Not for the Corvette or anything of that sort," he told *Hot Rod's* Jim McFarland, "but for research and development and future stuff."

After "fiddling on the side" (his words) in 1953 and 1954, Duntov was named Chevrolet's director of high-performance vehicle design and development in 1956, with his main focus on the division's highest-performance vehicle. Almost overnight he was recognized as *the* man with his thumb firmly planted on the Corvette's pulse. A few more years down the road and he was the father figure, although he wasn't officially named Corvette chief engineer until 1968, after some bureaucratic bumbling had temporarily cut him out of the loop. From 1968 to 1974, however, he reigned supreme.

For those who've always wondered but were afraid to ask, the Father of the Corvette got his name as a result of having two dads. The son of Russian

Zora Duntov joined General Motors in 1953 and later became the first of three Corvette chief engineers. He retired in January 1974.

parents, Zora Arkus was born in Belgium on Christmas Day, 1909. Later, after returning to her hometown, by then known as Leningrad, Zora's mother divorced Arkov and married Josef Duntov. Zora then took on the hyphenated last name out of respect to Misters Arkus and Duntov.

An avid speed freak from his youngest days, Mr. Arkus-Duntov drove for British sports car builder Sydney Allard at Le Mans in 1952. He drove again in France in 1953 despite Cole's insistence that he stay home and attend to his new position. His job was still there, of course, after the 24-hour race. It also remained intact following the class victories he scored while piloting a Porsche Spyder at Le Mans in 1954 and 1955. From then on, however, driving fast Corvettes remained his prime passion—and the faster the better.

As much as he always dreamed of building a supremely balanced, lightweight, midengine Corvette, Duntov didn't necessarily look down his nose at the beastly big-block cars that began

appearing in 1965. He loved horsepower, and thus he was fond of the 427. Furthermore, he was no fool; if GM wouldn't okay his dream, then he would make the most of the realities left to him. As a 1969 *Car Life* report explained, "We asked Duntov if he had considered a 2,000-pound, 300-horsepower Corvette." His reply? "He has, and the closest he's been able to come is a 3,500-pound, 435-horsepower Corvette."

Duntov still dreamed of the midengine Corvette, even after GM execs finally closed the book on it in 1974. He then carried on as a grand ambassador of sorts for America's Sports Car until his death in April 1996.

American V-8. "Here's an engine that can wind up tighter than the E-string on an East Laplander's mandolin, well beyond 6,000 rpm, without blowing up like a pigeon egg in a shotgun barrel," went one of his wackier word weavings. What a pigeon egg would be doing in a shotgun is anyone's guess, but you get the picture. We hope.

While winding out high and fast was a major key to the small block's initial success, there were other ways to enhance performance, and Cole's crew was more than willing to try every one early on. More cam, more compression, more carburetor represented the best choices back then to help maximize output, yet there was a simpler path to take toward making more horses. As the old

gearhead's adage goes, "there's no substitute for cubic inches." What this means is as plain as the beak on a pigeon's face: In the absence of any other upgrades, increasing displacement represents the quickest, easiest way to also increase horsepower.

Small-block displacement got its first boost in 1957 and with little fuss or muss. Those 4.40-inch-bore centers meant there was enough iron present in the block's cylinder walls to allow a bit of boring, an important fact considering Cole expected that the engine's rev-intensive stroke would be kept as short as possible through whatever growth stages lay ahead. Accordingly, cylinder diameter was punched out from 3.75 inches to 3.875, while the all-important stroke remained at 3.00 inches. The end result was the 283 V-8, offered along with the proven 265 (for one last year) in 1957.

Various progressive stages—some up, some down—followed for the first-generation small block after its initial growth spurt. Once the last usable pony had been squeezed out of the 283, it was superseded in 1962 by the bigger, better, badder 327, which then morphed into the 350 in 1967. Three years later, Chevy introduced the largest small block, the 400, which, despite its not-small-at-all cubic-inch tally, was never intended for big-time performance applications; nor were the yeoman 307 (built from 1968 to 1973), the short-lived, short-changed 262 (1975 to 1976), or the economical, environment-friendly 267 (1979 to 1981). Introduced for 1976, the little 305 V-8 tried to look tough at times but for the most part was more or less a shadow of former hot-to-trot small blocks. Chevrolet's 302, on the other hand, was a ridiculously raucous rodent bolted together for one purpose only—to transform the Camaro into the wildest pony car this side of the Pecos. For the tale of this race-ready screamer, offered exclusively for the Z/28 Camaro from 1967 to 1969, see Chapter 3.

As for the 327, it required just a little more sweat to create compared to its 283-ci forerunner. According to engineer Maurice Rosenberger, the 283 had barely hit the streets in 1957 when talk of even more displacement started. He had seen various racers that year running Chevy small blocks that been bored and stroked to as many as 342 cubic inches, and he suggested to Cole that they try a similar approach. A less-than-preferable stroke stretch was a must if more

The beautifully new Bel Air Sport Sedan—one of 20 new Chevies. Sweet and low—and longer for '57!

'57 CHEVROLET!
SWEET, SMOOTH AND SASSY!

Chevy goes 'em all one better for '57 with a daring new departure in design (looks longer and lower, and it is!), exclusive new Triple-Turbine Turboglide automatic drive, a new V8 and a bumper crop of new ideas including fuel injection!

Chevy's new and Chevy shows it—from its daring new grille and stylish lower bonnet to the saucy new slant of its High-Fashion rear fenders. It's longer, too, and looks it.

And new style is just the start. There are new V8 power options that range up to 245* h.p. Then, you've a choice of *two* automatic drives as extra-cost options. There's an even finer Powerglide, and new Turboglide with Triple-Turbine take-off.

Go see the new car that goes 'em all one better. Your Chevrolet dealer's got it! . . . Chevrolet Division of General Motors, Detroit 2, Michigan.

Chevy's new beauty wins going away! Body by Fisher, of course.

*A special 270-h.p. engine also available at extra cost. Also revolutionary Ramjet fuel injection engines with up to 283 h.p. in Corvette and passenger car models.

"Sweet, smooth, and sassy!" was
Chevrolet's new catch phrase for 1957.
After all, how hot could hot get?

1957 Fuel-Injected V-8

CONSTRUCTION:
**cast-iron block
w/cast-iron cylinder heads**

DISPLACEMENT (CUBIC INCHES):
283

BORE & STROKE (INCHES):
3.875 x 3.00

LIFTERS:
solid

COMPRESSION:
10.5:1

INDUCTION:
**Ramjet
fuel injection**

HORSEPOWER:
283 at 6,200 rpm

TORQUE:
290 at 4,400 rpm

cubes from the factory were going to happen, but that wasn't the worst of it. Cole wanted a 4.00-inch bore, and that extra cylinder diameter required some serious precision during the casting process to guarantee enough cylinder wall thickness at all eight holes.

Rosenberger's cohort, Don MacPherson, remembers seeing walls as thin as 0.018 inch, surely the limit. And, in fact, early 327s suffered from oil-burning maladies after casting deviations left some cylinder walls so lean that they deflected during the reciprocating process, allowing lubricants to make their way into the combustion area. Casting in a little more iron around the cylinder barrels solved this problem. The 4.00-inch bore then worked fine, and it combined with a 3.25-inch stroke to equal those 327 cubic inches.

Most other aspects and components of the 283 simply carried over for the 327 to keep costs down. But this share and share-alike attitude created another problem. Now with more cubes making it able to make even more horsepower, the 327 sometimes tore

itself apart on the bottom end, because the existing crankshaft simply wasn't strong enough to stand the strain of extreme use. Main bearing journals on that crank measured 2.30 inches in diameter, and this was stout enough for the 265 and 283, as were the shaft's 2.00-inch connecting rod journals. Chevrolet's bored-and-stroked small block, however, definitely needed a beefier crank with thickened journals, although it didn't arrive until 1968, one year before the 327 retired. Measurements for those enlarged main bearing and rod journals were 2.45 and 2.10 inches, respectively.

Another bottom-end improvement made to the small block in 1968 involved the crank's main bearing caps. From 1955 to 1967, all Chevy V-8s relied on typical two-bolt caps to hold the crank's five main bearings firmly in place. Beginning in 1968, all high-performance V-8s with a 4.00-inch bore (save the 327) received beefier four-bolt main caps for the three inner bearings, while the front and rear main bearing caps remained two-bolt

Run LIKE THE WIND

The small "dog dish" hubcaps on this 1957 fuel-injected air box Corvette were used in place of typical wheel covers when wider wheels were ordered. These rims were one of many race-ready options introduced that year. "Air box" referred to the fresh air induction equipment installed beneath the hood.

Four fuel-injected small blocks were listed for the 1957 Corvette, beginning with RPO 579A, made up of the 250-horsepower fuel-injected V-8 backed by Chevy's new four-speed manual transmission.

Trading that four-speed for a Powerglide automatic resulted in RPO 579C, while the 579B option featured the fabled 283-horsepower fuelie, offered only with the four-gear. Production totals were 713 for 579B, 182 for 579A, and 102 for 579C.

Rarest of the group was RPO 579E, a competition-conscious package known today as the Airbox option. Included in this deal was a special induction setup that allowed Chevy's 283-horsepower 283 to breathe in cooler, denser outside air instead of hot underhood atmospherics.

To do this, a plenum box was fabricated and mounted on the fenderwell panel on the driver's side. At the front, this box mated to an opening in the support bulkhead beside the radiator. Inside the box was an air filter. At the rear was a rubberized duct that ran from that filter to the injection unit. Outside airflow

Part of the RPO 579E air box package involved relocating the tachometer from the dashboard to the steering column.

entered through the bulkhead opening into the box and then on to the engine, resulting in the release of a few extra ponies on top end.

At $726.30, RPO 579E cost half as much again as the garden-variety 283/283 fuelie, leaving little wonder why so few were built. Airbox Corvette production was only 43 in 1957, bringing the total fuel-injected tally that year to 1,040.

Additional race-ready Airbox modifications included relocating the tachometer from the dashboard to the steering column and deleting the nonessential radio and heater. With the radio gone, ignition shielding wasn't required, which in turn meant that plug wires could run directly from the distributor to the spark plugs away from the hot exhaust manifolds. Plug wires on all other 1957 Corvettes ran the long way down below the exhausts, because this was the easiest place to mount the static-suppressive shielding.

Other hot parts debuted along with RPO 579E in 1957, beginning with a Posi-Traction differential and wide 15x5.5 wheels adorned with small hubcaps in place of full wheel covers. A heavy-duty suspension, RPO 581, entered the fray

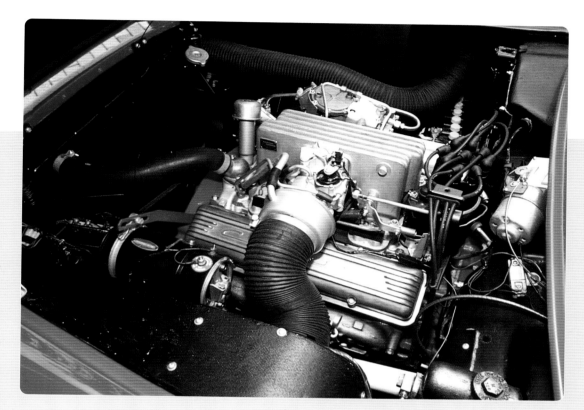

The air box plenum (black unit mounted just inside of driver's side fender) allowed cooler, denser ambient atmosphere to flow freely into the Ramjet fuel injection unit.

early on, but was quickly superseded by RPO 684, which combined the 581 underpinnings with a beefed-up brake package and also mandated the installation of the Posi rear.

RPO 684 brakes featured cerametallix linings, finned drums, and vented backing plates with scoops to catch cooling air. Delivering this air to the rear wheel scoops required an odd duct work arrangement that began at each side of the radiator, ran back through the

engine compartment and down around each front wheelwell, and made its way inside the lower rocker panels. At the trailing end of each rocker was a short, fiberglass deflector that directed the flow inboard toward the scoops on each vented backing plate.

The sum of RPOs 684 and 579E equaled the hottest Corvette to date—and the first of many great 'glass-bodied two-seaters able to hit the track right off the truck.

Did it get any sexier in 1957 than a fuel-injected Bel Air convertible?

The author can personally attest to this topless fuelie's appeal—he drove the car.

pieces. Additionally, the cylinder blocks for these four-bolt engines were recast with extra iron in their three inner bulkheads to allow all those bolts to torque up tight.

Like the Z/28's 302, the new 350 V-8 relied on the 4.00-inch bore. And, introduced as it was for 1967, the 350 also was the first small block to use the beefier crank, with its enlarged journals created especially to deal with an increased stroke. Again, Cole hoped to avoid any more stroking to create the 350, but when he told his engineers to achieve that displacement by increasing only bore, they had to laugh. As MacPherson later jokingly recalled, the only layout possible under these parameters had the pistons overlapping. There simply was not enough space left between the cylinders to meet the boss's demands.

Thus, Chevy introduced another new stroke for the 350, this one measuring 3.48 inches. And to more confidently handle the extra piston travel inherent in a lengthened stroke, the 350 was treated as well to beefed-up connecting rods. These stronger rods, in turn, were heavier; this meant, among other things, that the reciprocating process would put more stress on the crank. That brings us back to those widened journals, without which the 350 would have never held together at high rpm. Extra counterweights were required to balance the new crank; the added material, working in concert with the heavier shaft's longer throws, meant that the 350's block had to be modified to allow the heftier crank ample room to rotate.

It was the mixing and matching of these various strokes and bores that led to those additional small-block varieties. The Z/28's 302 resulted in 1967 after a 283 crank was

stuffed into a 327 block. And when the 283 V-8 finally reached retirement that year, it was replaced in 1968 by the meat-and-potatoes 307, created by planting the new widened-journal 327 crank into the existing 283 block. In turn, the 350's 3.48-inch stroke did extra duty inside the 267- and 305-ci small blocks. Exclusive bores for these two measured 3.50 and 3.736 inches, respectively. Both bore and stroke (3.671 x 3.100) were exclusive in the weak-kneed (it produced 110 net-rated horsepower) 262 V-8's case, and the same also could be said about the 400.

No simple remix of existing parts could have produced this supremely sized small block, which displaced more cubes than many big blocks of the 1960s. Making the 350 had already maxed out the existing

Both the proven 265 and enlarged 283 small blocks were offered for 1957. Notice the familiar "ram's horns" exhaust manifolds—they were introduced along with the 283 that year.

Optional fuel injection showed up in 1957
in various Chevrolet models, including the
Nomad sport wagon.

Compared to today's electronic injection setups, Chevrolet's Rochester-produced Ramjet unit was simplistic, to say the least. But it represented cutting-edge technology back in 1957.

cylinder block's bores, and its stroke too was about as long as established design parameters permitted. But Ed Cole wanted this big small block, and he wanted it badly. Apparently his goal was to prove that his beloved V-8 could do any thing that Chevy's Mk. IV big block could do, including expand into the displacement stratosphere. Why else would he make such a difficult demand of his engineers?

Developing the 400 V-8 proved far tougher than all previous expansions put together. Reaching the desired displacement required a supposedly impossible 4.125-inch bore coupled with an unprecedented 3.75-inch stroke, and these two excessive dimensions weren't achieved without some radical reformations. A shorter rod with material removed from its big-end bolt bosses was used to allow that long, long stroke to do its reciprocating thing without conflicting with the camshaft. But far more work was involved recasting the block to make room for those wide, wide bores. Engineers completely did away with the typical water jacket spaces between cylinder barrels, creating what they called "Siamesed" cylinders—it was the only way to preserve cylinder wall thickness around those gaping 4.125-inch bores.

Making these major changes produced various downsides. For starters, those bores were widened without relocating cylinder head bolt positions, with some bolts remaining perilously close to cylinder walls. Torquing down those bolts actually warped nearby walls, resulting in excessive (and incurable) oil consumption as the piston rings lost contact with those slight bulges during their travel up and down the cylinders. A more serious problem involved the trimmed-down

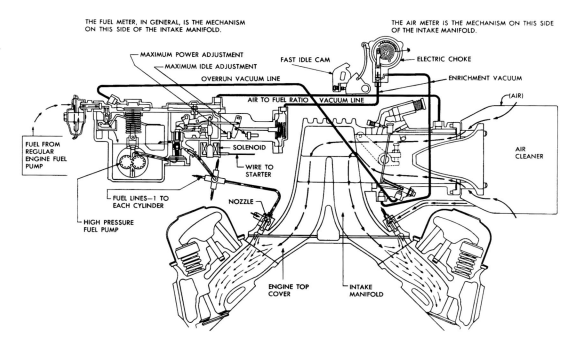

Zora Duntov proudly shows off the Corvette's new fuel-injected engine to *Mechanix Illustrated's* Tom McCahill in 1957.

Estimates claim that about 25
fuel-injected passenger car Chevrolets
were built for 1959.

rods, which predictably were weaker than the 350's. Even though the crankshaft was treated to even larger main bearing journals (now measuring 2.65 inches in diameter) and four-bolt bearing caps, engineers knew from the beginning that the 400 would never handle high-rpm use in high-performance applications.

Thus, when the 400 debuted for 1970, it was limited to "family car" and light truck installations. Specified further was an automatic transmission mating only—no way were engineers going to present buyers with an easy opportunity to overrev this engine in front of a manual gearbox. To say that horsepower hounds were disappointed was an understatement. Rumors of the 400's impending arrival had led many to believe that this would be the hottest small block yet. But perhaps *Car Craft* magazine said it best in 1970, when it called Chevrolet's new V-8 the "400-inch Bust."

Output for the four-barrel 400, RPO LF-6, in 1970 was a respectable 265 horsepower, but it was downhill from there. By 1973 the

net rating was 150 horses and wimpy two-bolt mains had replaced the preferred four-bolt caps. On the other hand, the 400 remained a major torque churn throughout its career—just what a customer needed to haul his or her four-door Caprice or Chevy pickup around. That career ended in 1980 on the truck side of the fence; Chevrolet had last built a 400-powered passenger car in 1976.

Fortunately, for every vanilla-flavored 400, there were more than enough spiced-up small blocks to go around during the Gen I V-8's long run. Dating back to 1957, the first 283 initially was upgraded to 270 horsepower with dual four-barrels, and that wasn't even the hottest package offered that year. Like Pontiac, Chevrolet introduced Americans to fuel injection in 1957, kicking off a legendary legacy that would enhance the Corvette's image up through 1965.

General Motors first began experimenting with fuel injection in the early 1950s, with engineer John Dolza doing the bulk of the work. Dolza's efforts were accelerated after Mercedes-Benz made Bosch fuel injection

ABOVE LEFT: Fuel injection was last offered as a passenger car option in 1959.

ABOVE RIGHT: Chevrolet's 1959 passenger car fuel-injected option received its own unique air induction ductwork. Two injected 283 V-8s were offered that year; one at 250 horsepower, the other at 290.

Improved heads helped boost the solid-lifter fuel-injected 283's output to 315 horsepower in 1961. The hydraulic cam version was rated at 275 horsepower. Notice the revised plenum with its smooth-textured top.

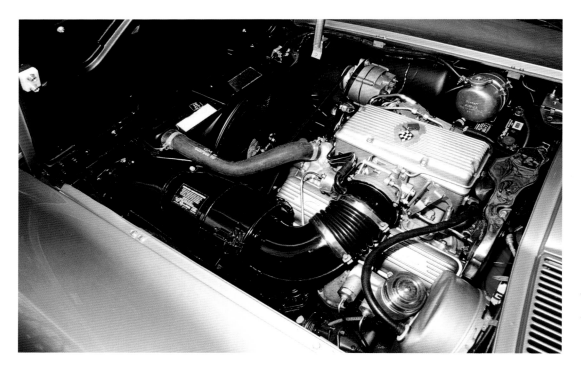

Output for the Corvette's fuel-injected V-8 hit 360 horsepower in 1962. This 360-horsepower 327 then carried over into 1963, taking on the new RPO code L84. Shown here is a 1963 Z06 Corvette's L84 small block.

standard on its stunning 300SL "gull-wing" coupe in 1954, and then Ed Cole put Zora Duntov on the project in 1955. A prototype injection installation was being tested on a Chevrolet V-8 by the end of that year. And not even a 1956 test track crash that put Zora in a body cast could keep him from finalizing the design, which was being readied almost right up to the date the new 1957 Corvettes were unveiled. Supplied by GM's Rochester Division, the resulting Ramjet fuel injection option was introduced for Chevy's two-seater and its passenger-car cousins that year. Its price in a Corvette was a hefty $484.

Ramjet injection featured a two-piece cast-aluminum manifold, with the valley cover section underneath incorporating "tuned" ram tubes running to the intake ports. The upper casting incorporated an intake plenum, and mounted on each side of this casting was air- and fuel-metering equipment. After gasoline was delivered to this equipment by a high-pressure fuel pump, it was precisely measured and injected continuously through eight injectors into the airflow just before it entered the cylinder heads. Thus Chevrolet's Ramjet setup was of continuous-injection design. Direct injection involved mounting the injectors inside the combustion chambers. Continuous injection didn't require nearly as much fuel delivery pressure as direct injection did.

The Rochester system delivered fuel more evenly in a much more efficient manner than dual four-barrel carburetors, and it did so instantly on demand, making unrivaled throttle response the "fuelie" Corvette's forte. According to *Road & Track*, "The fuel injection engine is an absolute jewel, quiet and remarkably docile when driven gently around town, yet instantly transformable into a roaring brute when pushed hard." The fuel injection equipment also eliminated flooding and fuel starvation common to the carburetors of the day whenever hard turns sent the gas supply in the bowl centrifuging off sideways away from the pickup.

On the downside, fuelies earned an early reputation for hard starts and finicky operation. Keeping everything in proper tune was a must, although that was difficult considering that so few local mechanics were qualified to tinker with an injected Corvette in 1957. Some frustrated owners even went so far as to replace the Ramjet system with conventional carburetors. Factory fixes and a little owner education soon helped rein in those gremlins.

Teething problems aside, the fuel-injected 283 V-8 helped put Corvette performance at the cutting edge in 1957. Two power levels were offered: 250 horsepower with hydraulic lifters or a healthy 283 horses with a solid-lifter cam. The latter package inspired promotional people's claims that the fuel injection small block was Detroit's first engine to reach the one-horsepower-per-cubic-inch plateau, this despite the fact that Chrysler had offered an optional 355-horsepower 354-ci hemi-head V-8 for its 300B in 1956. To this day history still commonly credits Chevrolet with this feat.

First or not, the "283/283" was certainly out in front on the street in 1957. *Road & Track* reported that a top-shelf injected Corvette could go from zero to 60 miles per hour in 5.7 seconds—a great number today, a simply stunning achievement back then. The car's quarter-mile time, at 14.3 seconds, was equally alarming. But the best was yet to come.

While the Ramjet option was last offered in Chevrolet passenger cars for 1959, it carried on proudly into the 1960s as the Corvette's supreme power source. After growing to 290 horses in 1958, top fuel-injected output hit 315 horsepower in 1961, followed by a jump to 360 horsepower when the 283 was traded for the 327 in 1962. In 1963, the injected 327 was given the RPO code L84, and L84 output next increased to 375 horses for 1964. The last fuel-injected Corvette was built in 1965—the same year the first big-block Sting Ray hit the streets. Priced a couple hundred dollars less than the last L84 small block, the 425-horse 396-ci Mk. IV V-8—fed by one large, less-complicated four-barrel carburetor—instantly made many fiberglass fans forget all about the fuelie.

1965 L79 V-8

CONSTRUCTION:
**cast-iron block
w/cast-iron cylinder heads**

DISPLACEMENT (CUBIC INCHES):
327

BORE & STROKE (INCHES):
4.00 x 3.25

LIFTERS:
hydraulic

COMPRESSION:
10.5:1

INDUCTION:
**single four-barrel
carburetor**

HORSEPOWER:
350 at 5,800 rpm

TORQUE:
360 at 3,600 rpm

L84 output peaked at 375 horsepower in 1964, and this same engine carried over into 1965. This 1965 fuelie Corvette also features power brakes and the rare electronic ignition option.

It was the development of bigger, better four-barrels during the early 1960s that also helped noninjected small blocks steal attention away from their Ramjet-equipped running mates, contributing as well to the latter's fall from grace. Still rated at 270 horsepower, the last dual four-barrel 283 was offered for 1961; in 1962 it was replaced by a 300-horsepower 327 topped by a single Carter AFB (aluminum four-barrel) carburetor. The 340-horse L76—basically an L84 with a Carter four-barrel in place of the Ramjet injection unit—appeared the following year, and this high-compression, solid-lifter small block was boosted up to a then-record (for carbureted small blocks) 365 horses in 1964. Along with being a relatively popular Corvette option, the L76 327 was briefly offered beneath Chevelle hoods that year; only a handful were built, however, before this clandestine combo was cancelled.

Much more successful in Chevelle ranks was the Corvette's L79 327, introduced for 1965. Essentially an L76 with a milder hydraulic cam in place of the 365-horsepower 327's cranky solid-lifter stick, the L79 produced its 350 maximum horsepower at a more usable 5,800 rpm, compared to the 6,200 revs required to bring on all 365 of the L76's horses. Without those clattering solid lifters, the L79 was quieter and idled much smoother than its L76 cousin and thus fit better in polite society. It also fit nicely between compact Nova SS fenders, where it became a supersweet option in 1966.

The hydraulic-cam L79 327 carried on as the Corvette's top small block choice after the solid-lifter L76 was cancelled along with the L84 in 1965. Even with the proliferation of Chevrolet's brutal big blocks, the L79

remained a strong-selling Sting Ray option up through 1968. It was replaced by the L46, simply a 350-cubic-inch translation. Still at 350 horsepower, the hydraulic-cam L46 was soon considered to be a poor man's version of yet another supreme small block, the LT-1, introduced for 1970.

This 370-horsepower 350 not only ranked as the new king of the carbureted mouse motors, it also represented the return of solid lifters to the Corvette small-block

Chevrolet built its last fuel-injected Corvette in 1965, the same year the big-block 396 was introduced. L84 Corvette production in 1965 was a mere 771.

What IF

Only a handful of 365-horsepower L76 Chevelles were built in 1964 before the option was unceremoniously cancelled. This example is a collector recreation; no restored models are known.

When Chevrolet General Manager Bunkie Knudsen introduced the Chevelle in August 1963, the car's hottest engine option was the 220-horse 283, a far cry from the 389-ci big-block Pontiac people were then planting between GTO fenders to create Detroit's first muscle car. No stranger to speed, Knudsen knew he had to keep up, even with his corporate cousins. But at the time, Chevrolet didn't have a suitable big block for its midsized A-body application; the venerable 409 was out of the question, and Chevy's then-mysterious "Mark motor" wouldn't debut until early 1965.

All that remained was Chevy's biggest small block. Accordingly, in December 1963, Knudsen's engineers announced that two 327s—the 250-horsepower L30 and 300-horsepower L74—would be available for the Chevelle. The L30's debut came in March 1964, the L74's three months later.

Also announced was the truly hot L76 327, the 365-horse Corvette V-8. An L76 Chevelle was first mentioned in assembly manuals in late January 1964 and at least one prototype was built—a roaring road rocket that apparently could hold its own with any muscle machine then running.

According to *Motor Trend* spies, "The 325-horsepower GTO and 365-horsepower Chevelle are very comparable in performance, giving 0–60 times of around six seconds flat. They're far and away the hottest of the new intermediates and quicker than most big cars with high-performance engines."

Full production of the 365-horse Chevelle, however, never got rolling. As *Motor Trend* again explained one month after first "scooping" the L76/A-body combo, "Don't hold your breath until you can buy a new Chevelle with a 365-horsepower engine. Chevrolet jumped the gun a little on the announcement of the '327' Corvette engine option for the Chevelle." Why? "They did this to counter big publicity for the GTO," added *Motor Trend*.

Why Chevrolet couldn't back up its premature promise involved various factors, not the least of which was a shortage of 327s that developed early in 1964 due to unexpected demand from full-sized Chevy buyers. "But the biggest problem," continued *Motor Trend's* report, "is that special exhaust manifolds are needed to clear the suspension in the Chevelle chassis. They're using the same manifolds from the 283 engine for the 250-horse '327' option, so you can order this one right away. But the 300- and 365-horsepower '327s' need bigger passages, and it's estimated that these manifolds won't be ready for assembly-line

The first official mention of L76 327 V-8 installations in midsized A-body chassis came in January 1964. The combo was then killed off in March.

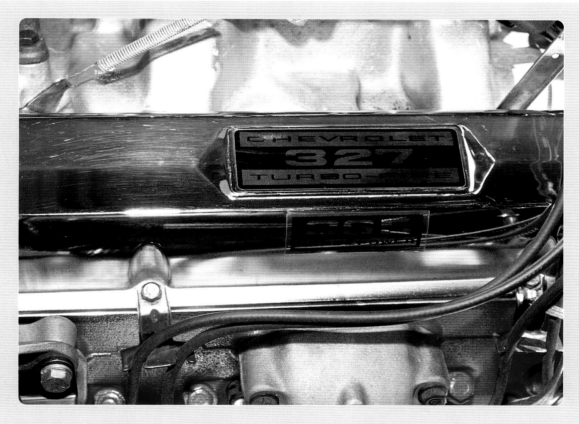

Basically a fuelie V-8 with a big four-barrel in place of the Ramjet injection unit, the L76 327 stood as the highest rated carbureted small block until the 370-horsepower LT-1 arrived in 1970.

to a product update memo (dated March 19) sent to Chevrolet dealers, the 365-horsepower Turbo Fire 327 had "been cancelled and will not be offered" to Chevelle customers for 1964. Nonetheless a few did escape into the wild. A couple tales of L76 Chevelle purchases have been heard. But, with an availability window of roughly two months, it's doubtful that these sales totaled more than a handful. Two, maybe three mysterious survivors are known today.

As for the fabulous 365-horsepower Super Sport shown here, it's actually a clone. Recognizing he'd probably never see the real thing, veteran Chevy restorer Scott Gaulter chose to recreate the little-known L76 Chevelle image himself as close as possible to original factory specs, right down to the K66 transistorized ignition—itself also a briefly listed Chevelle option for 1964. Unlike the Corvette small block, the K66 equipment did return to the Chevelle's RPO lineup in 1965.

A show-stopper from head to toe, Gaulter's 365-horse SS "reproduction"—Scott feels "clone" doesn't do the car justice—is an impressive representation of what might have been, had Chevrolet's Corvette-powered Chevelle not been stillborn.

installation until May." That delay helps explain why the 300-horse L74 Chevelle didn't show up until June, although engineers apparently gave up on the better-breathing manifold idea. None were ever cast for the L74 or L76.

As for the L76 Chevelle, it was killed off almost before it was born. According

Chevrolet's popular Impala SS could've been fitted with either six-cylinder or V-8 power in 1963. Six different V-8s were offered, beginning with the base 283 small block in this model. Two 327 small blocks and three 409 big blocks were optional.

lineup. And its debut instantly invited comparisons to previous mighty mice. According to *Car and Driver*, any other power source was "of little interest to the Corvette purist, the man who remembers the soul and vitality of the high-winding fuel-injected 283. Today's equivalent is the LT-1."

The LT-1 essentially was an enlarged version of another truly hot solid-lifter small block, although saying that begged the question of which came first, chicken or egg? As a June 1971 *Car and Driver* report explained it, the LT-1 "is probably even better known as the Z/28, which is what it is called when ordered in the Camaro. Corvette engineers originated the idea, so Duntov winces when you say the two engines are the same, but they are."

A second LT-1 350, this one rated at 360 horsepower, served as the heart and soul for the second-generation Z/28 Camaro, introduced early in 1970. As mentioned, previous Z/28s used the hellacious 290-horse 302 hybrid, which was the engine that laid the groundwork for the LT-1. Chevy small-block parts mixed and matched so easily, applying the proven Z/28 touch to the 350 V-8 in 1970 was as simple as turning a wrench—too bad there weren't enough parts to go around.

After serving two years beneath Camaro hoods, the 350 finally replaced the venerable 327 as the Corvette's standard power source in 1969, and RPO LT-1 was initially listed as an option that year. More than one press

The 1963 Impala Super Sport's base 283 V-8 relied on a two-barrel carburetor to help produce 195 horsepower. Compression was 9.5:1.

source also applauded its arrival. "If you're hung up on a Sting Ray and you want one that handles as well as it hauls, check out the new 370-horsepower LT-1 350-cuber, it's the only way to go," announced a headline in the May 1969 issue of *Cars* magazine. "Besides being a super-duty engine with high-rpm potential, it's also relatively light," continued the *Cars* review. "This factor, plus its high torque rating, makes for a dynamite handling and accelerating package."

Such announcements, however, proved premature, as the LT-1 never made it into a production Corvette in 1969. As a July 1969

Car Life report explained, "The factory listed the 370-horsepower 350-ci engine early in the model year, found they couldn't get all the pieces without depriving the Z/28 market, and cancelled. But before they did, the factory shop manuals came out. All the engine specifications were listed." It wasn't the first time a Corvette option was listed early on and then erased. And it wouldn't be the last time that the fiberglass faithful would be teased with a hot new engine only to see it yanked back out of their reach. But fortunately, in this case, the warmly welcomed LT-1 did debut the following year. Late was better than never.

continued on page 100

Boring and stroking the small block resulted in the 327 V-8, introduced in 1962. Shown here is the 1964 Corvette's 327, which was rated at 250 horsepower in standard form.

Small-block options were plentiful in A-body ranks during the 1960s. The 1965 El Camino up front features the hot 350-horsepower L79 327, while the 1965 Chevelle SS in back has the base 295-horsepower 283. A 220-horse 283, a 250-horse 327, and a 300-horse 327 also were available that year.

Super NOVA

This Nova SS is one of 5,481 Chevy II models built for 1966 with the 350-horsepower L79 V-8.

Image was initially the sole focus when Chevrolet bestowed Super Sport status upon its two-year-old Chevy II compact in 1963. Sure, that bucket seat interior was cool, as was the special trim inside and out. But from a performance perspective, there was nothing at all super about the first-edition Nova SS. Like all Novas that year, the Super Sport renditions were available with one power source only, the weak-kneed 120-horse 194-ci six.

Yet there was a way around this power shortage. Speed-conscious customers who noticed that the Chevy II engine bay had been designed all along to accept the ever-present Bowtie small block could have swapped in a 283 or 327 with relative ease. Or they could have paid their local dealer to install Chevrolet's own V-8 conversion kit, offered in 1963 for about $1,500, plus labor. Chevrolet did away with all the fuss and muss in 1964 when it finally listed an optional V-8 (the 195-horsepower 283) for its compact line.

Even more performance potential appeared in 1965 as two optional 327s, the 250-horsepower L30 and 300-horsepower L74, debuted in Chevy II ranks. The really big news the following year unveiled both a squeaky-clean restyle and another optional small block—the Corvette's L79 327.

Armed with 350 healthy horses, the L79 Nova SS instantly became one of Detroit's greatest "sleepers"—who could have guessed that such a polite-looking compact could get off the line in such a hurry? Rest to 60 miles per hour required

Only six L79 Novas were let loose in 1967 before the option was dropped from Chevrolet's compact ranks.

Chrome dress-up was included with the L79 327 V-8 beneath both Nova and Chevelle hoods.

only 7.2 seconds, according to a *Car Life* road test that also produced a 15.1-second quarter-mile. Breaking into the 14s was simply a matter of replacing those skinny standard treads with some real meat out back. Although the 350/327 installation mandated a switch from the Chevy II's typical 13x4 wheel to a 14x5 rim wearing 6.95-14 rubber, that upgrade still wasn't tough enough to suitably handle the L79's extra torque. Nor were the brakes—they were the same wimpy 9.5-inch

drums used on garden-variety four-cylinder Chevy II models in 1966.

But if stopping in a hurry wasn't among your worries, the L79 Nova represented just the ticket for the young, fearless set. At about $3,600, it was reasonably affordable. And its diminutive nature translated into notable nimbleness, while its hydraulically cammed heart was both nasty and nice.

"Unlike some samples from the supercar spectrum," concluded *Car Life's*

critics, the 350-horsepower Nova "maintains a gentleness along with its fierce performance potential; its power/weight ratio is second to none, and it is definitely better balanced than most."

Chevrolet sold 5,481 350-horse Chevy II/Nova models for 1966 before this killer combo was quietly cancelled early the following year. Reportedly, for 1967 a mere 6 of the L79 compacts were built.

The passenger car L79 327 became an
option for the Chevelle in 1965 and the
Chevy II/Nova in 1966. Chrome dress-up
for the valve covers and a dual-snorkel air
cleaner were standard.

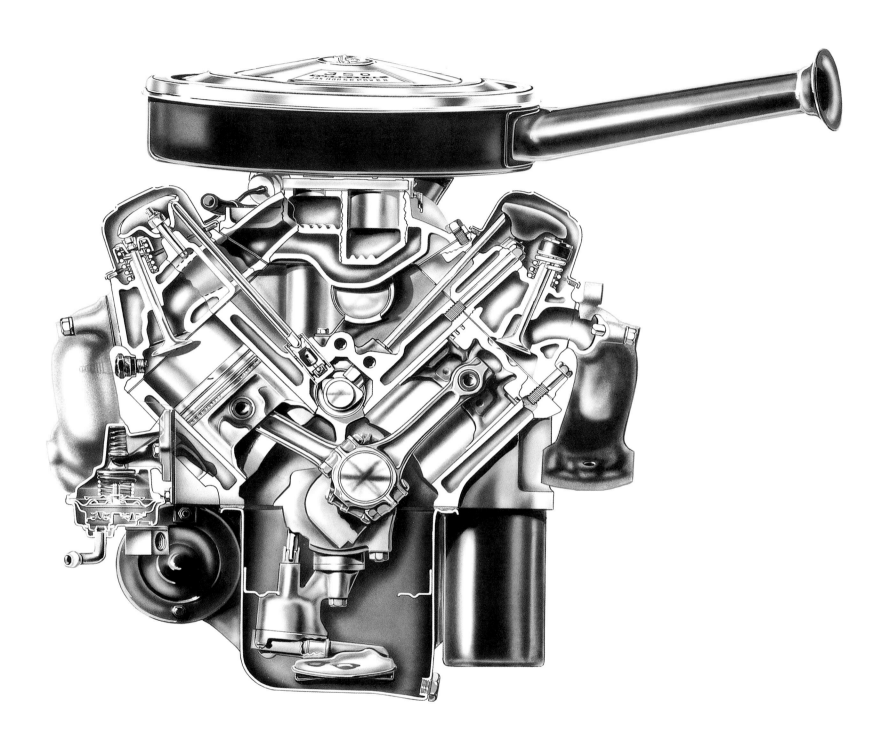

Stretching both bore and stroke to the limit resulted in the 350-cubic-inch small-block, introduced for 1967. Block modifications were required to make room for the new 3.48-inch stroke.

The solid-lifter L76 327 V-8 was introduced at 340 horsepower in 1963. Output then increased to 365 horsepower in 1964. The last L76 was offered in 1965.

IMPROVED 307-327-350 CU. IN. V-8 CYLINDER BLOCK

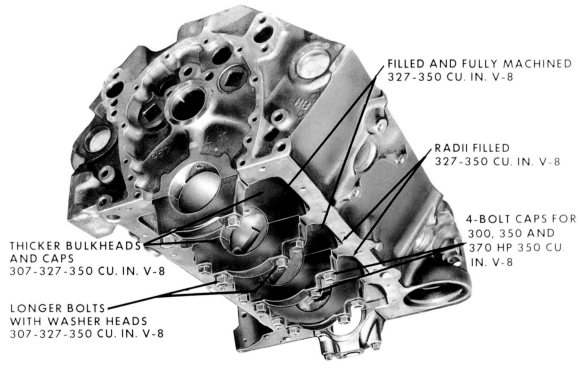

FILLED AND FULLY MACHINED
327-350 CU. IN. V-8

RADII FILLED
327-350 CU. IN. V-8

4-BOLT CAPS FOR
300, 350 AND
370 HP 350 CU.
IN. V-8

THICKER BULKHEADS
AND CAPS
307-327-350 CU. IN. V-8

LONGER BOLTS
WITH WASHER HEADS
307-327-350 CU. IN. V-8

Tougher four-bolt main bearing caps were among the various warmly welcomed improvements made to the small block's foundation during the late 1960s.

Chevrolet finally discontinued the 283 at the end of the 1967 model year. In its place for 1968 came the 307 V-8, created by inserting the 327 crankshaft into a 283 cylinder block.

This cutaway of the 400-cubic-inch small block reveals the Siamesed cylinder layout required to overbore the block to 4.125 inches.

continued from page 92

Included in the 1970 Corvette's LT-1 package were the big-valve cylinder heads that had been staples around Chevy's top-performance small-block parts bin dating back to the fuelie's days. Intake valves were 2.02-inchers, and exhausts measured 1.60 inches in diameter. These hot heads were also machined for screw-in rocker studs, and they used hardened-steel pushrod guide plates. Pushing those rods was an aggressive mechanical cam that dialed in at 317 degrees duration on the intake side, 346 for the exhaust, with 96 degrees of overlap. Valve lift was 0.459 inches intake, 0.485 exhaust.

Four-bolt main bearing caps held a forged crank in place at the block's bottom end. Connecting rods were also forged, as were the aluminum TRW pistons. An aluminum high-rise dual-plane intake went on top, crowned by a massive model 4150 Holley four-barrel rated at 800 cfm. LT-1 Corvettes delivered in California used a slightly different 4150 Holley (the front fuel bowl was vented) to work with the Evaporative Emission Control (EEC) equipment required by that state's clean air cops. At the other end of the process were the big block's 2.5-inch exhaust pipes in place of the 2-inch tubes normally found behind other 350 small blocks. Ignition was Delco transistorized.

There were a few downsides to the LT-1 deal, though real men probably couldn't have cared less. "Chevrolet is telling you something," explained a *Car Life* road test of the 370-horsepower Corvette. "You cannot get an automatic transmission, air conditioning,

1970 LT-1 V-8

CONSTRUCTION:
cast-iron block w/cast-iron cylinder heads incorporating screwed-in rocker studs and pushrod guide plates

DISPLACEMENT (CUBIC INCHES):
350

BORE & STROKE (INCHES):
4.00 x 3.48

LIFTERS:
solid

COMPRESSION:
11:1

INDUCTION:
single

HORSEPOWER:
370 at 6,000 rpm

TORQUE:
380 at 3,200 rpm

or power-assisted steering with the LT-1. It's hard to find mechanical reason for all of these exclusions. The same engine comes with an automatic in the Z/28, and the bigger Corvettes turn 6,500 rpm and come with the Corvette-only power steering. Our suspicion is that the keen types at Chevrolet just don't want to waste all their engine and chassis work on somebody who drives with his fingerprints."

Whatever the rationale, leaving off the air conditioning compressor was the only thing to do, considering all the cooling problems that had been inherent to the third-generation Corvette since its debut in 1968. Compounding that natural fact was the LT-1

V-8's own hot-blooded temperament, something any high-compression engine could demonstrate with little prodding back in the 1960s and 1970s. Keeping that blood from boiling was tough enough without a compressor pulley to crank, so why push its luck? As for the banned automatic, weren't sports cars supposed to have a stick?

Unfortunately, the LT-1 was introduced just as the great American muscle car's days were coming to a close. Tightening emissions controls, growing safety concerns, soaring insurance costs, and rising fuel prices all helped bring about this end. The first sign of impending doom came in 1971 when compression levels were cut drastically across

At 370 horsepower, the 1970 Corvette's LT-1 350 V-8 replaced the L76 as Chevrolet's most powerful non-injected small block.

Two-Horse RACE

Ford's pony car progenitor galloped about unchallenged for nearly three years before General Motors finally made it a multi-horse race. Both Pontiac's Firebird and Chevrolet's Camaro debuted for 1967, this after following two widely different development paths.

SS equipment included a special hood with simulated vents, wide oval rubber on widened wheels, and the ever-popular F41 heavy-duty suspension group.

Camaro roots can be traced back to the summer of 1964, when Chevrolet's F-car project, code-named XP-836, was born. With Dearborn's new Mustang then wowing the world, Henry Haga's styling studio wasted little time doling out a full-sized clay model that compared quite favorably to Ford's 1965 Mustang, a fact proven side-by-side in a GM factory photo from December 1964. Known as the Panther to insiders, the F-body proto-type evolved into a production reality that was officially unveiled to the press on September 12, 1966. In the words of Chevrolet General Manager Elliot "Pete" Estes, the '67 Camaro—offered in hard-top and convertible forms—was a "four-passenger package of excitement."

Like the Mustang, the new Camaro featured unit-body construction (with a

The SS-350 Camaro was initially the hottest pony car offered by Chevrolet in 1967, but it was quickly overshadowed a few months into that year's production run by the big-block SS 396 model.

front subframe) beneath an uncluttered, attractive shell laid out in the now-familiar long-hood, short-deck format. Comparable as well was the standard six-cylinder power, joined by a collection of optional V-8s that began with the tried-and-true 327. Then, in November 1966, the small-block Camaro was overshad-owed by the SS 396 rendition, a big-block

Chevrolet's 295-horsepower 350 small block was exclusive to the SS model in Camaro ranks in 1967. One could not be ordered without the other.

bully that acted more like a Clydesdale than a pony. But in between was another Super Sport model that bridged the gap between the 327-powered Camaro and its SS 396 alter ego.

Called the SS 350, this Super Sport Camaro, like base models, was available with or without a top. Standard SS equipment in 1967 included a special hood with simulated vents, red-stripe wide-oval tires on wider 14x6JK wheels, and Chevy's renowned F41 heavy-duty suspension. Additional dress-up touches consisted of a color-keyed (black or white) accent stripe around the nose and

familiar SS identification on the grille, fenders, steering wheel, and fuel filler cap.

Only up front did the badge actually read "SS 350," this in honor of the Super Sport Camaro's exclusive small block. One couldn't be had without the other; thus the whole package was listed under RPO L48, identified as the "Camaro SS w/295-horsepower Turbo-Fire 350-ci engine." With its hydraulic cam, the L48 350 was better suited for civilized operation than the Camaro's super-duper big block, yet at the same time it was no mild-mannered machine. As *Hot Rod*

magazine's Eric Dahlquist explained, "The new extension of the mighty-mite 265 will pull Chevrolet's fat out of the fire, if indeed it ever fell in." Mildly tweaked, the SS 350 Camaro that Dahlquist tested managed an impressive 14.85-second quarter-mile pass, topping out at 95.65 miles per hour.

Throw in another snazzy option, the Rally Sport group (available on any model Camaro in 1967), and a Chevrolet customer instantly had his Mustang-owning neighbor turning green with envy. A purely cosmetic package, the RS option (RPO Z22) among other things added hideaway headlights and various pieces of exclusive trim. Appropriate badges were included, too, though these were superseded whenever RPO Z22 was ordered for an SS 396 or SS 350 Camaro—"SS" took precedence over "RS."

Fully loaded with both pizzazz and performance, a Camaro SS RS convertible easily outshone its established rival from Ford in 1967. Was there a better way to see the U.S.A.?

Introduced midyear for 1970 (thus the "1970-1/2" tag), the next-generation Z/28 Camaro was called a poor man's Corvette by some critics, and why not? Both cars shared the LT-1 small block.

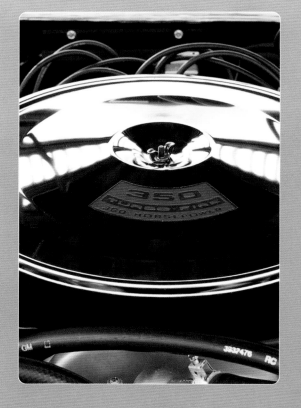

The LT-1 350 produced 360 horsepower beneath a 1970-1/2 Z/28 Camaro's hood.

the board in Detroit. The LT-1 was no exception—its sky-high 11:1 squeeze fell to 9:1 that year. Output dropped to 330 horsepower in 1971, and it shrank again, to 255 horsepower, when gross output numbers were replaced by net figures in 1972, the last year for the LT-1.

At least LT-1 buyers were treated to one last surprise just before the car's demise. In July 1971, a build order was issued for an "air conditioning and engine cooling development vehicle" to test whether or not an A/C compressor could peacefully coexist with the solid-lifter small block. This car was built in September and delivered to the Engineering Center in Warren, Michigan, "to be used for experimental purposes and/or industrial processing." From there it went to GM's Mesa Proving Grounds in Arizona for some serious testing under the sun.

With its relatively tame 9:1 compression, the 1972 LT-1 was not nearly the same hothead it had been in 1970. Basically all engineers did was add deep-groove pulleys to resist throwing the accessory drive belt at high rpm. The typical LT-1 tach, with its 6,500-rpm redline, was also deep-sixed in favor of a rev counter redlined at 5,600 rpm to remind drivers that they needed to keep cool on the throttle to stay cool behind the wheel.

Following the LT-1's retirement, standard Corvette power quickly sank to all-time lows: 190 horsepower for the base 350 in 1973 and a mere 165 horses in 1975. Mind you, these were net ratings, but they still represented a major downturn compared to 1972's 200 SAE net standard horses.

The LT-1's failure to return for 1973 meant the end of the road for solid lifters,

those noisy, rev-sensitive mechanical tappets that for more than 15 years had reminded Corvette drivers that the engine beneath that fiberglass hood did indeed mean business. "At first it seems unthinkable," began *Car and Driver's* December 1972 obit. "High-winding engines and valvetrain clatter have been Corvette trademarks since 1956. To the enthusiast, it was those solid lifters that separated the Corvette engines from their weaker passenger car siblings. And now, with the passing of the LT-1, it is reasonable to say that The Corvette Engine no longer exists."

Yet even without the LT-1 around, Corvette buyers still had three V-8s to choose from in 1973, as in 1972. Joining the base 350 and the optional LS4 454 big block was a new

1970 LF6 V-8

CONSTRUCTION:
cast-iron block w/cast-iron cylinder heads; Siamesed cylinders within block

DISPLACEMENT (CUBIC INCHES):
400

BORE & STROKE (INCHES):
4.125 x 3.75

LIFTERS:
hydraulic

COMPRESSION:
9:1

INDUCTION:
single four-barrel carburetor

HORSEPOWER:
265 at 4,400 rpm

TORQUE:
400 at 2,400 rpm

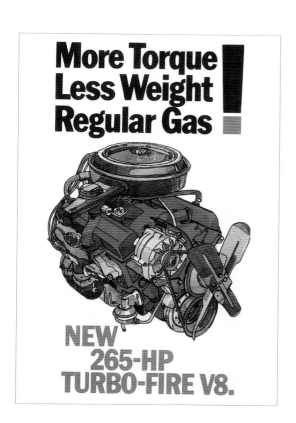

With compression down to appease
the clean air cops, the 1972 LT-1
V-8 was able to share under hood space
with an air conditioning compressor
without overheating.

RPO code—L82. Though it filled in the space left behind by the LT-1, the L82 small block was actually a descendant of the hydraulic-lifter L46. Featuring 9:1 compression, big-valve heads, and a relatively aggressive cam, the L82 350 produced 250 horses, which still stood tall despite *Car and Driver's* claim that Corvette-style performance had blacked out. L82 compression never slipped during the 1973 to 1977 run, and in fact it topped all Corvette engines built in those years. L82 output in 1974 was again 250 horses. But power dropped to 205 horsepower in 1975 and then leveled out at 210 net horses in 1976 and 1977. The reason for that drop was no mystery.

The compression cuts made in 1971 represented a first step toward the federally mandated use of lower-octane unleaded gasoline, which reportedly ran cleaner than the tetraethyl lead-laced jet fuels previously used to keep high-compression Corvette engines alive and well. But the real reason behind the 1971 introduction of low-lead fuels involved a preparation for the next wave of Washington-ordered clear-air requirements, scheduled for 1975. In order to comply with these more stringent emission-control standards, Detroit engineers concocted the contaminant-burning catalytic converter, which didn't mix at all with leaded gasoline. Thus began ethyl's swan song.

Chevrolet offered its last LT-1 Corvette in 1972. This 1972 LT-1 served duty as a test mule for the installation

of optional air conditioning, which couldn't be ordered with the solid-lifter

small block in 1970 and 1971.

Mighty MOUSE

A four-speed stick was the only choice behind the LT-1 during its three-year run as a Corvette option.

Built from 1970 to 1972, Chevrolet's original LT1 Corvette probably came the closest to garnering real world-class respect prior to the ZR-1's arrival in 1990. In 1970, *Car Life's* critics called it "the best of all possible Corvettes." Earlier that year, *Motor Trend's* Chuck Koch concluded that the LT1 was "much closer to its German competitor than most Porsche owners care to admit."

The LT1 earned this praise by combining ratlike muscle with the nimbleness inherent in mouse-motor Corvettes. Weighing about 150 pounds less than Chevy's Mk.IV big block, the 350-ci small block didn't compromise handling the way the hot, hefty 427 did. Nose-heavy big-block Corvettes could eat up a straight line but were no match for their better-balanced brethren in the twisties. With its 370 rip-snortin' horses, the nimble, nasty LT1 Corvette could do both. According to *Sports Car Graphic's* Paul Van Valkenburgh, rest to 60 miles per hour required only 6.7 seconds, and the quarter-mile pass went by in 14.17 clicks. As for the road-handling side of the coin, Koch came away floored after comparing the LT1 to a Porsche 911E: "The Corvette was just as fast as the Porsche through the corners, if not faster."

Ordering the $447.60 LT1 option in 1970 added, of course, a stiffer suspension along with the muscled-up mouse. Not included—no way, no how—were air conditioning or an automatic trans. Offered behind the 370-horsepower 350 was either a wide-ratio or close-ratio four-speed. And for those with fatter wallets, there was an even meaner version of the LT1 Corvette, the race-ready ZR-1.

With its 370 healthy horses, the 1970 LT-1 Corvette combined big-block muscle with small-block nimbleness.

It was no coincidence that David Hill's gang later revived this moniker for its legendary killer Corvette in 1990. In 1970, the first-edition ZR-1 stood as one of the best 'Vettes yet up to that point. Yet, unlike its 1990s counterpart, the original ZR-1 Corvette attracted little fanfare. This too wasn't coincidental—Chevy people in no way wanted to draw undue attention to what was basically a racing machine let loose on the streets. Nor did they care about promotion; they knew only a select few buyers would dare try this baby out, and even fewer would be able to afford the ZR-1 option's $965.95 asking price. It was no mystery that only 25 LT1/ZR-1 Corvettes were sold in 1970.

Along with the 370-horsepower LT1 small block, the ZR-1 package added transistorized ignition, an aluminum radiator, heavy-duty power brakes, a truly stiff suspension (with nearly doubled spring rates), and Chevrolet's gnarly M22 "rock crusher" four-speed. The ZR-1 option was available each year the LT1 was. News in 1971 included introduction of a big-block running mate, the ZR-2, which was matched up with the LS-6 454 V-8. The 12 LS6/ZR-2 Corvettes built that year were joined by only 8 LT1/ZR-1s. ZR-1 production for 1972 then "soared" to 20.

"Standard" LT1 Corvette production was 1,287 in 1970, 1,949 in 1971, and 1,741 in 1972. Of that 1972 tally, as many as 240 were equipped with optional air conditioning as a final consolation to customers who loved cool cars. Although some magazines spoke too soon concerning the arrival of a fourth LT1 in 1973, anyone with eyes could've recognized that the days of solid lifters and huge Holley four-barrels were over.

Understanding why the 454 big block was cancelled in 1974 is equally simple. The Corvette's first catalytic converters came in 1975 to further help choke off high performance. Chevrolet's initial "cat" system featured a single large-capacity converter; a design featuring two smaller units failed durability tests. Two Y-pipes were used to at least preserve the appearance of sporty dual exhausts. The first one funneled exhaust flow from both cylinder banks together into one tube to enter the converter. From there, a reversed Y-pipe did the opposite in back to deliver the cleansed spent gases to twin mufflers. True dual exhausts wouldn't make a comeback until the LT5-powered ZR-1 debuted for 1990. Standard Corvettes were finally refitted with real duals as part of

the second-generation LT1 upgrade made for 1992.

The restrictive single exhaust setup severely crimped power in 1975, explaining the base 350's abysmal 165-horsepower rating and the L82's corresponding output drop. Fortunately some extra tinkering brought both these ratings back up—180 horses for the former, the aforementioned 210 for the latter—for 1976 and 1977. And with the 454 in the archives, the Corvette was left with the standard 350 and the optional L82 in 1975—the first time in 20 years that only two power sources were offered.

For some Americans there was only one choice in 1976 and 1977; the L82 was not offered during those years for Corvettes sold in California, because the optional performance V-8 did not meet that state's tougher emissions standards. Four-speed transmissions were also "banned" out west for those years, meaning the only combo a Californian could buy was the 180-horsepower 350 backed by the Turbo Hydra-Matic automatic.

Fortunately the L82 was still around as the Corvette celebrated its 25th birthday in 1978. Output that year actually increased from 210 horsepower to 220, thanks to the addition of a less-restrictive exhaust system and a dual-snorkel air induction setup that improved breathing on the top end. Engineers were just then figuring out how to reverse the downward performance spiral created by ever-tightening emissions standards and demands for better fuel economy. Results of this roller coaster ride up a new learning curve even included a power boost for the standard L48 350, which went from 180 horsepower in 1977 to 185 in 1978.

1979 L82 V-8

CONSTRUCTION:
**cast-iron block
w/cast-iron cylinder heads**

DISPLACEMENT (CUBIC INCHES):
350

BORE & STROKE (INCHES):
4.00 x 3.48

LIFTERS:
hydraulic

COMPRESSION:
8.9:1

INDUCTION:
**single four-barrel
carburetor**

HORSEPOWER:
225 at 5,200 rpm

TORQUE:
270 at 3,600 rpm

L48s sold in California and high altitudes that year were rated at 175 horses.

L48 or L82, the quarter-century-old Corvette remained the country's top performance automobile, or so said *Car and Driver* in a turnabout of opinion late in 1977. "After a number of recent Corvette editions that prompted us to mourn the steady decline of both perform-ance and quality in this once-proud marque, we can happily report the 25th exam-ple of the Corvette is much improved across the board. Not only will it run faster now—the L82 version with four-speed is certainly the fastest American production car, while the base L48 automatic is no slouch—but the general drivability and road manners are of a high order as well."

Additional tweaking increased L82 output to 225 horsepower in 1979. The L48 that year received the L82's dual-snorkel induc-tion equipment and open-flow mufflers, which helped up its output ante to 195 horses. Although the L82 received another boost to 230 horsepower in 1980, it was the end of the line for the C3 Corvette's last optional "hi-perf" V-8. After the L82 option was cancelled, Corvette buyers in 1981 were left with one and only power choice, a 190-horsepower 350.

Similar power outages occurred in the Camaro lineup during the late 1970s, and

Chevrolet officials even temporarily shelved the Z/28 after 1974 to avoid any further fuss with federal smog standards. When the Z28 then surprisingly returned midyear in 1977, it was promoted more as a great all-around performer as opposed to a tire-melting road rocket. Standard power came from a 185-horsepower 350, which dipped to 175 horses in 1979.

Chevrolet's two top performers, the Z28 and Corvette, were somehow still around as the 1970s wound down, and they would continue rolling on into the next new decade. But things then looked bleak from the small block's perspective, as far as making muscle was concerned. Luckily, engineers would find a way to work the mouse motor back into shape soon enough.

After being cancelled in 1974, the Camaro Z/28 made a triumphant return midyear in 1977. With small-block power on the wane, more emphasis was put into making the 1977-1/2 Z/28 handle like a champ.

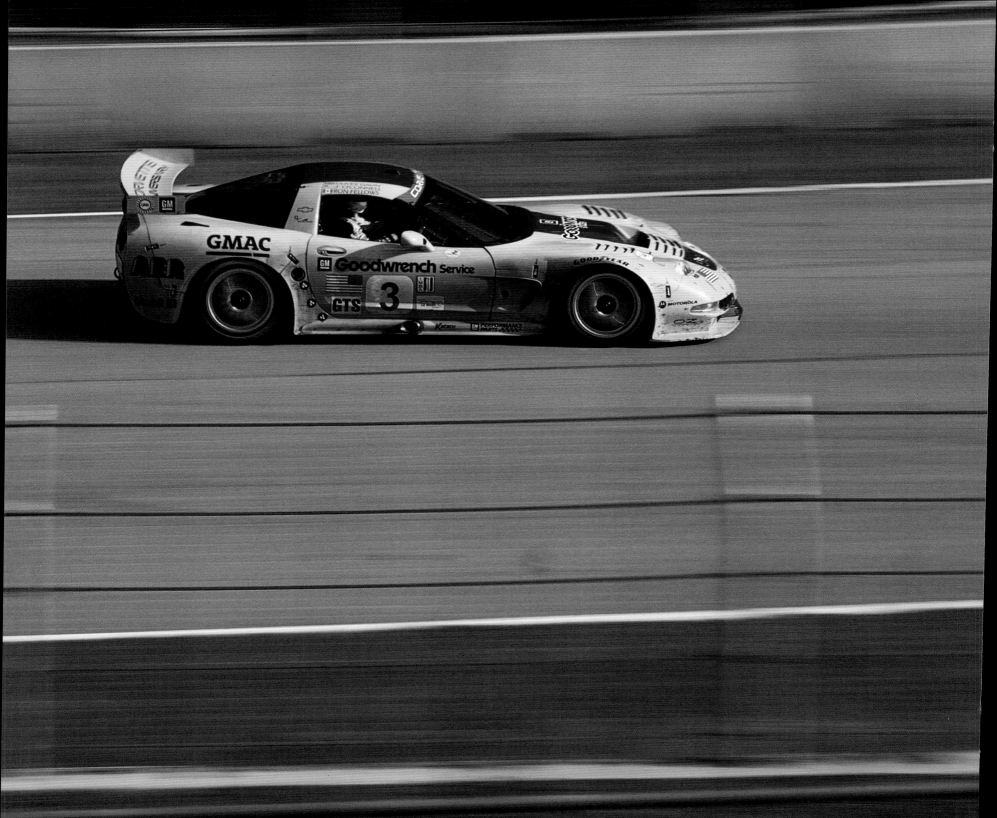

Chapter 3

COMPETITIVE NATURE:
Racing Chevy's Small Block

Introduced in 1999, the brutal C5-R is the latest in a long line of racing Corvettes and has dominated IMSA's American Le Mans Series. Here a C5-R tours Road Atlanta on the way to the 2002 ALMS title.

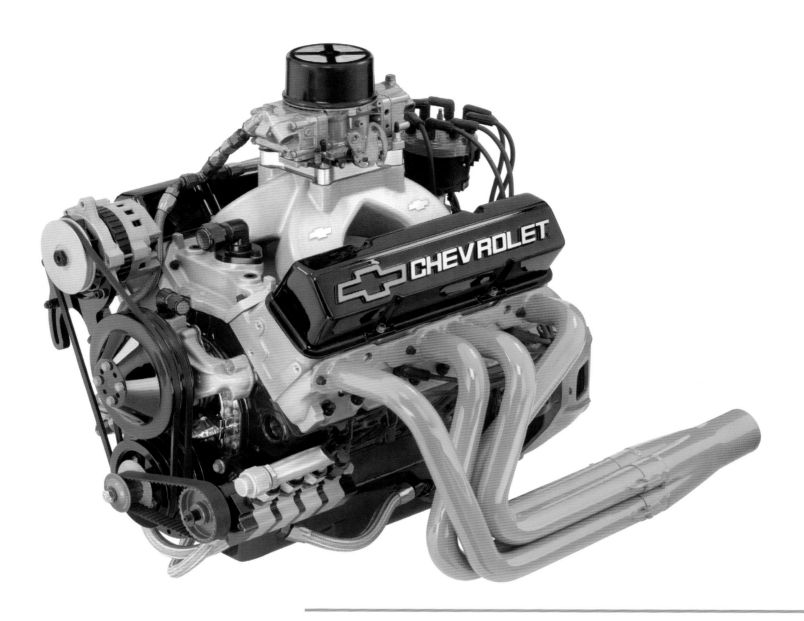

Chevrolet's small-block V-8 easily ranks as the most successful production-based competition engine ever built. This is the NASCAR-targeted SB2 engine, first seen in 1998.

THEY DIDN'T CALL IT THE HOT ONE FOR NOTHING. Who cared that Detroit's horsepower race was already heating up well before the small-block V-8 debuted in 1955? This truly was one for the weatherman's record books. Just a year before, Chevy's yeoman Stovebolt six had been quietly rolling along doing its sales-leading thing with the utmost pragmatism. Then, bam! Along comes this blood-warming '55 model with its beautiful body and so much sizzling power—all at a price so low

that Average Joe and friends couldn't help but flock down to their local Chevy store for a look, or maybe even a buy or two. And just when Joe thought it was safe to go back into his friendly neighborhood showroom, wham! The attraction grew even hotter for 1956.

Dual four-barrel carbs and 225 horses in a Chevy—were they kidding? Not at all; nor were those promo guys just blowing smoke. Numbers alone could've told the tale, but *Mechanix Illustrated*'s Tom McCahill just had to throw in a few extra words for good measure after road testing the 225-horsepower

The 2002 C5-R was powered by an LS1 that was bored and stroked to almost 7.0 liters. Output was more than 600 horsepower.

V-8. "Zero to 30 averages 3.2 seconds, 0–60 in 8.9 seconds, and in 12 seconds, you're doing 70," he began. "This is just about May, June, and July faster than the Chevrolets of just two or three years ago." He wasn't joking either. Nor was he simply tossing raves about when he concluded that the Chevy small block "might very well be rated the greatest competition engine ever built." What a prophet.

And to think that the 225-horsepower 265 wasn't even the hottest mouse-motor offered that year. On the Corvette side of the fence, Zora Arkus-Duntov and his friends were busy transforming Chevrolet's disappointing two-seater into a dashing

dream machine, and that dual-carb V-8 was just a start. Appropriately nicknamed for its creator, the legendary "Duntov cam" also debuted in 1956, although few mild-mannered customers noticed. Listed under RPO 449, this solid-lifter bump stick reportedly boosted unofficial output to 240 horses. Why unofficial? Because Chevrolet paperwork never posted an advertised number—Ed Cole's guys didn't want just anybody lining up to buy this bit of hot hardware. What those papers did mention was that this "Special High-Lift Camshaft" option was recommended "for racing purposes only."

Whatta ya know? A firm named after a famous race driver actively supplying racers

with the right parts to go racing? Brickyard veteran Louis Chevrolet surely would've been proud, had he not turned his back on the firm bearing his moniker in September 1913. He had wanted to build fine, fast automobiles, but company founder Billy Durant knew that competing directly with Henry Ford with cheap, practical transports represented the only way to fly. Durant won out and Chevrolet walked, leaving his contractually bound surname behind. The rest is automotive history.

Chevrolet sure sold a lot of cars (and trucks) during the decades that followed, so there wasn't much need to use racing as a promotional tool, not like a young Henry Ford had done while founding his own business around the turn of the century. Who in their right mind, prior to the 1950s, could have imagined the old, reliable Bowtie brand actively backing racers all the way from factory to track?

That all changed with The Hot One's arrival. Suddenly car buyers were able to associate the Chevrolet name with real factory-supplied power and speed. And there were no reasons why Chevy officials shouldn't take full advantage of all that performance potential to build a winning reputation, which in turn would help move even more cars (and, hopefully, trucks) off dealers' lots. Race on Sunday; sell on Monday—what a concept.

Today that concept is surely embraced as much by Chevrolet as by any other American make. You name the competition venue, and the Bowtie boys are present and accounted for—Monte Carlo coupes in NASCAR's Nextel Cup Chase; pickups in NASCAR's Craftsman Truck league; C5-R Corvettes in IMSA's American Le Mans Series; Chevrolet's high-

tech Indy V-8 on the IRL's IndyCar circuit; big-block-powered Cavaliers in NHRA Pro Stock drag racing. Currently Chevrolet is the only manufacturer actively involved annually in the "Triple Crown" of international motor sports: the 24 Hours of Le Mans, the Daytona 500, and the Indianapolis 500, all this clearly demonstrating just how important on-track activities are to General Motors' entry-level division.

"Racing is an integral part of Chevrolet's brand promise that says 'We'll be there,'" explained General Manager Brent Dewar in 2004. "It's a promise from Chevrolet to its owners—past, present, and future—to provide some of the most spirited, most dependable products on the road." Winning, too, is an integral part. No other Detroit firm can come close to the number of NASCAR, NHRA, road racing, and off-road championships racked up by Chevy over the years.

Yet trophies aren't the only things Chevrolet people take home after a race; lessons learned are valued every bit as much, if not more. "There is a two-way exchange of both technology and knowledge between motor sports and mainstream vehicles at Chevrolet," began a 2004 media report on the present state of GM racing affairs. "Engineering advances developed in racing have practical benefits for Chevrolet's road-going vehicles. The aerodynamic profile of the Monte Carlo coupe is an example of the interaction between racing and production. The production Monte Carlo's front brake cooling ducts were inspired by a similar design on NASCAR race cars. Racing does indeed improve the Chevrolet breed."

And doing the bulk of that racing for 50 years now has been the ever-improving small-

continues on page 121

Daytona Beach speed freak Smokey Yunick was the key to Chevrolet's early on-track efforts. His engines powered Chevy's first NASCAR winners and the Corvettes that made headlines at Daytona and Sebring in 1956 and 1957.

Factory BACKED

Estimates claim about a dozen or so "Black Widow" Chevys were created to roll right onto NASCAR tracks. Race-ready modifications included beefed suspension parts and heavy-duty truck rims.

Full-fledged factory involvement in sanctioned racing is taken for granted today, and has been for decades. But family ties between production line and finish line were clandestinely flimsy when Chevrolet's Black Widows appeared late in 1956. Known back then more simply (and understandably) as Black & Whites, the two-tone race-ready machines represented

Chevrolet's first really big factory-backed push into Bill France's NASCAR circuit, which at the time was still welcoming truly "stock" cars.

Indeed, much of a Black Widow's makeup was true-blue Bowtie, right down to the door handles, bench seat, and windshield wipers. The sinister stockers began life, in most cases, as bare-bones 150-series utility sedans (some

convertibles were built for NASCAR's drop top division) with pieces of plywood planted in place of their back seats. Between those black fenders up front was Chevrolet's new 283-horsepower fuelie V-8 or its 270-horsepower dual-carburetor cousin. Before being shipped from Detroit to SEDCO's shop in the Atlanta area, a basic Black Widow was stripped of any and all unnecessary equipment like hubcaps, spare tire, and so on.

At SEDCO, these '57 Chevys were modified for NASCAR competition with special emphasis on beefing up areas that had proven prone to failure on nearly all early stock cars. Keeping wheels rolling represented one of the biggest problems during NASCAR's formative years, as steering gears, spindles, bearings, and even the stock steel rims themselves regularly self-destructed, sometimes with spectacular end-over-end results. One of the most important modifications made at SEDCO involved fabricating stronger, longer spindles using truck pieces in place of the weaker passenger-car parts. The rear axle was a half-ton pickup piece, as were the heavy-duty six-lug wheels.

Additional beefs included tubular crossmembers added between the front frame horns and behind the rear axle.

Either Chevrolet's 270-horsepower dual-carb 283 or the new fuel-injected small block were installed in the Black Widows. Notice the special induction equipment added to this Black Widow's fuelie V-8.

Look, ma—no back seat. Various non-essentials were left off the Black Widow cars before being shipped to Atlanta for modification.

Lower A-arms in front were boxed, stiff stabilizer bars went on at both ends, a transverse track rod was added to the axle, and dual shock absorbers were bolted on at all four corners. Reinforced motor mounts held the 283 small block in place and brakes were gnarly cerametallix units, the same type used on the competition Corvettes that ran at Sebring and Daytona in 1956 and 1957.

SEDCO began building Black Widows in September 1956, but rolled out only a few before complications closed things down. First, NASCAR banned superchargers, fuel injection, and multiple carburetors in April 1957. That was followed by the infamous AMA ban on factory racing involvement two months later and SEDCO's eventual shutdown in August. A best guess for total Black Widow production comes in at about a dozen, including six or seven convertibles and two station wagon tow cars—the latter pair apparently created to convince NASCAR rules moguls that the Black Widow conversion was indeed a factory option from Chevrolet.

Though Chevy would continue to support certain racers—much more secretively, of course—after 1957, the days of such plain-as-day backing in black and white were over just like that. Over, that is, until racing stopped being a dirty word around GM.

Both racing's famous Unser family and Chevrolet's small-block V-8 were regular winners at Colorado's annual Pikes Peak Hillclimb during the 1950s and 1960s. Indy veteran Bobby Unser and his Chevy-powered Sproul Homes Special set a new "Race to the Clouds" record of 12 minutes, 30.6 seconds in 1963. It was Unser's seventh Pikes Peak victory, then second only to uncle Louis Unser's nine titles. PIKES PEAK AUTO HILL CLIMB EDUCATIONAL MUSEUM COLLECTION

continued from page 116

block V-8. Apparently Tom McCahill did know whence he spoke in 1956—Chevy's mighty mouse now stands tall as the most successful production-based competition engine ever built, having powered more race-winning cars and collected more championships than any rival-built mill. Along with NASCAR and NHRA, racing circuits conquered by the small block during the last half-century have included SCCA Trans-Am, Can-Am, Formula 5000, USAC (sprint car and hillclimb), World of Outlaws (more sprints), SCORE (off-road), and even APBA offshore boat racing.

All told, though, it has been in NASCAR that the small block has made the most hay, and that's also where it got its start in sanctioned racing. A V-8 Chevy first won a NASCAR race at Columbia, South Carolina, in March 1955. But far more historic was the victory scored that September by Herb Thomas at the prestigious Southern 500 in Darlington, South Carolina, before a sell-out crowd of 50,000. The Chevy that Thomas drove that day had been prepared by noted speed freak Henry Yunick at his "Best Damn Garage In Town" in Daytona Beach, Florida.

Yunick, better known as "Smokey," was enlisted by Ed Cole that summer to make

They weren't part of the small-block family, but these mighty mites still deserve mention for the glory they brought Chevrolet at Indianapolis. From 1986 to 1993 these turbocharged 2.65-liter Indy V-8s helped 11 drivers score 86 wins, including six straight victories at The Brickyard.

Veteran driver Herb Thomas scored Chevrolet's first big NASCAR win at Darlington, South Carolina, in September 1955. Thomas and his Yunick-built '56 Chevy ran strong the following year only to narrowly miss out on the Grand National championship to Buck Baker's Chrysler.

Chevrolet a big winner in stock car racing, just as he and Thomas had done for Hudson earlier in the decade. Smokey at first balked at the idea, then only agreed to a meeting with Cole after NASCAR founder Bill France personally asked him to help "get Chevrolet hooked on stock car racing." Yunick then allied with Chevrolet, but not until he had Cole also hire former Hudson performance parts manager Vince Piggins to handle Chevy's hot parts department.

Yunick was initially sheepish about Chevrolet's new V-8 after winding it out himself for the first time. "That was a pretty good engine, but the valvetrain was for (expletive deleted)," he said to *Chevy High Performance* magazine's Jim Resnick during the small block's 40th anniversary celebration in 1995. "It had that slip 'n slide, wiggle 'n jiggle motion up there. Above 5,800 rpm, the pistons and valve gear flew all to hell faster than I could fix it. To their credit, Chevy was willing to fix it." One of the earli-

est lessons learned by both racers and rodders about the small block was that its pressed-in rocker arm mounting studs needed to be replaced by more firmly fastened down screw-in pieces to negate some of that wiggle 'n jiggle.

At Darlington, Thomas' first-place finish was backed up by Jim Reed's Chevy in second, and Reed eventually copped NASCAR's Short Track title that year. Both drivers' achievements translated into some serious promotional fodder for GM's advertising crew, which then—as Chevy General Sales Manager W. E. Fish would later tell *Motor Trend* in 1956—had the public thinking Chevrolet had invented stock car racing. Cole's men indeed were hooked.

Escalation quickly followed. Late in 1956, Cole, at Piggins' urging, began bankrolling the Southern Engineering Development Company near Atlanta, an organization responsible for overseeing all the division's competition ventures in NASCAR and USAC.

Chevrolet's Monte Carlo returned to NASCAR racing in 1995 after a brief hiatus during which time Chevy's Lumina was the weapon of choice on stock car tracks.

On paper, SEDCO was a division of Atlanta dealership Nalley Chevrolet; in public, SEDCO manager Hugh Babb continually denied any ties to Warren, Michigan.

But if Chevrolet wasn't involved, why did it release its "Stock Car Competition Guide" early in April 1957? This 22-page booklet was "prepared for Chevrolet dealers, to assist individuals who plan to participate in this challenging American sport. It is advisory only, with material obtained from some of the top professional racing experts, performance engineers, and independent mechanics whose skill and dedicated effort have made Chevrolet a leader in open competition."

According to *Motor Trend*, Chevrolet budgeted $750,000 for its racing efforts in 1957. Most of that money was spent through SEDCO, which among other things became home to a special run of race-ready '57 Chevys known today as "Black Widows." Yunick never liked the factory-supplied Black Widow, nor did he agree with Piggins' plans for an "official factory team," as SEDCO was in fact. At first he opted to instead keep his own Chevy racers running by his hand. Then he walked away from Chevrolet completely, jumping over to Ford in 1957 for what he claimed to be four times the money Cole had paid him.

As it was, Chevrolet's first well-financed motor sports program didn't last all that long anyway. The new NASCAR rules in April 1957 banned fuel injection, superchargers, and multiple carburetors from Grand National racing, a move that crimped SEDCO's style. That was followed in June by an edict sent down by the Automobile Manufacturers Association that effectively banned factory-backed racing, supposedly so that America's automakers could concentrate instead on promoting automotive safety. Of curious note was the fact that the AMA's chairman at that time was GM President Harlow "Red" Curtice, who was especially aware of Ford coming up strong on the outside to perhaps finally beat Chevy in the sales race that year. It was Curtice who recommended the infamous AMA "ban," which Ford immediately obeyed to the letter, thus again falling back behind Chevrolet. A mere coincidence? You decide.

Chevrolet, too, abided by the AMA ruling, at least on the surface. Though SEDCO

Chrysler's big bad Hemi has dominated professional drag racing dating back to 1957 when Big Daddy Don Garlits' "Swamp Rat 1" (foreground) started setting records. But even Garlits couldn't resist giving the small block a try. His Chevy-powered "Swamp Rat Too" (back) was briefly campaigned in 1958.

Less IS MORE

Lead-footed speed parts merchant Dean Moon was always more than willing to prove the merits of his go-fast goodies in the real world. "Moon feels that the best way to test his products is in actual use, so he built an immaculate dragster specifically for just such a purpose," explained a report in the September 1961 issue of *Hot Rod*. "It is scheduled to be used to test everything from foot pedals through engines."

The engines in question were of the same breed: Chevy small-block V-8. As for the rolling test bed mentioned, that was Moon's classic *Mooneyes* rail job, a beautiful gas dragster built in 1959, as Moon Equipment brochures later put it in 1964, "to show all Chevy-lovin' customers just what one of their small-displacement bears will do to the big-bore competition."

What the Bowtie small block lacked in size at the strip it almost made up with "rev-ability." Moon used uncharacteristically short rear gears, reportedly as low as 4.86:1, in *Mooneyes* to take full advantage of the 283 Chevy's inherent ability to rev out the way no big block could. A dizzying 9,000 rpm was the norm at both ends of a *Mooneyes*' run.

Moon parts, of course, were plentiful throughout *Mooneyes*' 283 V-8, which was bored out to 300 cubic inches. Stored in a polished Moon tank, its NHRA-mandated gasoline was delivered to a Hilborn four-port injection setup by way of a Moon hydraulic throttle kit controlled by a Moon foot pedal. A Potvin-modified 6-71 GMC blower driven directly off the crank via a Potvin front-mounted drive system supplied extra pressure. Moon initially marketed the cool-looking Potvin parts, and then acquired the company.

The most prominent of many cams used during *Mooneyes*' brief career was another Potvin piece, an Eliminator roller stick that activated Moon racing valves. Moon breathers and Moon "no-name" valve covers gleamed away on top, and family ties showed up again when the small block's maximum output—560 horses at 6,500 rpm—was measured on a Moon dynamometer.

This muscled-up mouse was bolted into a Dragmaster chassis, a popular choice at the time but also the right one for Chevy's small block. It was more than strong, yet amazingly lightweight, just what the doctor ordered when a 300-ci mill was doing the hauling at the strip.

Its first time out, *Mooneyes* burned up the quarter-mile in 10.29 seconds at 147 miles per hour. After a switch to a conventional top-mounted blower in 1962, the car ran 9.52 seconds at 153.06 miles per hour to cop A/Gas Dragster laurels at Pomona. *Mooneyes* was the first rail to win at both of the NHRA's main events, the Winternationals and U.S. Nationals, and it also was the first big-time Yankee dragster to compete in international competition, this coming after its retirement in 1963.

In September that year, Dean Moon and driver Dante Duce took *Mooneyes* to England on the invitation of noted British speed merchant Sydney Allard. Allard's goal was to compare his latest creation, a

Behind that unique front-driven Potvin supercharger are 300 cubic inches of small-block muscle. Moon's crew bored out a 283 to help produce 560 horsepower from this mighty mouse.

Built in 1959 by Dean Moon to showcase his speed parts business, the legendary *Mooneyes* gas dragster could torch the quarter-mile in the low-10-second range using a Potvin-blown small block.

blown Chrysler dragster, to one of America's best. Refitted with its original Potvin blower, now boosting a 375-cubic-inch Chevy small block, *Mooneyes* smoked its way down a makeshift strip at Silverstone Raceway to the delirious delight of a few thousand enthusiastic Brits. Duce managed a run of 9.48 seconds at 166.60 miles per hour, earning honors as the first driver to break the 10-second barrier on a British quarter-mile.

A badge commemorating that run still can be found on *Mooneyes*, proudly displayed today at Don Garlits' Museum of Drag Racing, near Ocala, Florida, along with countless other milestone dragsters.

Moon Equipment accessories were plentiful back in the 1950s and 1960s; most popular were gas tanks and wheel discs.

The late Pete Robinson (right) was perhaps the small block's biggest fan as far as NHRA competition was concerned. Here he launches his Chevy-powered rail off the line at the Winternationals circa 1962. PAT GANAHL COLLECTION

at least on the surface. Though SEDCO immediately ceased operations and Vince Piggins returned to Warren, a convenient rear entrance to Chevy Engineering remained open for various preferred racers, who did a damn good job of keeping the small block—and, later, its big-block brother—running strong at the track. Piggins did his best to keep this performance pipeline flowing, however clandestinely, as the head of the division's Product Performance Department, which eventually took on the name "Product Promotion." During Vince's tenure at Product Promotion, Chevrolet commonly copped annual Manufacturers' Championships in NHRA drags (14 titles), NASCAR (9 crowns), and SCCA Trans-Am road racing (9, too). Another coincidence? Again, your call.

Herb Fishel took over at Product Promotion after Piggins' 1983 retirement, just as GM execs were changing their minds about motor sports. All through the 1960s and 1970s they had continually claimed that their divisions weren't "in racing." Meanwhile, Chevrolet products continually crossed finish lines first. "If you can't see that Chevrolet is racing, you are blind in your good eye," wrote *Car and Driver* magazine's Larry Griffin in 1984. "Not only does all the famous backdoor hanky-panky continue to

continues on page 135

The Dragmasters' "Two Thing" rail smokes 'em at the 1960 NHRA Nationals in Detroit. Power came from two Chevy small blocks mounted side by side. Elapsed time was 9.24 seconds at more than 180 miles per hour. PAT GANAHL COLLECTION

Old PRO

Grumpy Jenkins—with his trademark cigar—toys here in 1982 not with a V-8, but with Chevrolet's "3/4 small block," a V-6. *Pat Ganahl collection*

Many drag fans still love to watch "their cars" pound the quarter-mile, perhaps because they like to dream about doing that pounding themselves. Whatever the attraction, these devotees remain faithful to good old "door slammers," cathartic machines that in many ways hark back to the glory days of Super Stock competition in the early 1960s. In many minds, that glory has been kept alive for 30-odd years by the NHRA's Pro Stock league.

Forget about funny cars. Though they do promote brand awareness (in name alone), they long ago slipped away from whatever feeble family ties to the factory that they had to begin with. Indeed, it was the funny's rapid transformation from 1960s factory-experimental to 1970s flopper that originally led to Pro Stock racing's formation.

Some early F/C pilots, like Don Nicholson, didn't like the direction this new breed was taking. In Dyno Don's case, he was turned off by the increasing danger, sparked by the exploitation of exotic fuels and fanned by the unpredictable aerodynamics of the flimsy fiberglass shells. Nicholson proposed to stop the insanity by limiting engine displacement and sticking with gas-fed carburetors. He also preferred stock bodies and chassis, as did the renowned Ronnie Sox/Buddy Martin duo from North Carolina and a not-so-well-known dour driver/builder from Pennsylvania called "Grumpy."

Although Nicholson, Sox & Martin, and others made their own contributions to pro stock racing's quick rise, it is Bill "Grumpy" Jenkins who is remembered as the main man behind its birth. In 1975, Jenkins was tabbed by *Car Craft* magazine as one of "The Ten Most Powerful Men in Drag Racing," an acknowledgment of his tireless promotion of the Pro Stocks. Jenkins was unquestionably the field's first really big name. Pro stockers were first officially recognized by the NHRA in 1970, and it was "Grumpy's Toys" that were soon winning everything in sight in Pro Stock ranks.

In 1972, Jenkins won 11 Pro Stock events with a tiny Toy, a Chevy Vega powered by a surprisingly stock 327 small block. "All" Jenkins did was add Sealed Power pistons, forged aluminum rods, a General Kinetics cam, Air Flow Research-tweaked heads, and a modified Edelbrock tunnel-ram intake sporting two 660-cfm Holley four-barrels. According to Grumpy, this mighty mouse put out 540 horsepower, which translated into both ends of the Pro Stock record that year: a 9.42-second elapsed time and a top speed of 146.82 miles per hour. With an even mightier small block in 1973, Jenkins became the first Pro Stock driver to break into the 8s.

Born William Tyler Jenkins in December 1930, Grumpy began his career building race engines, with Dave Strickler's "Old Reliable" 409 Chevys

benefiting greatly from his expertise, starting in 1961. Four years later, Jenkins took up driving himself, at first relying on a Hemi-powered Plymouth. But he was back with his beloved Bowtie brand in 1966, running the first of countless Grumpy's Toys, a '66 Chevy II fitted with an L79 327. He moved up to a big-block Camaro in 1967 and switched back to small blocks five years later.

Success became Jenkins' middle name during the 1970s. All those wins in 1972 not only gave him the Pro Stock title, but they earned him more than $250,000, a figure he also reached in 1973, 1974, and 1975. For four out of five years prior to 1974, Jenkins was honored as the Pro Stock Driver of the Year. That year he started turning over driving chores to other drivers and, in 1976, his Grumpy's Toy Monza began running a 494 cubic-inch big block.

There may be no substitute for cubic inches, but there was no stopping Bill Jenkins' small-block Chevys during Pro Stock's formative years.

The Two Thing's twin 354-ci small blocks were joined together by the starter-gear teeth on each flywheel. The V-8 on the left was modified to run backwards.

TOP: Dave Rudy's black small-block '32 roadster garnered a best-appearing-car award at the 1964 NHRA Nationals in Indianapolis. It was powered by a 364-ci Chevy V-8.

BOTTOM: Zora Duntov took a team of three Corvettes to Daytona Beach in February 1956 to compete in NASCAR's annual Speed Week trials. He ran 150.533 miles per hour to set a new sports car flying mile record.

Duntov was joined at Daytona in 1956 by veteran racer John Fitch and Betty Skelton.

Skelton's beach racer, shown here, was later restored by noted Corvette collector Bill Tower.

Zora Duntov examines some of the
innovative components of his beloved
Corvette SS race car, built late in 1956.

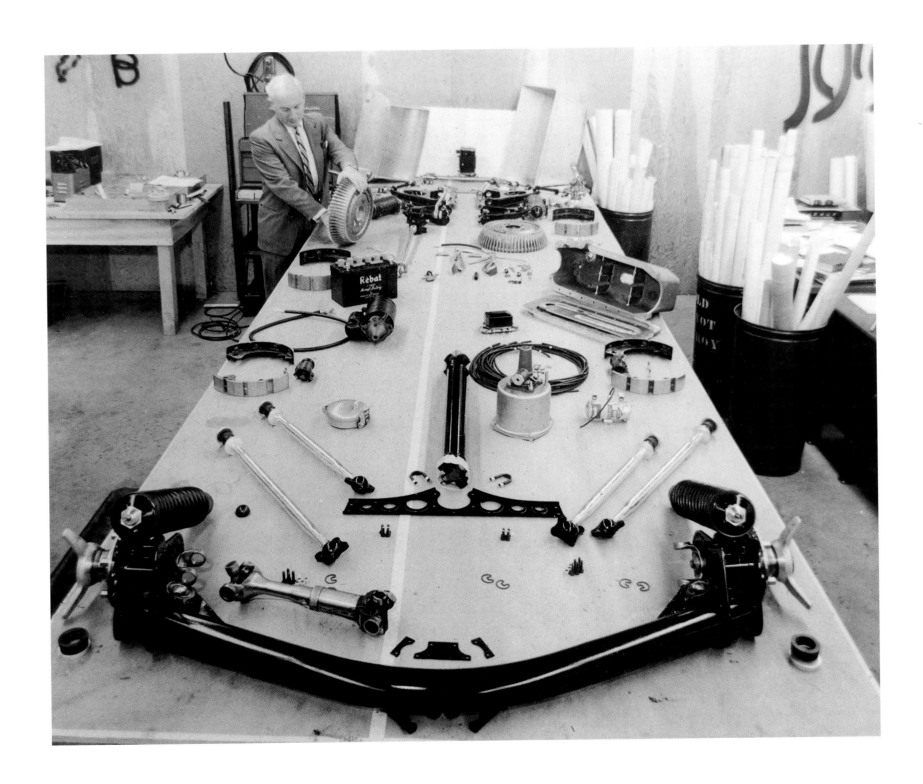

continued from page 129

but now the front door has been flung open for the first time in two decades."

Apparently GM management finally decided to just step out of the closet. Their coming-out party was held in October 1984 at the annual SEMA extravaganza, where the Chevrolet display first unfurled the "Chevy Thunder: The Heartbeat of America" banner. At the same time, Chevy General Manager Robert Burger was announcing plans to openly compete at Indianapolis with a new Indy V-8, created through a partnership with Ilmore Engineering and Roger Penske's Penske Racing. Though it certainly featured a diminutive cylinder block (displacement was a tidy 2.65 liters), this 700-horsepower, four-valve, DOHC V-8 was by no means considered part of Chevrolet's small-block family. But whatever its species, it was a merciless competitor; from 1986 to 1989 it won 32 of 58 races, and it also powered every Indy 500 winner from 1988 to 1993.

NASCAR competitors felt the impact of GM's newfound enthusiasm for racing as Chevrolet scored nine consecutive Manufacturers' Championships from 1983 to 1991. The car that earned the bulk of those titles was the Monte Carlo, a seemingly unbeatable machine that won 95 of 193 (52 percent) Winston Cup events from 1983 through its retirement after the eighth race of 1989. Chevy's new Lumina took over from there.

A new name for Product Promotions also arrived in 1989: "Chevrolet Raceshop," a more appropriate shingle, considering that Fishel's job was to supply racers with only the best race-ready pieces. Three years later Herb became director of the new Motorsports Technology Group, an organiza-

THE REAL McCOY

Here is the most remarkable car made in America today — the new Chevrolet Corvette.

Why remarkable?

Because it is *two* cars wrapped up in one sleek skin. One is a luxury car with glove-soft upholstery, wind-up windows, a removable hardtop (with virtually 360° vision), or fabric top, ample luggage space, a velvety ride and all the power assists you could want, including power-operated fabric top* and Powerglide transmission*.

The other is a sports car. And we mean the real McCoy, a tough, road-gripping torpedo-on-wheels with the stamina to last through the brutal 12 hours of Sebring, a close-ratio trans-

mission (2.2 low gear, 1.31 second) matched to engine torque characteristics, razor-sharp steering (16 to 1) that puts *command* into your fingertips.

Other people make a luxury car that has much the same dimensions as this. That's not so tough. And the Europeans make some real rugged competition sports cars—and that's considerably tougher. But nobody but Chevrolet makes a luxury car that *also* is a genuine 100-proof sports car.

It's a wicked combination to work out, and we didn't hit it overnight. But you'll find, when you take the wheel of a new Corvette, that the result is fantastic — the most heart-lifting blend of all the things you've ever wanted a car to be.

If you find it hard to believe that one car could combine such widely different characteristics we can't blame you. And no amount of talk can tell you half so much as 15 minutes in a Corvette's cockpit — so why don't you let your Chevrolet dealer set up a road test of the most remarkable car made in America today? . . . Chevrolet Division of General Motors, Detroit 2, Michigan.

*Powerglide and power-operated fabric top optional at extra cost.

MOTOR TREND/JULY 1956 3

After Duntov, Fitch, and Skelton made headlines at Daytona, Fitch took four Corvettes to Sebring in March 1956, supplying ample fodder for GM advertising people.

Two Corvette SS chassis were tested in 1957; the other was a fiberglass-bodied mule that was later rebodied into GM styling chief Bill Mitchell's Stingray racer.

Beneath the Corvette SS's beautiful blue magnesium body is a purpose-built tubular space frame. This ill-fated racing machine resides today in the Indy 500 museum in Indiana.

tion created to consolidate all of GM's competition activities beneath one roof. Today, Fishel's group is known simply as "GM Racing."

NASCAR news for 1995 included the Monte Carlo's return and the appearance of yet another small-block milestone. First presented for review before NASCAR officials in October 1995, Chevy's awesome SB2 (for Small Block—Second Generation) V-8 eventually was approved for Winston Cup competition starting in 1998. This sensational 358-ci small block produced 775 maximum horsepower at a dizzying 8,400 rpm for the Monte Carlo. Another SB2, this one pumping out 725 horses at 7,800 rpm, was approved for Craftsman Truck racing.

"The SB2 marked the first time in the history of the GM small block that a package of engine components was specifically developed for a single four-barrel NASCAR racing engine," said Jim Covey, GM Racing's NASCAR engine development manager. "With the SB2 program, we had an opportunity to make a significant improvement over existing racing engines." Armed with the SB2, veteran driver Jeff Gordon grabbed his third Winston Cup crown in 1998. Though the name in 2005 is Nextel Cup, the results are similar—50 years old and Chevy's small block remains a force to be reckoned with on NASCAR tracks.

The Corvette, of course, is also in its 50s now, and it too was still running around tracks in 2004 like an Olympic sprinter in his prime, thanks to the venerable small block. The latest in a long line of loud, proud racing Corvettes, Chevrolet's screaming yellow C5-R models are powered by a heavily modified LS1 V-8 bored and stroked to just a tad short of 7.0 liters. Output is upward of 610 horsepower.

The heart of the SS racer was a fuel-injected 283 small block fitted with aluminum heads. Among additional weight-saving touches was a special magnesium oil pan.

Trans-Am PONY CAR

Before GM cancelled its long-running F-body platform, Pontiac's venerable Trans Am stood as the only factory hot rod to roll uninterrupted from the muscle car's heydays in the 1960s into the new millennium. Chevrolet's Z/28 (or Z28, depending on your perspective) Camaro would also fill this bill if not for a brief "retirement" in 1975 and 1976. Had it not sat out those two years, the Z/28 could've claimed the title as America's longest-running muscle car. Pontiac's first Trans Am Firebird had appeared in 1969—by that time, Chevy's first-generation Z/28 was entering its third year and had already proven itself both on the street and at the track.

Introduced to the automotive press on November 26, 1966, at Riverside, California, the first Z/28 Camaro was little more than a street-going extension of Chevrolet's Sports Car Club of America racing effort. Earlier that year, SCCA officials had kicked off their inaugural Trans-American Sedan Championship racing season, which ended up being a one-horse show as Ford's Mustang beat up on a bunch of Plymouth Barracudas and Dodge Darts. The series almost didn't return for an encore, as fans apparently weren't too keen on watching Mustangs win all day long. Not until Chevrolet's Vince Piggins convinced SCCA officials that his company would honor Trans-Am competition with its presence did a 1967

race schedule become reality.

On August 17, 1966, Piggins, then an assistant staff engineer in charge of performance product promotion, issued a memo to upper brass outlining his plan to build an SCCA-legal factory racer based on Chevrolet's new pony car. Once approved, Piggins' proposed package was given

Fifteen-inch Rally wheels—offered by Chevrolet in 1967 only with front disc brakes—were standard for the first Z/28 Camaro.

All Z/28 Camaros built from 1967 to 1969 featured the exclusive 290-horsepower 302 small block. This 302 is fitted with the extremely rare cowl-induction ductwork option.

RPO code Z28, a label that stuck despite Piggins' pleas for the name "Cheetah."

To meet SCCA homologation standards, Piggins' hot-to-trot pony had to have a back seat, a wheelbase no longer than 116 inches, and an engine no larger than 5 liters (about 305 ci). Additionally, Chevrolet had to sell at least 1,000 of them to the public. The first two requirements were a cinch, as was, apparently, the production quota. "The sales department anticipates a volume of 10,000 such vehicles for 1967," wrote Piggins in his memo. As for the displacement limit, the cleverly destroked 327 met that challenge with little fuss or muss.

But Chevrolet built only 602 Z/28 Camaros for 1967. How then was it legalized for the SCCA circuit? Chevy officials played a little numbers game by homologating the more plentiful 350-ci Camaro under Federation Internationale de l'Automobile (FIA, the world governing body over SCCA racing) Group I rules, and then qualified that car equipped with RPO Z28 under Group II specifications. Don't understand? You're not alone; just nod your head in mock recognition.

Along with the exclusive 302-ci small block, RPO Z/28 also included a fine

supporting cast: Chevrolet's superb F41 suspension, a quick-ratio Saginaw manual steering box, and 3.73:1 rear gears. A Muncie four-speed (with 2.20:1 low) was a mandatory option, as were the front disc brakes with power assist. Thrown in along with those discs were four 15x6 Corvette Rally wheels. Other than these bright rims, the only other outward sign of a '67 Z/28's presence were twin racing stripes on the hood and rear deck. The legendary "Z/28" emblem didn't debut until midway through 1968.

On the street, Detroit's first Trans-Am pony car was a big winner. "With the Z/28, Chevy is on the way toward making the gutsy stormer the Camaro should have been in the first place," proclaimed a *Car and Driver* review. Trackside witnesses were also impressed as Z/28 Camaros dominated Trans-Am racing in 1968 and 1969, results that in turn helped sales soar. More than 7,000 Z/28s hit Main Street, USA, in 1968, followed by another 19,000 the following year.

A legendary legacy continued for more than 30 years before coming to a close.

Also at Sebring in 1957 was Bill
Mitchell's SR-2 racing Corvette, built the
previous year. Here, Mitchell's SR-2
tours the Sebring course on the way to
a 16th-place finish.

First let loose on unsuspecting GTS competitors in IMSA's American Le Mans Series (ALMS) in 1999, Chevrolet's fully factory-backed Corvette Racing program has built a winning reputation like no other ever witnessed during the fabled half-century history of America's Sports Car. An impressive 2001 season was kicked off with an overall win at the Rolex 24 Hours of Daytona, "probably the most significant victory in the history of the marque," in Herb Fishel's opinion. An equally historic 1-2 finish in class followed that summer at Le Mans, and the C5-R team repeated that result in France in 2002. In between, Corvettes ran away with the 2001 ALMS Manufacturers' Championship, winning six of eight races. Two more ALMS titles followed in 2002 and 2003.

"Somewhere, Zora Duntov is smiling, as are more than a million Corvette owners worldwide," said brand manager Rick Baldrick after the milestone Daytona win in 2001. "This victory signals that the Corvette heritage is stronger than ever."

The Corvette's long, legendary competition heritage dates back to the Duntov cam's appearance in 1956. With this and other race-ready parts in hand, Zora himself set out to prove that his reborn baby could run with the hottest performance machines out there. In February 1956 he took a three-car team to Daytona Beach, Florida, for NASCAR's annual Speed Week trials, where he established a new sports car flying-mile standard of 150.533 miles per hour.

Veteran racer John Fitch then led a four-car effort farther south to Sebring for the 12-Hour endurance event in March. Two of the Sebring Corvettes failed to survive the day in March 1956, as did 35 rivals. But

Fitch's entry finished tops in its class. That achievement was all promotional people needed; immediately came the famous "Real McCoy" magazine ad, which described the revamped Corvette as "a tough, road-gripping, torpedo on wheels with the stamina to last through the brutal 12 Hours of Sebring."

A Chevrolet team returned to Sebring in 1957, but early Corvette competition efforts
continues on page 146

The Corvette SS lasted only 23 laps at Sebring in March 1957 after overheating problems and rear suspension breakage forced its retirement.

The SR-2 Corvette initially featured
a small, centrally located tail fin, but this
appendage was soon replaced by the offset
"high fin" shown here. This historic
racing machine also belongs to Bill Tower.

Duntov tried racing again in 1963 with his Corvette Grand Sports, of which only five were built before GM clamped down on such shenanigans. The first two Grand Sport coupes built were later converted into roadsters. The fifth built, shown here, resides in Bill Tower's impressive collection.

Three SR-2 Corvettes were built in 1956—two racing models and one street-going showboat. The street machine (center) was built for GM President Harlow Curtice. Bill Mitchell's (right) was the first completed, followed by another created for the son of GM styling guru Harley Earl.

continued from page 141

weren't limited to production-class racing. The distinctive SR-2 "prototype racer," created the year before, was there, too, as was Duntov's dream machine, the Corvette SS. Both featured hopped-up fuel-injected small blocks and modified bodies.

Conceived by Harley Earl for his son Jerry, the first Corvette SR-2 initially wore a blue shell capped by a small tailfin in back. That centrally located airfoil was traded for a larger, reshaped fin, offset to the driver's side, in 1957. This SR-2 won an SCCA B-Production championship in 1958. A second red-and-white SR-2, this one built for Styling Chief Bill Mitchell, debuted in February 1957 during Daytona's Speed Week trials. A flying-mile speed record of 152.886 miles per hour was established there, and then Mitchell's SR-2 finished 16th at Sebring a month later.

Far more exotic, the purpose-built Corvette SS incorporated a low-slung tubular space frame and lightweight magnesium body. Weight-saving aluminum heads also graced its tweaked 282 fuelie V-8. Coil-over

shocks were at all four corners, independent de Dion suspension was in back, and the brakes were finned drums with the rear pair mounted inboard on the differential to reduce unsprung weight. Along with the one beautiful blue SS built in Chevrolet Engineering, Duntov's crew also fashioned a crude fiber-glass-bodied test mule counterpart.

On paper, the SS certainly looked promising. Problems, however, appeared almost immediately at Sebring in March 1957, forcing an early retirement from the 12-Hour endurance event. Then any hopes of going back to the drawing board and trying again at Le Mans later that summer were dashed, once the AMA ban went into effect that summer.

A year or so later, the SS mule was acquired by Bill Mitchell, who then used its chassis as a base for his Stingray racer, a car that provided more than one styling trick later used on the regular-production Sting Ray in 1963. With Dr. Dick Thompson at the wheel, Mitchell's Stingray roared to an SCCA

LEFT: An all-aluminum 377-ci small block was originally planned for the Grand Sport Corvette, but production delays left Zora Duntov with no choice but to install this 377 V-8 instead early on. It features a special nickel-alloy block and conventional cast-iron heads topped by a set of 48-millimeter Weber side-draft carburetors. Aluminum versions of this engine eventually found their way into the Grand Sports once they were available.

RIGHT: Along with the Grand Sports, Jim Hall's Chaparrals also relied on the aluminum 377 small block. With no clearance problems in Hall's racers, the engine could use the larger 58-millimeter Weber down-draft carburetors. Both this lightweight small block and its red-painted counterpart belong to collector Bill Tower.

The five Grand Sports raced in various forms for various owners during their short careers, with the last major appearance coming in 1966. Both small-block and big-block power were used, and various body modifications came and went.

C-Modified championship in 1960. Thompson was one of the supposedly "independent" drivers who benefited greatly from Chevy Engineering's backdoor support during the years immediately following the AMA ban. A Thompson-driven Corvette first claimed an SCCA production-class championship in 1956. Others followed in 1957, 1962, and 1963.

AMA ban be damned, Duntov took another shot at building a dominant racing Corvette in 1963. This time the name was Grand Sport. Highlights included a tubular-steel, ladder-type frame fitted with big 11.75-inch Girling disc brakes at the corners. On top was a weight-saving handmade fiberglass body with superthin panels. Initial specifications called for a 377-ci small block fed by four Weber carbs. Early proposals also mentioned a production run of 125 or so Grand Sports. Neither plan became reality.

The first Grand Sport was fitted with an aluminum 327 fuelie, while awaiting the 377 V-8 still in development. But before that work could be completed, GM officials stepped in with a ban of their own. As of January 1963, all General Motors divisions would cease immediately any and all racing projects. Only five Grand Sports escaped Chevrolet Engineering before that order came down. From there each went through a progression of race teams, and each also underwent various mechanical and exterior modifications, with both small blocks and big blocks installed over the years. Additionally, two of these coupes were later converted into roadsters for competition at Daytona in February 1964.

GM officials, however, intervened once

The SCCA Corvette Challenge series pitted 50 identical Corvettes against each other in 1988 and 1989. Chevrolet built 56 special Corvette Challenge cars that first year, followed by another 60 in 1989.

'Round AND 'ROUND

The late Dale Earnhardt Sr. won back-to-back NASCAR Winston Cup titles in this Monte Carlo Aero Coupe in 1986 and 1987. Today it's owned by collector Bill Tower of Plant City, Florida.

The late Dale Earnhardt Sr. drove various brands during his record-setting Winston Cup career: Dodge, Pontiac, even a Thunderbird from Ford for Bud Moore in 1982 and 1983. But he was, first and foremost, a Chevy man, with the bulk of his lifetime win total coming at the wheels of Monte Carlos and Luminas.

Introduced on Main Street, USA, in 1970, Chevrolet's somewhat upscale Monte Carlo coupe quickly evolved into the hottest thing going on the NASCAR circuit. Nothing could beat it by decade's end. Then along came Ford's aerodynamically superior Thunderbird— the machine that almost overnight vaulted Bill Elliott to the head of the NASCAR pack—in 1983. Once "Million Dollar Bill's" T-bird started running up

around 210 miles per hour, Chevrolet people recognized a dire need to develop similar speed to fend off the Ford threat. A more slippery body shell was a must.

They already had the Monte Carlo SS, introduced for 1983 with an aerodynamic sloped nose, a modification that reminded some witnesses of the wind-cheating snout that Ford had grafted onto its race-ready Talladega models in 1969. Yet as much as the revised front end helped reduce drag, it couldn't compensate for the Monte Carlo's nearly vertical rear glass, which created some seriously dangerous lift on the tail at high speeds. Elliott's sleeker Ford dominated in 1985, sending the Bowtie boys back to their drawing boards.

They returned to the track in 1986 with the Aero Coupe, a somewhat strange-looking concoction that

retained the Monte Carlo's familiar formal roofline in back but capped it off with a large, sloping rear window. Only 200 of these fastback Monte Carlos were built for the street that year, making them desired collectibles today. As for their value on NASCAR super speedways, Geoff Bodine proved that right out of the chute in February 1986 by winning the Daytona 500 in convincing fashion. Sixteen of the 42 starters at Daytona that day were Monte Carlo Aero Coupes, including Bodine's on the outside pole.

Archrivals Darrell Waltrip and Dale Earnhardt also drove Aero Coupe Chevys in 1986, with Waltrip and his slick Monte Carlo winning three races and scoring 21 top-five finishes that year. Earnhardt, though, got the last laugh, taking five checkered flags and finishing in the top five another 16 times at the wheel of his famous Wrangler-sponsored, Richard

Earnhardt's No. 3 Wrangler Chevrolet began life as a Junior Johnson-built Buick in 1981. The car was rebodied as a Monte Carlo in 1983. Darrell Waltrip drove it to Winston Cup championships in 1981, 1982, and 1985. It was sold to Richard Childress Racing (RCR) after the 1985 season.

Key to Chevrolet's dominating success on the 1986 NASCAR circuit was the new Aero Coupe body. The RCR No. 3 Monte Carlo was one of the first to be fitted with this new fastback body.

Chevrolet: 358 cubic inches fed by an unrestricted four-barrel carburetor to produce between 600 and 650 horses. Handling all that muscle is a Borg-Warner Super T-10 four-speed gearbox. Suspension is by heavy-duty coils and single gas-charged shocks at all four wheels—an impressive package, to say the least.

Dale Earnhardt Sr. may have driven a Ford in 1983—but once he got behind the wheel of this slick Monte Carlo three years later, he never looked back.

Childress Racing Enterprises Monte Carlo. That bright-blue-and-yellow No. 3 Chevy brought Earnhardt his second Winston Cup championship (following his initial title in 1980) and the first of back-to-back crowns.

Restored and still owned today by noted collector and Chevrolet racing nut Bill Tower, Earnhardt's 1986 NASCAR-champion Wrangler Monte Carlo looks as slippery as ever nearly 20 years after the fact. Beneath that aerodynamic exterior is a tubular chassis typically featuring various Blue-Oval-based components, including Ford's tough 9-inch rear end. But power, of course, is genuine

This NASCAR-spec 358-ci small block produced about 650 horsepower in 1986.

1967 Z/28 V-8

CONSTRUCTION:
**cast-iron block
w/cast iron cylinder heads**

DISPLACEMENT (CUBIC INCHES):
302

BORE & STROKE (INCHES):
4.00 x 3.00

LIFTERS:
solid

COMPRESSION:
11:1

INDUCTION:
**single four-barrel
carburetor**

HORSEPOWER:
290 at 5,800 rpm

TORQUE:
290 at 4,200 rpm

Chevrolet claimed it wasn't in racing during the 1960s. Yet there were oil man Jim Hall's Chaparrals flying the Bowtie banner high in Can-Am competition. Hall's shop in Midland, Texas, was home to some serious research and development, most of it factory backed by Chevrolet.

Duntov's grand scheme in 1963 involved building as many as 125 Grand Sport racing Corvettes. GM execs thought otherwise, though; they shut down all its divisions' competition projects in January 1963.

more before those two roadsters could reach Florida. Clearly, Chevrolet Engineering was still supporting much of the Grand Sport racing effort, despite orders to the contrary. This time Chevy General Manager Bunkie Knudsen was instructed to end these activities or risk his annual bonus. The five Grand Sports were then sold off. The Grand Sport's last significant on-track appearance came in 1966.

From January 1963 on, Chevrolet supposedly wasn't involved in racing. Yet Duntov still managed to give Corvette racers something

to play with that year. Listed under RPO Z06 was the Special Performance Equipment group, consisting of pretty much every hot part on the Corvette shelf. Mandatory features included the L84 fuelie 327, backed by its close-ratio Muncie four-speed and a Posi-Traction axle. Initially listed were heavy-duty suspension parts, special "cerametallix" power brakes with unique cooling features, an oversized 36.5-gallon fiberglass fuel tank, and five cast-aluminum knock-off wheels. In December 1962, Chevrolet temporarily withdrew the knock-off option due to production difficulties and removed the big tank from the package to help whittle down RPO Z06's original $1,818.45 asking price. The 36.5-gallon tank remained a separate option, available for any Sting Ray coupe. The sum of these parts left little doubt as to the original Z06 Corvette's intentions. And the same could be said when Chevrolet brought the Z06 back in 2001.

A similar all-encompassing competition

While the Grand Sport couldn't slip past corporate killjoys in 1963, Corvette buyers still could've picked up the race-ready Z06. Along with a hot fuel-injected small block, the Z06 package added special racing brakes and an oversized gas tank.

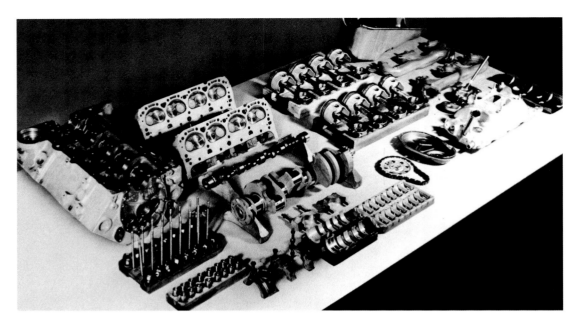

Though it was beefed throughout, the Z/28's first 302 still used the typical two-bolt block. Stronger four-bolt main bearing caps appeared in 1968.

A big 800-cfm Holley four-barrel fed the Z-28 Camaro's 302 V-8.

package appeared for the small-block Corvette in 1970, and it too used an RPO code later revived for another hot two-seater: ZR-1. Available only with the LT-1 350 V-8, Chevy's first ZR-1 package added a long list of heavy-duty parts and a seriously beefed suspension, all the better to go racing with. This rare, expensive option was offered all three years during the LT-1 run.

Still another purposeful suspension option, RPO Z51, debuted in 1984 and was

soon helping C4 Corvettes win everything in sight the following year in the SCCA's new Showroom Stock endurance series. After watching the best 'Vettes yet conquer every event on this schedule from 1985 to 1987, SCCA officials finally concluded that the only real competition for Chevrolet's sports car was another Chevy sports car. Thus, the Corvette Challenge emerged in 1988, pitting 50 identical L98 Corvettes against each other for a $1 million purse. Chevrolet built 56 two-seaters specially equipped (roll bars were added, among other safety features) for the Corvette Challenge series that year. Another 60 Challenge cars followed in 1989, some fitted with hotter 5.7-liter V-8s.

Back in the "no-racing" days, Chevrolet officials in Michigan also tried their products out on the track by way of the Lone Star State. Oil man Jim Hall's race shop in Midland, Texas, and Chevy's Research and Development center in Warren might as well have moved in together during the 1960s. Anyone with eyes could see that Hall's operation was more or less an outsourced laboratory for some of Chevrolet's hottest competition developments of the day.

Hall was no dummy when it came to race car innovation—his beautiful Chaparrals pioneered various competition concepts, including fiberglass monocoque construction, aerodynamic spoiler and wing arrangements, and automatic transmission use, to name a few. And when fitted with all-aluminum versions of Chevrolet's 327 small block (making as much as 420 horsepower), Hall's Chaparral 2 racers were hard to beat. His 2C model won 16 of the 21 races it entered in 1965. The Can-Am circuit, founded by Jim Kaser for unlimited-displacement sports

cars, was new that year, and Hall's small-block Chaparrals kicked some serious butt in this series until the rich Texan started playing with aluminum versions of Chevrolet's equally new Mk. IV big-block V-8.

The emergence of big-block brute force may have left the mouse motor out in the cold in some competition venues after 1965, but not all sanctioning bodies were so willing to concede that size matters. Such apparently was the case at the Sports Car Club of America's offices. SCCA officials in 1966 kicked off their first Trans-American Sedan Championship series, specifying that qualified contestants show up sporting no more than 5 liters (about 305 cubic inches) of displacement.

Vince Piggins recognized a great opportunity to take Chevrolet's new Camaro racing in this league in 1967, but there was a catch. The Camaro's 283 small block didn't take full advantage of that displacement limit, and the 327 obviously was too big. No problem—Chevy engineers simply bolted the 283 crank into the 327 block, with the end result equaling 302 cubic inches. Piggins then paired those cubes with a package called "Z/28" to create a true Mustang-killer. From 1967 to 1969, the 302 small block was built exclusively for Chevrolet's Trans-Am pony car.

Although the 302's cylinder block was a conventional passenger car unit with two-bolt main bearings (stronger four-bolt mains came along in 1968), the rugged crank was made of forged steel instead of nodular cast iron. L79 big-port heads, 11:1 pistons, a rather radical solid-lifter cam, and an 800-cfm Holley four-barrel carb on an aluminum intake heated things up further. Advertised output was 290 horses. Seat-of-the-pants readings, however, went much higher, some as lofty as 400 horsepower.

Whatever the true number, the 302 impressed the press to no end. "The very-

Chevy's 302 small block was created solely to make the 1967 Camaro legal for SCCA Trans-Am racing. This hot little rodent was conservatively rated at 290 horsepower.

Z/28 Camaro popularity soared on the street in 1969 with production topping 20,000. This high-performance pony car ranks as one of the muscle car era's greats.

RIGHT: This famous badge didn't appear until early in 1968, and the name was later translated into simply "Z28." No matter how you spelled it, though, the Camaro behind the name was a hot one.

The INTIMIDATOR

The late Dale Earnhardt Sr., shown here in a 1996 GM Motorsports press photo, lost his life at Daytona in 2001. He will be remembered forever as one of NASCAR's all-time greats.

The greatest name in Chevrolet racing may also, in many minds, be NASCAR's greatest: Earnhardt.

Three generations of Earnhardts have torn it up on stock car tracks, with young gun Dale Jr. right in the running for perhaps his first NASCAR championship, now known as the Nextel Cup, as these words were being written late in 2004.

Junior's grandfather, Ralph, got things rolling on the dirt tracks of North Carolina back in the 1950s, but never did break into the big time—basically because he didn't fancy leaving the Carolina area. Traveling wasn't for him, thus neither was Bill France's high-dollar Grand National circuit. Though he did run up and down the East Coast on the way to a NASCAR Sportsman title in 1956, Ralph for the most part chose to stick close to home, and he piled up countless wins on dusty local tracks. According to 1970 NASCAR champ Bobby Isaac, Junior's granddad was one of the best short-track racers ever. Ralph Earnhardt fell victim to a heart attack in September 1973. He was only 45.

Ralph's son, Dale, was 22 when he lost his father. Having grown up around dad's race cars, Dale Earnhardt Sr. always knew where he wanted to go, and he also was well aware of how much hard work was needed to get there. Like his father, young Dale Sr. didn't have the money to simply buy his way into NASCAR's major leagues, by then known as the Winston

Cup series. So he made his start the old fashioned way: He earned it.

In his heyday, Dale Sr. became known as The Intimidator, and a rocket scientist wasn't required to identify the reasons why. If you were in his way, say at Martinsville or Bristol, he'd either blow by you or through you—nothing was going to stop him from winning, from being the best. Along with his intimidating style, his gritty determination and toughness (both mental and physical) helped make him unquestionably NASCAR's Number One driver of the 1980s and early 1990s—and arguably the greatest ever, better even than maybe The King himself, Richard Petty.

Like Sir Richard, Earnhardt Sr. won a record seven NASCAR seasonal championships during his Winston Cup career, which began humbly in 1975 (he ran one race) and ended in his fatal wreck at Daytona in February 2001. That the new king was dead was almost too much to believe for many fans, who had watched him run so strong for so long. Perhaps his career was winding down by 2001; he was still the invincible one, The Intimidator, right up to that tragic end.

His NASCAR totals include 675 starts (648 straight at one point), 76 wins (sixth all-time), 22 poles, and more than $41.6 million (Number One all-time) in earnings. His first win came at Bristol's Southeastern 500 in 1979, the year he became a Winston Cup full timer. His last came in 2000 at Talladega's high-banked

super speedway, the track where he won the most: 10 times. Speedways (measuring between 1 and 2 miles) and superspeedways (longer than 2 miles) were where he made the most hay. His 23 victories at the former and 18 at the latter are both NASCAR records.

Yet as good as he was at high-flying venues like Pocono and Atlanta, it was the sport's greatest track that continually denied him. Not that he wasn't successful at Daytona—he won 34 times there during his career in Busch Series events, IROC races, Bud Shootouts, the Twin 125 qualifiers, and the Pepsi 400. But prior to 1998 he never grasped NASCAR's hallowed crown, the Daytona 500. Twenty-five times (3 of them on the pole) he started down in Florida in February, and 25 times he failed to finish first before he finally got the monkey off his back. On February 15, 1998, he won the 500, earning sincere congratulations from fellow drivers he had fought so fiercely with throughout his career.

Almost three years later to the day, he was gone. But fortunately his legend, as well as his name, carries on.

Chevy's Z/28 Camaro dominated Trans-Am racing in 1968 and 1969.

Dirt tracks have been especially friendly to the small block. Originally built in 1955 by Chet Wilson, the open-wheel machine shown here is recognized as the first successful Chevy-powered sprint car. Nicknamed "Offy Killer," it is driven here by Jud Larson at Muskogee, Oklahoma, in 1963. LEROY BYERS, SPENCER RIGGS COLLECTION

Chevrolet's Camaro served as the main attraction of the International Race of Champions for some 15 years. IROC competition pitted drivers from different types of races against each other in their Camaros, resulting in an all-star event of sorts. See how many of the famous faces you can identify in this 1989 IROC lineup—yes, that is Dale Earnhardt fourth from the right.

backdoor word is that 'destroking' the 327 has resulted in a happy and extremely potent screamer," wrote *Sport Car Graphic's* Jerry Titus. Meanwhile *Car and Driver* simply called it the "most responsive American V-8 we've ever tested." That was big talk for a small block. Was it any wonder then that this

mouse-motored machine quickly evolved into one of Detroit's most feared and revered muscle cars? Either on the street or on SCCA tracks, the Z/28 Camaro was hard to beat during the late 1960s. Plain and simple, "hot" just wasn't fiery enough to describe this one.

Chapter 4

TAKIN' IT TO THE STREETS:
Mouse Motor and
Hot Rod—A Perfect Match

The Chevy small block has been the street rodder's prime choice for nearly as long as the mouse motor has been around. Greg Stallmeyer's GS Customs, working in concert with Joe Kern's Custom Fab (both of Seymour, Illinois), was responsible for Jeff Wingo's beautiful bare chassis in the foreground, which will be topped soon by a 1950 Studebaker pickup body. In back is Judi Barrows' small-block-powered '48 Chevy convertible, also the work of GS Customs.

I T SEEMED A LITTLE ODD AT FIRST. TOURING THE VARIOUS AUTO SHOWS WITH ALL OF CHEVROLET'S NEW-FOR-1995 PRODUCTS WAS A YELLOW 1955 210 TWO-DOOR SEDAN. A very attractive 210 sedan to be sure, but it was still a 40-year-old car displayed right along with the company's fresh-off-the-line hardware. Were Chevy people nuts?

Damn straight! They were nuts about their little small-block V-8, which, in 1995, was celebrating its 40th anniversary. To mark this momentous milestone, GM Motorsport engineers had taken one of Chevrolet's first small-block models from 1955 and updated it with a thoroughly modern version of the mouse motor that just wouldn't scurry away. The idea was to honor the past while simultaneously promoting the present.

"The small block revolutionized automobiles when it was introduced in 1955," said Mark McPhail, the GM engineer who spearheaded the project. "More than 60 million Chevys built since then have the same essential engine. We

Beneath the hood of the Raceshop's sedan was an emissions-legal 265-cubic-inch L99 V-8 that produced 329 maximum horsepower at 6,500 rpm. This machine was both kind to the environment and a killer on the quarter-mile: its best elapsed time read 14.19 seconds at 94.71 miles per hour.

did this project to demonstrate the versatility of the small block in today's world."

Though the V-8 of choice seen between those classic fenders belonged in a 1995 Caprice, it too represented a salute of sorts to those that came before it. It was an L99 small block, an engine that demonstrated that at least some things old apparently can be new again. Introduced in 1994, the L99 displaced 4.3 liters—or 265 cubic inches, same as the old Turbo-Fire V-8 from 1955. That measurement, though, was about the only thing the two distant cousins shared.

Inside the L99 was the latest in Chevrolet hot hardware: among other things, powdered-metal connecting rods, a single roller timing chain, and a prototype hydraulic cam with more than 1/2 inch of valve lift. Heads were aluminum LT1 units borrowed from the Corvette parts bins. On top was an electronic sequential fuel injection system that used a Camaro LT1's 77-millimeter mass airflow meter. Compression was 8.8:1, compared to the 1955 Turbo-Fire's 8.0:1 squeeze. At 329 horsepower, output was double that of the first small block, actually more considering

Chevrolet Raceshop put together this 1955 Chevy hot rod in 1995 to help commemorate the small-block V-8's 40th anniversary. The car rolled on Goodyear radials mounted on Chevrolet pickup wheels.

Smokin' the hides is no problem for this 1957 street/strip Chevy. Beneath its hood is a nitrous-boosted 427-ci small block.

that those 329 ponies were net rated, while the '55 Turbo-Fire's 162-horsepower rating was a gross number.

Along with being stronger than dirt, this modified L99 was also real fine from the EPA's perspective. As McPhail explained further in June 1995, another of his project's goals was to prove that Chevy owners could have their cake both in hand and mouth at the same time. "A complete emission control system, including dual catalytic converters, brought the car up to smog-legal 1995 standards," he said. "From there, we moved on to ensure the car had the kind of performance expected by today's enthusiast." That performance was reported as 14.19 seconds at

94.71 miles per hour in the quarter-mile, more than enough smog-legal speed to make most enthusiasts happy these days.

By "enthusiast" McPhail meant "hot rodder," two words that are still dirty in many minds around Detroit, as well as around America. Back in the 1950s, hot rodders were prominently portrayed in movies (nearly all of them bad, yet still fun to watch in some cases) as hell-bent, leather-wearing hoodlums who terrorized law-abiding drivers. Though that image has dimmed considerably, today's occasional street-racing tragedies remind us all of rodding's darkest side. For many, though, "hopping up" (as old timers put it) a street machine or building a hot rod

Ford's good ol' flathead V-8 was the top rodder's choice before the Chevy small block came along to steal its thunder. On the left is a blown flattie; to the right is a rare Ardun-head OHV conversion, created by Zora Arkus-Duntov a few years before he went to work for General Motors.

remains a relatively wholesome hobby, and it was the wrench-bending guys and gals that McPhail's group was embracing—even if he couldn't bring himself to actually utter those two words—at least at first.

"Many enthusiasts enjoy purchasing used cars and upgrading them," continued McPhail. "In this age of environmental regulations, this project is an example of how enthusiasts can enjoy a smog-legal vehicle without sacrificing the spirit and soul that they value in hot rods and street performance cars." There, he said 'em.

No one really knows who first spoke the words, though hot rods in essence have been around nearly as long as the automobile itself. No one person can be identified as the hot rod's father. But if we had to pick one significant figure, only one, to pay homage to as the venerable grandfather of today's hot rodding, it might as well by Henry Ford.

Why? Because, prior to 1928, ol' Henry unknowingly had done the primordial hop-up set a major favor by flooding the market with 18 million Model T "flivvers" These cheap, lightweight, simple machines lent themselves

Dick Scritchfield's red roadster was one of the first hot rods converted to small-block Chevy power. Here it is circa 1963 during one of its many movie/television appearances. PAT GANAHL COLLECTION

Outta SIGHT

Dean Moon (center with trophy) pauses proudly with his lovely little *Mooneyes* dragster, the first challenger to win at both the National Hot Rod Association's (NHRA) U.S. Nationals and Winternationals. *Greg Sharp, NHRA Motorsports Museum collection*

Though its creator, Dean Moon, is no longer with us, his unforgettable "Mooneyes" logo still soldiers on, whether on a decades-old sticker barely stuck to the windshield of a '64 Impala SS or from modern promotional paperwork for his surviving speed parts business, now named Mooneyes USA.

Like his beloved logo, Moon himself remains a revered hot rodding icon. He was a pioneering member of the West Coast jet set whose resume included everything from setting speed standards at El Mirage and Bonneville to photographing feature cars for *Hot Rod* magazine. Legend has it Moon was the first SoCal hot rodder thrown in the clinker for illegally drag racing on the street, and he then became a big winner early on after the drags went straight in 1950. He had been actively involved with the Southern California Timing Association since its dry lakes beginnings in the 1930s, and in 1963 he was instrumental in the formation of the Speed Equipment Manufacturers Association, later renamed the Specialty Equipment Market Association, known more simply now as SEMA. In 1964, Moon was named SEMA's second president. He was inducted into the group's Hall of Fame not long after his death in June 1987.

It was behind his father's restaurant, Moon's Cafe, in Santa Fe Springs, California, that Dean first began toying with speed parts, a hobby that quickly evolved into a business. After serving in the U.S. Air Force during the Korean War, he officially opened the Moon Equipment Company on South Norwalk Avenue in Santa Fe Springs, where Mooneyes USA still resides today. Moon Equipment's mainstays early on included Dean's trademark fuel blocks, gas tanks, those kooky foot pedals, and, of course, his "Moon discs." By 1960, Moon's shop was *the* place to stop for hot rodders and racers alike.

Apparently the "Mooneyes" thing started during Dean's college days when he would type his name with a back-spaced comma plunked inside each "O." Next came two eyeballs painted on the side of a drag car sponsored by Moon's shop in 1953. Four years later, a commercial artist put the finishing touches on the official logo that quickly came to stand for the best in the speed parts business.

Dean Moon was always proud of his company's quality and integrity, and that pride showed up prominently each time he built one of his superbly crafted competition machines. His cars ran everywhere, from Pomona to Bonneville, and even to England. By winning races and breaking records, Moon's many four-wheeled screamers also promoted the home office back in Santa Fe Springs. You couldn't help but notice them, even when standing still; like his world-famous shop, his cars were all painted in the brightest shade of yellow this side of the sun. And they all ran as hot as they looked, thanks to Moon's favorite power source—the Chevy small block.

When Moon took his legendary mouse-motored *Mooneyes* rail to England in September 1963, he himself couldn't help noticing the impact he had already made there. "We saw Mooneyes emblems all over the place," he exclaimed in a *Drag Racing* magazine report on the trip. "Some of the British fellows wore Moon T-shirts that we hadn't sold since 1956! Many of the cars had the eyes painted on them for lack of decals. That's a real vote of confidence."

Along with being impressed with England's enthusiasm for American drag racing, Moon was quick to recognize a tempting opportunity. "They only lack the availability of specialized speed equipment," continued the man who dotted the eyes. And he knew just the remedy.

Six Stromberg 97 carburetors mounted atop a full-dress Chevy small block represented a rodder's dream during the early 1960s. Also notice the Vertex magneto and aluminum four-speed transmission. PAT GANAHL COLLECTION

relatively easily and affordably to speed-sensitive tinkering. By the 1930s, Model Ts were flooding salvage lots, too, making it easier still to try the hop-up thing. The lighter the better when boosting top end, so it was only logical that the most popular junkyard finds then were the T roadsters—the lightest of the light. Somewhere, sometime, someone later made the translation from "hot roadster" to "hot rod."

The great American hot rod was already around prior to World War II. Yet it didn't become an official candidate for American dictionaries by most accounts until after peace broke out in 1945. No one knows who received the rodding club's first membership

Featured on the January 1962 Hot Rod magazine cover, this 1929 Ford pickup was powered by a 1961 Corvette small block topped by two four-barrel carburetors. This rod ran 110 miles per hour in the quarter-mile. PAT GANAHL COLLECTION

card, but the lingo itself obviously was established in the car-culture mainstream—at least in Southern California—by the time Robert Petersen founded *Hot Rod* magazine early in 1948 in Los Angeles.

Sixteen years before, Henry Ford had given hot rodding pioneers another gift, his fabled flathead V-8, a Detroit milestone that

put real power into the hands of the people for the first time. The nickname came from this valve-in-block engine's simple cylinder heads: they were little more than flat iron covers slapped on top of the bores. Nonetheless a V-8 was a V-8, and rodders just couldn't pass up the chance to double up on their old four-holers from Ford (and

The Greens' 1923 Model T is powered by
a bored 350 small block topped by a Dyer
6-71 blower and a Predator variable-venturi
carburetor. Behind the 350 is a
Turbo Hydra-Matic automatic transmission.

Chevrolet) or jump two holes above a Chevy
Stovebolt. So what if it was decidedly low
tech? Like the Model T before, the flathead
V-8 was inexpensive, compact, and so
damned easy to play with. And it too was
plentiful. About 12 million "flatties" hit the
streets before Ford finally introduced a
modern overhead-valve V-8 in 1954.

Prior to the popularization of OHV V-8s,
there was nothing hotter behind a rod's
radiator than a Ford flattie, especially one
tweaked with all the latest go-fast goodies
offered by the speed equipment suppliers,
who had started springing up as rodding
gathered more and more momentum. High-
compression heads were supplied by the
likes of Earl Evans, Ed Almquist, and the well-
known Offenhauser shop. Among many
others, Vic Edelbrock and Phil Weiand developed improved-flow intake manifolds able to
mount multiple carburetors. Then there were
the cams, so many cams. Aftermarket lobe
grinders were plentiful as well by 1950,
including such luminaries as Ed Iskenderian,
Chet Herbert, and Jack Engle, to name just
a few.

These folks also manufactured hot parts
for the bigger, more powerful, much more
modern OHV mills from Cadillac, Olds, and
Chrysler during the 1950s. But they and
most of their countless cohorts concentrated
on the flathead, plain and simply because it
was the one V-8 that the grassroots guys
could afford to work on.

Then along came Chevrolet's new V-8 in
1955. Henry Ford may have helped the hot
rod get rolling, but it was the company
named after race driver Louis Chevrolet that
revolutionized rodding, much as it had the
automotive industry's entry-level market. By

There are few things more traditional in the street rodding world than a Chevrolet-powered T-bucket.

This blown '23 T belongs to Randy and Tanya Green of Champaign, Illinois. Nostalgic Cragar S/S wheels add to this rod's appeal.

Movie STAR CAR

One of the non-human stars of the 1973 George Lucas film *American Graffiti* was a yellow '32 Ford, driven by hot rodder John Milner (played by Paul Le Mat). The familiar Deuce coupe today is owned by Rick Figari of San Francisco, California. *Pat Ganahl*

Easily among the best supporting roles ever played by a hot rod in a movie was that by a yellow 1932 Ford in the 1973 film *American Graffiti*. Also starring Ron Howard, Richard Dreyfuss, and Cindy Williams, this wonderful tribute to 1960s teen land, Southern-California style, is perhaps remembered best for its golden oldies soundtrack and the cameos made by legendary disc jockey Wolfman Jack and a then-unknown starlet named Suzanne Somers. A young Harrison Ford also got his face in the Hollywood race in this one.

Other cars too were stars. Along with the old Ford driven by John Milner

(played by Paul Le Mat), there were two cool Chevys: a mildly customized 1958 Impala and a "wicked '55" that ran like a bat out of hell. The latter belonged to Ford's character, a cocky, cowboy-hat-wearing stud who challenges Milner's "Deuce" to a drag down Paradise Road. *American Graffiti's* climactic scene features this race, which Milner wins after his overconfident opponent rolls off into a ditch. No one is hurt, no citations are issued, and everyone lives happily ever after, save, eventually, for Milner. Film-ending credits tell us he is a killed by a drunk driver a few years later—so much for teenage innocence.

Reportedly, director George Lucas and partner Garry Kurtz put nearly as much effort into casting the "Milner coupe" role as they did its human counterparts. Various candidates were considered before Kurtz finally picked the '32 Ford, primarily because it already had a chopped top. Lucas wanted the quintessential hot rod and what better choice than a chopped Deuce? Kurtz paid $1,200 for the car, which also featured a 327 Chevy V-8 backed by a Borg-Warner four-speed transmission. Bob Hamilton's shop in Ignacio, California, then converted the coupe into a highboy with cycle fenders up front and bobbed fenders in back. Chromed headers and four Rochester 2G carburetors were added to the 327, and Orlandi's Body Shop in San Rafael, California, applied the yellow lacquer paint.

All the *American Graffiti* cars were put up for sale after filming was completed, but the Chevy-powered Ford rod, now priced at $1,500, went unsold. It was stored outside on a Universal Studios back lot until it was dusted off, freshened up (with a yellow acrylic enamel repaint) and put back to work in a sequel, *More American Graffiti*, released in 1979. After making a few promotional tours, the

The movie's transportation manager, Henry Travers, chose this particular Deuce because he liked its chopped top. Travers recalls that it was in grey primer with red fenders when the film crew purchased it for about $1,200. *Pat Ganahl*

at the corner of Van Ness and Mission in San Francisco. Many of *American Graffiti's* scenes were filmed at Mel's not long before it was torn down. A major fan of the Milner coupe dating back to the first time he saw *American Graffiti* around age 8, Figari had collected anything and everything involving the car before he became its second owner. And he still owns it some 20 years later.

Some stars never fade away.

Milner coupe was offered up again a few years later in a closed-bid auction for studio employees only. The winning bidder was Steve Fitch, who coincidentally already owned the '55 Chevy used in the first film.

Fitch let the car collect dust once more before he sold it to 20-year-old Rick Figari in 1985. As fate would have it, Figari's mother had worked as a carhop during the early 1960s at Mel's Drive-In

Milner is ticketed for a burned-out taillight during the film. He then files the citation (with countless others) in a pouch added to the passenger-side door specifically for this scene. *Pat Ganahl collection*

the early 1960s, the Bowtie boys had run away with the attention of younger rodders, while some grizzled veterans continued to hang on to the past. Even today the good ol' flathead isn't forgotten; yet few on the streets now can remember its days as king of the drive-in. When another movie, George Lucas' not-bad-at-all *American Graffiti*, premiered in 1973, the star of the 1962 SoCal cruising scene it depicted was a "piss-yellow/puke-green" '32 Ford coupe—fitted not with a flathead, but a hot little small block from Chevrolet.

An old Ford jalopy using a Chevy small block was already a common sight on the rodding scene by 1962 and quickly became the staple, and remained so until Dearborn's High Output 5.0-liter V-8 started attracting some rodding interest in the 1980s. But while Ford-powered street rods did gain some ground during the 1990s, the mouse motor still remains far and away the most popular choice, regardless of the brand of sheet metal it's wrapped up in. Fold up the hood

panels on any candy-colored Deuce today, and odds are there'll be a Bowtie down in there.

Like the flathead before it, the Chevy small block became the rodder's favorite because it was cheap, plentiful, lightweight, and easy to work with. Beyond that, however, it also was already so damned hot in stock form. Getting serious horsepower out of a flathead required a whole mess of boring, stroking, porting, and relieving, none of which was easy or cheap. The right small block, however, with the right high-performance factory parts needed nothing more than a set of free-flowing tubular headers (or maybe not) to dust the doors on nearly every flattie rod out there, be it chopped coupe or T-bucket.

Again like Ford (in 1932), Chevrolet's intentions in 1955 were to deliver mucho horses to the masses, and it was this unprecedented offering of low-priced high performance that made the small block a Detroit milestone. But Ed Cole and crew surely knew that everyday drivers wouldn't be the only ones to benefit from this breakthrough. If any engineering staffers weren't aware of this early on, they hopefully were clued in after December 16, 1953, when newly hired Zora Arkus-Duntov sent a memo to his bosses titled *Thoughts Pertaining to Youth, Hot Rodders, and Chevrolet*. "Since we cannot prevent the hot rodders from racing Corvettes or Chevys, maybe it's better to help them do a good job of it," concluded Duntov's legendary discourse. That's exactly what Chevrolet did.

As plentiful as the engines themselves were, the countless parts made the small block so much fun to play with. New performance pieces seemingly popped out of the

John Milner's yellow Deuce coupe (right) squares off on Paradise Road against the sinister black '55 Chevy in the climactic scene of the 1973 George Lucas film *American Graffiti*. Powering this famous movie-star rod was a 327 Chevy V-8.

PAT GANAHL COLLECTION

A custom-painted 1958 Chevrolet Impala also played a prominent role in *American Graffiti*. According to the script, it too was powered by a multi-carb 327 Chevy V-8.

PAT GANAHL COLLECTION

Chevy-BAKER

Splicing a Chevy Nova front frame section onto the original Studebaker foundation helped make this truck's way-down-in-the-weeds stance possible.

cool for school, even without a chopped top or any other major sheetmetal sculpturing.

Witness this 1946 "Stude" pickup, owned by David and Joy Clark of Urbana, Illinois. Modern wheels and tires, monochromatic paint, and a filled joint or two transformed this half-ton hauler into a real head-turner, as David discovered back in 2000. A card-carrying rodder dating back to the early 1970s, Clark already owned two hopped up Chevrolets (a 1937 and 1957), but he couldn't resist adding the glowing green Studebaker to his stable after just one look. Once in his garage, Clark's Stude was treated to a

Street rodders basically know no rules, save for the long-standing (though now somewhat softening) stipulation that a "true" street rod can't get any newer than 1948. Other than that, pretty much anything goes. Modifications range from mild to wild, and any vehicle, car or truck, is fair game, be it Ford, Chevy, or Chrysler.

Or Studebaker. . . Fat-fendered flights of fantasy always have been street rodding's main attractions, and they just don't come much heavier than the plump-looking pickup trucks built in South Bend, Indiana, from 1941 to 1948. These babies just beg to be dropped into the weeds per common rodder's practice; once down there they can't help but look too

Various body seams have been filled and a custom cargo box fashioned for this 1946 Studebaker pickup, owned by David and Joy Clark of Urbana, Illinois.

Left: Nestled way down in there is a late-1970s vintage 350 small block.

Below: Studebaker never built a truck cockpit as plush as this. Modern features include comfortable buckets, air conditioning, a tilt steering column, and cruise control.

little bodywork spruce up courtesy of buddy Don Patton. The two longtime comrades chose to leave things beneath the skin well enough alone, however. After all, why fix something that wasn't broken?

Like nine out of 10 street rods out there, Clark's Studebaker is powered by a Bowtie small block—in this case a late-1970s four-barrel-fed 350 backed by a Turbo Hydra-Matic automatic transmission. Built primarily with comfort in mind, the truck also sports air conditioning, cruise control, and a tilt steering column.

Let the other guys belch fire and smoke the tires. When the Clarks make the scene in their "Chevy-Baker," they do so low and slow, content in the knowledge that no one ever said all rods have to be frighteningly fast. Remember, on the street, there are no rules.

woodwork every year as The Hot One grew progressively hotter. According to drag racing legend Bill "Grumpy" Jenkins, the rodding world was truly rocked in 1957 when the dual-carb 283 V-8 was boosted up to 270 horsepower. "The 270-horse version really launched this engine," said Jenkins to *Chevy High Performance* magazine's Jim Resnick in 1995 during the small block's 40th birthday party. "It was the buy-it-and-build-it era wherein hot rodders accepted the engine, and you could buy just about anything you needed to make it a competitive piece. Credit should be given to the factory high-performance parts that established the engine, even without its expensive fuel injection system."

Chevrolet asked nearly $500 for its new Ramjet fuel injection option in 1957. For that kind of heavy green, your garden-variety speed freak probably could've built up two equally strong, carbureted small blocks for his hot rod, relying on the many aftermarket speed parts already available by then for the Chevy V-8. Among others, rodding legend Dean Moon wasted little time shifting his Southern California speed shop's focus over

Started by Dick Dean and finished by Joe Bailon, this Chevy-powered "barber shop" was created during the early 1970s, when "the crazier, the better" motto dominated the show-rod circuit.

Did it come much crazier than
a Chevy-powered Roman chariot?
PAT GANAHL COLLECTION

Aaron Grote of Cisco, Illinois, built this retro rod using a '34 Chevy truck chassis and radically customized 1960 Buick tail. The rear section of the frame was shortened 4 inches and "re-arched" to allow the installation of a Ford 9-inch axle.

to the small block after its 1955 debut and quickly became one of the mouse motor's best friends. One of those "others," Vic Edelbrock, was by August 1957 getting 279 horsepower out of the noninjected 283. Top advertised output for the factory's fuelie that year was only 4 horsepower more.

Modifying the small block for more power was nowhere near as tough a job as in the flathead's case. Those interchangeable cylinder heads breathed well enough on their own, but massaging the ports for more flow was almost child's play in comparison to the valve-in-block Ford. Or you could've simply stuck with certain stock units, which were first treated to enlarged port areas (for high-performance applications) in 1956. Those ports grew even larger for the 1961 fuel-injected 283, and bigger valves (2.02-inch

intakes, 1.60 exhausts, compared to 1.72/1.50) were installed in the injected 327 in 1964. Indeed, it was the post-1961 fuel injection head that became the rodder's dream, and one misguided rocker—black leather jacketed Bruce Springsteen—later even tried bolting a pair of fuelie heads atop a 396 big block, in one of his hit ballads, that is. Maybe Bruce shoulda stuck to motorcycles.

Like the small-, medium-, and large-port heads, the classic small-block crank came in three different sizes as the main journals were widened to improve durability. Small journals measured 2.30 inches; medium, 2.45; and large, 2.65. That latter measurement was reserved only for the Siamesed-cylinder 400, introduced in 1970; this crank (with its long 3.75-inch stroke)

Grote narrowed the 1960 Buick sheet metal by 26 inches to mate with the '34 Chevy cab. The Buick's roof supplied the metal for the lower quarter panels, and the roll pan in back was fashioned from a 1953 Oldsmobile grille turned upside down.

became a favorite for 1970s rodders building the popular 383-cube small block.

Car Craft may have called Chevy's largest mouse the "400-inch Bust," but this low-performance V-8 apparently did offer some attraction to horsepower hounds. Sprint car racers were especially fond of the 400's large-journal block, which represented a damn good start on the way to wringing the small block for every cube it could manage. The 400's fragile connecting rods, however, were best left to the pickup truck crowd.

Though the famous Duntov cam was lumpy enough in many cases, early rodders could have just as easily chosen an aftermarket stick—there were so many offered by the early 1960s, and the heavy competition

made for some tidy prices. From the beginning, speed shops represented the best choice when it came to improving the small block's stock valve gear for hot rodding applications. Screw-in rocker arm studs (with pushrod guide plates) were highly recommended, even more so whenever valve spring pressure and lift were increased. Roller-tipped rocker arms were also a major plus and helped minimize the valvetrain maladies that Smokey Yunick encountered in 1955. Chevrolet Engineering addressed some of Yunick's early complaints with stronger pistons in 1956. Friction-cutting roller lifters, too, became a common rodder's tweak well before Chevy began offering them on the Corvette's L98 V-8 in 1987.

TOP: Power for Grote's '34 Chevy comes from a modern 350 crate motor dolled up vintage-style with three Rochester carburetors on an Edelbrock intake.

BOTTOM: A mixture of stock Chevrolet performance parts and aftermarket go-fast goodies, this dressed-up 270-horsepower 283 was fitted into a 1957 Chevy and given away as part of a *Hot Rod* magazine promotion in 1984. PAT GANAHL COLLECTION

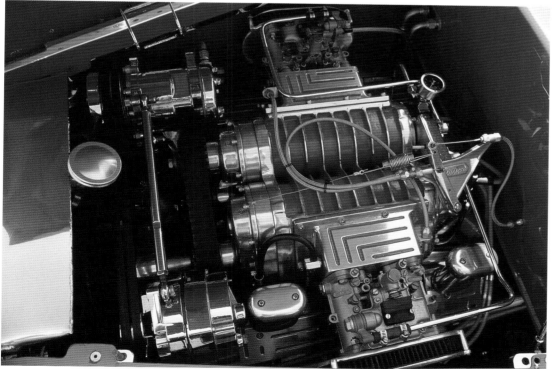

TOP: You name the speed parts and you'll see them fitted to a hopped-up small block. The setup shown here is a Moon Cross-Flow manifold topped by Weber-style throttle bodies. The car is a 1950s-era Rambler station wagon. PAT GANAHL COLLECTION

BOTTOM: Jerry Magnuson developed his three-lobe Roots-type blower for motorcycles. Here, two pint-sized Magnuson superchargers appear atop a modified stock four-barrel intake on a Chevy small-block V-8 in a '32 Ford roadster. PAT GANAHL COLLECTION

Road WARRIOR

Chevrolet's 1957 Bel Air probably ranks as the most readily recognized automobile in Detroit history, matched perhaps only by Ford's two-seat Thunderbird of 1955 to 1957. "Icon" doesn't do this one justice; even a blind man knows a '57 Chevy when he sees one. So popular is this modern neoclassic that you're almost likely to find more examples rolling around today than were originally built nearly a half-century ago. Recreating one complete from scratch has long been possible thanks to the vast collection of reproduction parts made available over the years, a plain fact not missed by restorers, racers, and rodders alike.

Longtime '57 fan Bill Frye may well represent all three of these factions at once. Save for its nonstock Firethorn Red paint, American Racing mags, and customized grille work, Frye's beautiful Bel Air coupe appears predominantly original on the outside. But underneath that unmarred sheet metal beats the heart of a real ground-pounder, an alter ego given away at a glance by those fat, sticky competition tires in back. Yet as much as this baby loves to run, it also looks super sweet standing still on a show field or cruising low and slow down Main Street. Whatever the venue, Frye's Chevy is a real winner inside and out.

Frye and his crowd-pleaser go way back. A rust-free West Coast Chevy when he bought it (minus engine and transmission) in 1969, his beloved Bel Air was first brought back to life as a drag queen fitted with a 370-ci small block topped by twin four-barrels on a tunnel-ram intake. Running one quarter-mile at a time remained the coupe's only duty until the late-1970s, when Frye found he no longer could afford to compete at the drags. He then rebuilt his ride from the ground up as a street machine and repainted it with the acrylic lacquer that still shines on some 25 years later. Car and owner next "did the show thing for about three or four years" before boredom set in.

Frye put his Bel Air back to work on the drag strip during the 1980s running seven or eight races a season. And he still trips the lights occasionally today, though you'd never know it at a glance considering the car's pristine condition. Its best times on local 1/8-mile tracks in Illinois and Indiana run down around 6.5 seconds, and it has recorded 9.90s in the quarter-mile. That's fast in anyone's book.

Beneath the hood is a super small block stroked up to 427 cubic inches and boosted with a little nitrous injection. The transmission is a Turbo Hydra-Matic 400 automatic (with trans brake) and the rear end is a narrowed 12-bolt containing 4.33:1 gears. The sum of these parts equal one '57 Chevy that you're not likely to overlook—as if that was possible.

Owned by Bill and Joyce Frye of Paxton, Illinois, this '57 Bel Air street/strip car still wears the Pontiac paint applied 25 years ago. Bill Frye bought the car in 1969.

Beneath the spit and polish is a nitrous-injected 427-ci small block that makes as much as 700 horsepower. Compression is 13:1.

A narrowed 12-bolt rear and street-going slicks are the only outward concessions to this Bel Air coupe's nasty nature at the drag strip. It has run as fast as 9.90s on the quarter-mile.

With so many factory parts that mixed and matched in seemingly endless possibilities, and with so many companies like Crane, Crower, Hooker, etc., making so many performance-enhancing products, was it any wonder that, by 1970, the small-block Chevy V-8 had left all other hot rodding power possibilities buried in the dust? And even during the trying 1970s, when horsepower and hot rodding both became truly taboo subjects on the automotive scene, there were still many diehard hot rodders out there massaging their mouse motors.

It was that hands-on attitude that came back into focus around Chevrolet Engineering during the 1980s. In 1989, Chevrolet introduced its High Output 5.7-liter V-8, a "crate-motor" option created with hot rodders in mind. (Named because a customer could simply take it home in a crate to be installed in any vehicle his heart desired.) Included in the deal were a four-bolt block, a forged crank, a hydraulic cam with roller lifters, aluminum heads, and an aluminum high-rise dual-plane intake manifold. With a 750-cfm Holley four-barrel, a heavily advanced High Energy Ignition (HEI) distributor, and tube headers in place, the 350 HO produced 345 horsepower, making it a real steal.

After it was introduced at the SEMA show late in 1988, the 350 HO brought 'em running like nobody's business. Early on, Chevrolet couldn't keep up with demand as about 350 crates a month were being loaded out of parts departments across the country. Apparently, people will forever tinker with their toys, no matter what gas costs.

"Performance enthusiasts are accustomed to working on their own cars," reiterated Mark McPhail in 1995. "Project cars (like his '55 sedan) show them not only how to do that, but to do such upgrades in smog-legal form and let them know that GM Performance Parts are available through franchised dealers."

Those dealers began offering another crate motor, the ZZ430 5.7-liter V-8, in 1998. The "430" in that tag came from this engine's output: Both maximum horsepower and torque ratings were 430. Features included "Fast Burn" cylinder heads and a big 750-cfm Holley four-barrel carburetor. Looking at this race-ready small block, it's easy to understand why General Motors presently supplies about 60 percent of the crate motors being sold today to both racers and rodders alike. While some of those are big blocks, the majority are small blocks.

Chevrolet's mouse motor and the great American hot rod—a match made in heaven? No, in Warren, Michigan.

Chevy-powered Ford rods certainly are alive and well in the new millennium. Here, Elmer Lash (left) plants a modern LS1 small block into his '40 Ford in his shop in Champaign, Illinois, while comrade Bob Ogle tinkers with the 350 V-8 in his '40.

Chapter 5

WEIRD SCIENCE:
The Injected Eighties

Fuel injection helped make the Corvette famous in 1957. Throttle body injection (TBI) then helped save the small block from possible extinction. Introduced in 1982, Chevrolet's Cross-Fire Injection TBI V-8 was the heart and soul of the redesigned 1984 Corvette.

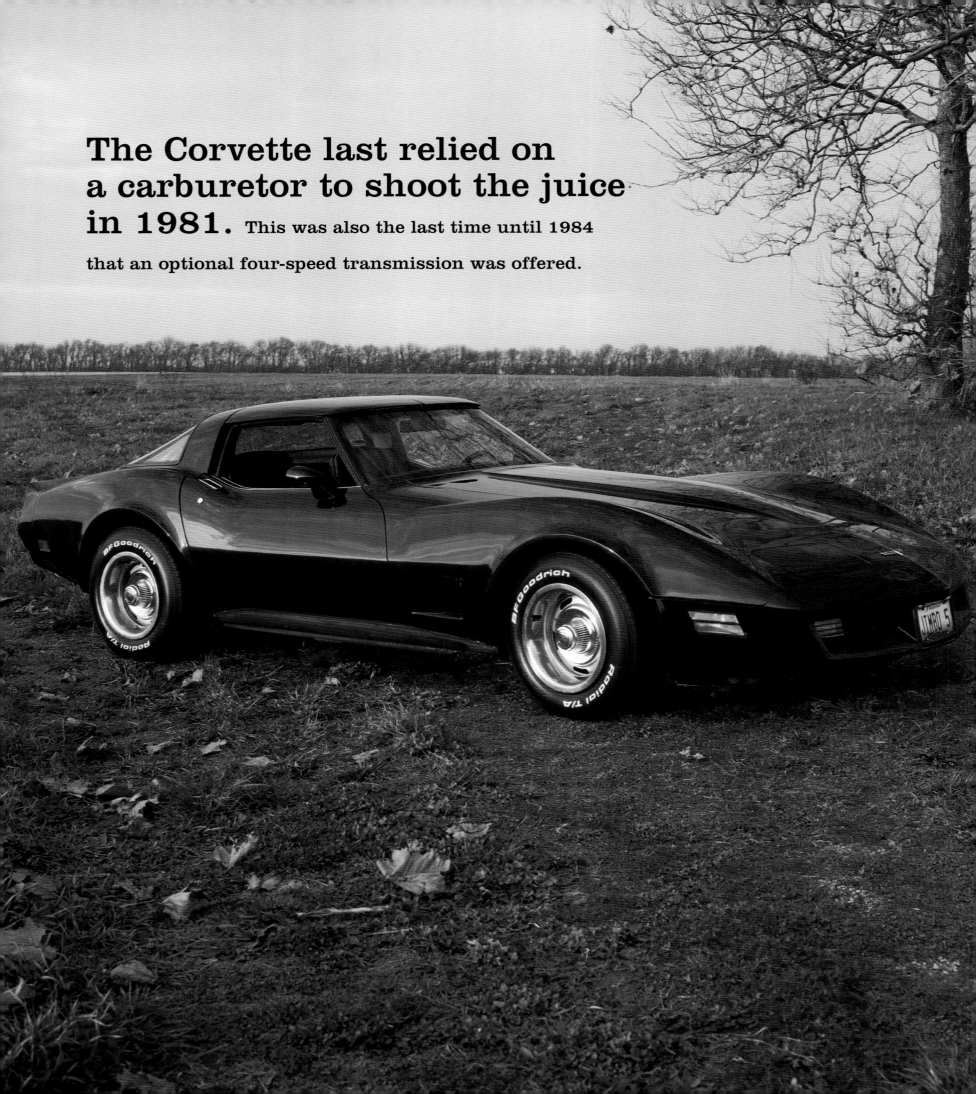

The Corvette last relied on a carburetor to shoot the juice in 1981. This was also the last time until 1984 that an optional four-speed transmission was offered.

THINGS WERE LOOKING PRETTY BLEAK AROUND SMALL BLOCK LAND AS THE 1970S COUGHED AND CHOKED TO A CLOSE. Cleaning up the internal combustion engine's act by federal order had pretty much wiped out real high performance by mid-decade. And that wasn't all. Some Detroit-watchers began discussing a future without V-8s entirely, and a small group of extremists even predicted the end of the road for all gas-fired engines regardless of cylinder count. In many environment-conscious minds, battery-powered transports were surely right around the corner.

An entirely new attitude encompassed the marketplace by the time the 1980s arrived as car buyers then had nearly forgotten all about acronyms and abbreviations like "mph" and "hp." Instead, they had become painfully familiar with the likes of "EPA," "mpg," and "CAFE"—the latter letters referring to the Washington-mandated corporate average fuel economy standard that demanded an automaker deliver a minimum miles-per-gallon

The only engine available for the 1981 Corvette was the L81 350 V-8, rated at 190 horsepower. Behind this L81 is a Turbo Hydra-Matic 350 automatic transmission. Fuel-conscious 2.87:1 gears bring up the rear.

rating in its cars or suffer a penalty tax. Along with catalytic converters and low-octane unleaded gasoline, the 1970s had also brought us sky-high fossil-fuel prices, which on their own undoubtedly would've been enough to transform the 10-mile-per-gallon (and less) muscle cars into dinosaurs.

It was this newfound need to skimp on fuel consumption that inspired Chevrolet engineers to introduce the 262-cubic-inch V-8 with its meager 3.5-inch bore, the smallest in small-block history. This 110-horsepower weakling proved a dismal failure, lasting only one year after its 1975 introduction. In its place came the bigger, better 305 V-8 in 1976, and this reasonably successful small block was then "de-bored" in 1979 to create the more efficient 267, which stuck around up through 1981. Additional efficiency resulted in 1978 when Chevrolet put together

The Camaro Z28 was named as the honored pace car for the Indianapolis 500 in 1982. Chevrolet built 6,000 "Commemorative Edition" pace car replicas for public consumption.

a new V-6, described by some as a "three-quarter small block." It was this fuel-conscious six that laid the groundwork for the later arrival of the truck line's popular Vortec engine series.

As for a truly hot small block, it truly was hard to come by as the 1980s dawned. Although engineers did manage to keep the Corvette running as America's most exciting (translated: fastest) production car, there was little else left over for Average Joe, who never could save up enough pennies and dimes to put himself behind the wheel of one of those 'glass-bodied beauties. More to Joe's liking was the Z28 Camaro. But by the 1980s this muscle car survivor had become very much a mere shadow of its former sexy self. After returning it to Chevrolet's perform-ance lineup midway through 1977, engineers had concentrated mostly on improving han-dling, the only right thing to do, considering that they had so few horses to work with. Standard power for the 1981 Z28 came from a 175-horsepower 350.

At least most press critics at the time did love what engineers had done with the latest Z28's chassis. After testing a 1982 Z28, *Car and Driver*'s Don Sherman described the top-shelf Camaro's road-hugging nature as a "take-home Bondurant instructional course," in reference to Chevy racing legend Bob Bondurant's equally famous driving school in Arizona. "Handling will clearly be the new Z28's claim to fame," continued Sherman, "just as it was 12 years ago when the General's engineers last had a serious go at this car."

Too bad he couldn't say the same for straight-line performance. "This car has no motor, or at least none that's really appropriate

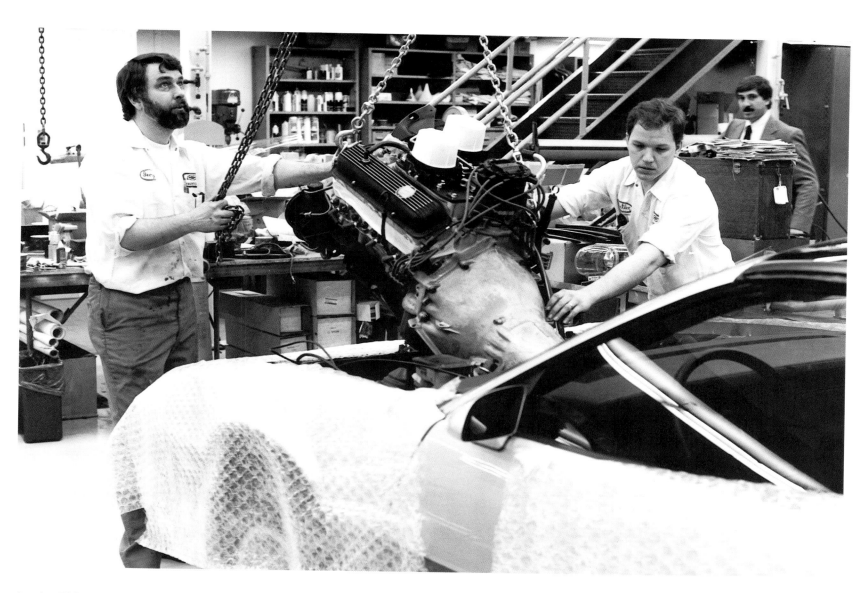

for the Z28. We'll leave the small-block Chevy V-8 to the aftermarket tuners. It has virtually no future at GM, other than near-term Corvette and Camaro/Firebird applications, and the necessary funds are not likely to be allotted to bring this 27-year-old engine up to date." Sherman's own humbly offered solution to this power shortage involved the development of a really hot aluminum-head, single-overhead-cam V-6 with electronically controlled "port-type" fuel injection. In response, the "General's" engineers probably politely thanked Don for his suggestion then went back to work in the real world. Or back to sleep.

While aluminized, electronically injected OHC engines are quite common today, they had yet to reach much more than a dream stage back in the early 1980s. Switching to weight-saving aluminum (and magnesium) pieces would come soon enough, but potentially powerful overhead cam designs at the time still represented too costly a proposition. Enhancing both performance and efficiency with the use of improved fuel delivery systems, on the other hand, was already in the works.

Forced induction, in the form of turbocharging, had helped some companies to pump out a few more horses, mostly from

Chevrolet Engineering technicians lower a special all-aluminum small block into one of the two '82 Camaros built specially to actually pace the Indy 500.

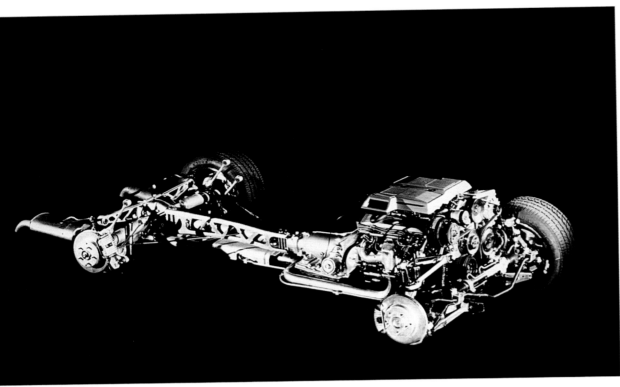

1984 Corvette V-8

CONSTRUCTION:
**cast-iron block
w/cast-iron cylinder heads**

DISPLACEMENT (CUBIC INCHES):
350

BORE & STROKE (INCHES):
4.00 x 3.48

LIFTERS:
hydraulic

COMPRESSION:
9:1

INDUCTION:
**Cross-Fire Injection
(throttle body injection)**

HORSEPOWER:
205 at 4,300 rpm

TORQUE:
290 at 2,800 rpm

four-cylinder engines, beginning in the late 1970s. But the bulk of these early turbo applications served only to barely bridge the gap between efficiency and performance in budget buggies that almost couldn't get away from your mother-in-law and her walker. A "Turbo" badge in the 1980s by no means signified the presence of a hot car.

Chevrolet engineers preferred fuel injection—after all, they had pioneered the automotive application of this proven technology in America in 1957. That Ramjet equipment, though, had been of mechanical design; that is, it relied solely on inherent functional inputs (airflow, vacuum pressure) to control fuel delivery. While more precise than contemporary carburetors, Chevy's original injection system still could stand some serious improvement from a performance-maximizing point of view. But, more importantly from a 1980s perspective, was the fact that Chevy's Rochester fuel injection installation had done nothing to control emissions, basically because it didn't have to: Washington's first influential Clean

Air Act arrived just as the last fuelie Corvette was being built in 1965.

Even more precision through computerized electronic controls eventually emerged to better address the clean air issue. By 1970, Pontiac engineers were testing a Bendix-built electronic fuel injection (EFI) system on one of their V-8s with wonderfully clean-running results, inspiring *Motor Trend* magazine's Karl Ludvigsen to conclude that this advancement "could be the vital link in enabling the internal combustion engine to meet stringent emission standards." Unfortunately another decade arrived before General Motors made an EFI V-8 available.

It was Germany's Bosch company that helped introduce a regular-production EFI automobile in America, creating its Jetronic system for Volkswagen's 1600 engine in 1968 to help "Vee-dubs" imported into this country comply with the latest emissions standard update made that year. Various other European makes, including Saab, Volvo, and Mercedes, were also soon onboard the EFI bandwagon. GM, meanwhile,

Featuring Chevrolet's stock Cross-Fire Injection setup, the Indy pace car small block featured 11:1 compression and tubular headers. Output was about 250 horsepower.

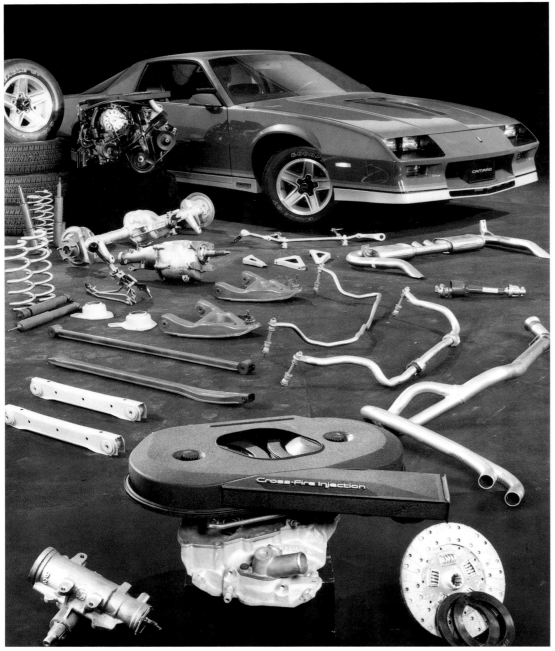

choice but to make major leaps in innovation only when they absolutely had to. For the most part, small steps marked engine technology advancements made during the 1970s. And if not for California's always-tougher emissions standards, those advances probably would've been even longer in coming.

Keeping the Corvette running strong across America was tough enough back then; making it run at all on the West Coast represented the true test. California's superstrict smog standards meant that, beginning in 1976, Corvette buyers in that state could drive off a Chevy lot with one engine only, the base 350. There were even tighter restrictions in 1980. Chevrolet failed to certify its 350 V-8s for sale in California that year. So in place of the 190-horsepower L48 (and in exchange for a $50 credit), Corvettes came with the LG4 305-ci V-8. Although it was taken right from the mundane passenger car parts shelf, the 1980 Corvette's California-legal LG4 still produced only 10 horses less than the L48 thanks to the use of stainless-steel tubular headers and a "Computer Command Control" system that automatically adjusted carburetor mixture and ignition timing on demand. A small step, maybe, but this "brain box" did represent real progress.

Both the LG4's lightweight headers (with oxygen-sensor smog controls) and computer controls were transferred to a new 350 small block, the L81, in 1981. This 190-horsepower V-8 not only was certified for sale in all 50 states, it also became available in California with either an automatic transmission or a four-speed, making it the first time since 1975 that a bushy, blond beach boy could buy a Corvette with a stick. Bitchin'!

continued to tinker its way along with a few tweaks here and there to hopefully keep customers convinced that progress indeed was being made.

Cost constraints surely represented the prime factor behind Detroit's seeming hesitancy to get its own EFI designs up and rolling sooner. Tight budgetary strings left American engineers in those days little

Along with Cross-Fire Injection, the 1982 Z28 also was treated to various chassis upgrades.

Chevrolet closed out the C3 Corvette's run in 1982 with the "Collectors' Edition," priced at about $4,000 more than the garden-variety 1982 Corvette coupe. Exclusive wheels, paint, and upholstery set the Collectors' Edition apart, as did a unique hatchback rear window.

SYSTEM OVERVIEW

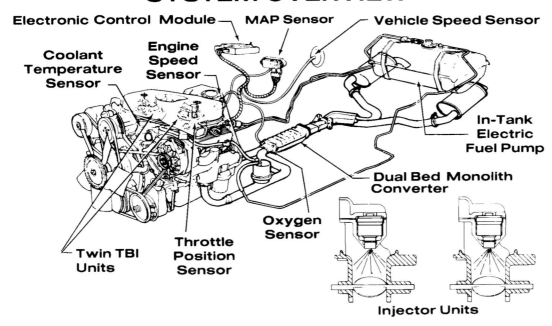

Electronic Control Module — MAP Sensor — Vehicle Speed Sensor

Coolant Temperature Sensor

Engine Speed Sensor

In-Tank Electric Fuel Pump

Dual Bed Monolith Converter

Oxygen Sensor

Twin TBI Units

Throttle Position Sensor

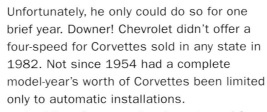

Injector Units

ABOVE LEFT: All 1982 Corvettes were fitted with the Cross-Fire Injection small block, which worked in concert with a special four-speed automatic transmission to help improve efficiency along with performance.

ABOVE RIGHT: Press critics may have scoffed at the name, and its throttle body injection technology was quickly overshadowed by more refined advances, but one thing was certain—the Cross-Fire Injection package certainly looked cool.

Unfortunately, he only could do so for one brief year. Downer! Chevrolet didn't offer a four-speed for Corvettes sold in any state in 1982. Not since 1954 had a complete model-year's worth of Corvettes been limited only to automatic installations.

Luckily, a four-speed option returned for the redesigned fourth-generation Corvette in 1984. And various other "new" C4 features also made return appearances that year. During the early 1980s, Dave McLellan's engineers more than once had let some of the developing C4 technology slip into the latest C3 Corvette, with examples including the lightweight magnesium valve covers that first appeared on the L81 V-8 in 1981. Cutting unwanted pounds was a main goal of the C4 design, and other weight-conscious pieces created during this process—a new differential housing and corresponding mounting member, both made of aluminum—had been released early for the 1980 Corvette.

But easily the biggest cat let out of the bag was the C4's innovative powertrain.

While Corvette fans would have to wait more than half a year to finally see the redesigned C4 in the spring of 1983, they got to try out the engine and transmission in the best 'Vette yet some 18 months earlier. Designated L83, the '82 Corvette's 350 V-8 used refined versions of the LG4 California V-8's tubular-header exhausts and Computer Command Control system. The real attraction, however, came up top in the form of Cross-Fire Injection.

Cross-Fire Injection was Chevrolet's high-performance variation on GM's throttle body injection (TBI) design, introduced in 1980 for Cadillac's Eldorado and Seville. Less complex (and thus less costly) than EFI designs, GM's TBI system didn't require the high-pressure fuel pump and low-pressure boost pump (incorporated inside the fuel tank) common to EFI setups. EFI required lots of fuel-feed boost (up to 79 psi), while TBI did not. According to engineer Lauren Bowler's SAE paper, titled "Throttle Body Fuel Injection—An Integrated Control System," "The motivating factor behind the hard work

Super DAVE

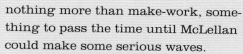

David Ramsay McLellan needed about eight years to make his own mark on America's Sports Car after replacing Zora Duntov in January 1975, to become the Corvette's second chief engineer. McLellan's baby, the redesigned C4 Corvette, debuted in March 1983, more than six months later than initially planned, a lag that allowed public anticipation to reach a fever pitch. McLellan himself helped to fan those flames by letting some developing technology slip out ahead of time, most notably the L83 small block, introduced for the final C3 Corvette in 1982.

"It's a harbinger of things to come," said McLellan about the car that preceded his real claim to fame. "For the 1982 model is more than just the last of a generation; it's stage one of a two-stage production. We're doing the power team this year. Next year, we add complete new styling and other innovations." "Next year" ended up being 1984 in official model-year terms, but who was counting?

As for Dave McLellan, his engineering career began in 1959 after graduation from Wayne State University. His first job was in the noise-and-vibration laboratory at GM's Milford Proving Grounds, and he was at Chevrolet working on the second-generation Camaro by early 1969. A brief assignment in 1971 took McLellan to GM's Technical Center, where he contributed to John DeLorean's proposed K-car, a platform that would have combined the Nova, Camaro, and Corvette. After the K-car was rightly shot down, McLellan remained at the Technical Center as a full-time chassis engineer for the Camaro/Nova group.

He spent most of 1973 and 1974 at the Massachusetts Institute of Technology's Sloan School of Management on GM's dime—clearly he was being groomed for something big. With his MIT master's degree in hand, McLellan returned to Chevrolet in the summer of 1974 as one of Duntov's staff engineers. Zora stepped down six months later, and McLellan expectedly took his place. Filling his shoes, however, didn't come so quickly.

The 1976 Corvette was already cast in stone when McLellan took over, and much the same could be said about the 1977 model. McLellan's regime didn't make a noticeable impact until the Corvette was fitted with fastback rear glass in 1978. But this minor makeover represented nothing more than make-work, something to pass the time until McLellan could make some serious waves.

C4 development began in 1978, a time when Duntov's long-considered midengine proposals were still fresh in the minds of GM decision-makers. Though retired, Zora still dropped by McLellan's offices in Warren, Michigan, about once a month. The Corvette's father figure not only couldn't walk away, he also couldn't quite forget the one dream that was never fulfilled, even though by then GM execs had finally squelched his midengine idea.

McLellan did dabble with a midengine mule early on, but he undoubtedly was more of a realist than Zora. McLellan knew his bosses never would fund such radical innovation, especially considering how well the conventional design was selling as the 1970s were winding down. McLellan's legacy, like Duntov's, would be traditionally rear-driven—via the traditional small-block V-8—when he handed the Corvette's reins to David Hill in 1992.

The second of three Corvette chief engineers, Dave McLellan pauses with his sculpted self during the National Corvette Museum's grand opening party in September 1994.

Weird science was the 1984 Corvette's calling card, inside and out. What seemed like a great idea at first—that Star Trek dash—quickly became the butt of jokes among the automotive press.

to obtain an acceptable low-pressure fuel system was the elimination of the precision high-pressure fuel pump and its associated cost." Now it was Chevrolet's turn to save pennies and dimes.

Chevy people kept even more cash in their wallets while developing the TBI setup's foundation. Eagle-eyes might have noticed that the Cross-Fire Injection equipment looked an awful lot like the rare twin-carb option found on some Z/28 Camaros in 1969. This was no coincidence. According to technician Louis Cuttitta, the L83's intake manifold was simply an updated version of the aluminum "cross-ram" casting used 13 years before.

New were the two Rochester-supplied, computer-controlled throttle body injector units mounted diagonally on that intake in place of the twin four-barrel carburetors seen in 1969. In command of those twin units was an electronic control module (ECM) that was capable of adjusting up to 80 variables (ignition timing, fuel/air mixture, idle speed, etc.) per second to maximize both performance and efficiency. According to Bowler, additional benefits included "hardware simplicity, reduced evaporative emissions, excellent hot fuel handling characteristics, a single metering circuit to calibrate per throttle bore, elimination of ignition-off dieseling (run on), full fuel range scheduling including cold start, and the flexibility to expand to a closed loop with an exhaust sensor."

In truth, Cross-Fire Injection didn't do all that much more for small-block performance.

1985 Corvette L98 V-8

CONSTRUCTION:
**cast-iron block
w/cast-iron cylinder heads**

DISPLACEMENT (CUBIC INCHES):
350

BORE & STROKE (INCHES):
4.00 x 3.48

LIFTERS:
hydraulic

COMPRESSION:
9:1

INDUCTION:
**Tuned-Port Injection
(TPI)**

HORSEPOWER:
230 at 4,000 rpm

TORQUE:
330 at 3,200 rpm

Late DATE

Delays bringing the next-generation C4 Corvette to market left Chevrolet officials with little choice but to skip the 1983 model year. The first C4 was introduced in March 1983 as a 1984 model.

In the rush to proclaim the fabulous C5 as the best 'Vette yet, few witnesses seemed to recall a similar sensation seen nearly 15 years before. Like the all-new fifth-generation Corvette, the first C4 garnered *Motor Trend*'s prestigious "Car of the Year" award, and rightly so. Granted, the C5's trophy didn't come until the convertible version was introduced in 1998, but that's only because the Targa-topped sport coupe initially unveiled in January 1997 appeared too late to make *Motor Trend*'s 1997 balloting.

Chevrolet's first C4 was tardy for its coming-out party, too. Bowling Green rolled out its last C3 in 1982. Dealer

introductions for the third-generation's long-awaited replacement didn't begin until March 1983, by which time Chevrolet officials had already decided to simply forego an official 1983 model run.

No '83 Corvettes were sold to the public, and the first C4 emerged as a 1984 model.

Various factors contributed to this late arrival. C4 roots dated back to 1978, with the plan then being to introduce the latest, greatest Corvette as a 1982 model. Meanwhile, the C3 rolled into the 1980s still selling like proverbial hotcakes. After reaching an all-time record of 53,807 in 1979, Corvette production stayed above 40,000 for both 1980 and 1981. If it wasn't broken, why fix it?

On top of that, Chevrolet officials also didn't want to tackle start-ups for both a new assembly line and a new model at the same time. The production facility in Kentucky had only started rolling itself in June 1981, with the venerable C3

An extended model year run for the 1984 Corvette resulted in near-record sales of 51,547, all sport coupes. Only the 1979 Corvette, at 53,807, was more plentiful.

While the C4 was considered "all new" for 1984, its 5.7-liter Cross-Fire Injection engine was already familiar by then. It had debuted beneath the 1982 Corvette's hood.

improved markedly with a five-link design in place of the old three-link setup. Topping things off was a totally fresh restyle, incorporating a large clamshell hood that allowed easier engine access.

Appearing as it did in the spring of 1983, the '84 Corvette then enjoyed an extended production run, allowing it to nearly surpass that 1979 record. The final tally read 51,547. Chevrolet clearly had itself another winner.

remaining the focus. Various development gremlins then surfaced, as they do so often, to help delay the C4's introduction further. Most agreed, however, that the end result was worth the wait.

While awarding the Car of the Year trophy, *Motor Trend's* editors concluded that the C4 had risen to a new plateau: "The ('84) Corvette has the highest EQ (Excitement Quotient) of anything to come out of an American factory. Ever. Its

handling goes beyond mere competence; call it superb, call it leading edge, call it world class. *We* certainly do."

Indeed, it was the C4's new chassis that set it apart from its forerunners. Highlights included transverse, mono-leaf fiberglass springs front and rear, Girling four-wheel disc brakes, revised suspension locations at both ends, and the liberal use of aluminum components throughout to save weight. Independent suspension continued in back, but it was

Beneath this air cleaner are twin diagonally mounted throttle body injectors. Advertised output for the TBI 350 small block was 200 horsepower in 1984.

America's fastest production car made more than one major leap ahead during the 1980s. The 1984 model (right) featured a new chassis and body and the 200-horsepower Cross-Fire Injection small block. The Cross-Fire experiment was all but forgotten by the time the 1989 model (left) appeared. Top output in 1989 was 245 horsepower from a TPI V-8.

At 200 horsepower, the L83's advertised output was up only 10 horses compared to its L81 predecessor. Yet that figure still was nothing to sneeze at. As a 1982 *Road & Track* review explained, the L83 represented "a far cry from the 400 horsepower-plus days of the L88 (427 V-8), but not exactly a shrinking violet by today's wheezing standards." What Cross-Fire Injection did do was allow a slight power boost to happen alongside both a major emissions reduction and a tidy fuel economy gain. Sounds like the best of all worlds, no?

Enhancing the 1982 Corvette's all-around appeal further was the new 700-R4 four-speed automatic transmission, which also was electronically linked to the L83's TBI system. Shifting and the torque converter's lockup clutch feature were all precisely controlled by the ECM depending on varying speed and load data inputs, and it was this control that helped improve fuel efficiency. Wags may laugh today, but the entire Cross-Fire Injection package clearly represented the highest tech seen to that point between fiberglass flanks.

If only Chevrolet could have come up with a better name. The term "Cross-Fire" inspired snickers right off the bat in 1982. "One test driver commented that this sounds more like a malfunction than a sales feature ('Stand back, kid, that engine's about to cross-fire!'), but the system works very well nevertheless," concluded the *Road & Track* test of the '82 L83 Corvette. Guess you can't always judge a book by its cover—or an engine by its air cleaner.

Along with the Corvette, the restyled 1982 Camaro also was treated to Cross-Fire Injection, but only as an option for the Z28's

5.0-liter (305-ci) V-8—the 350 small block had been dropped from the Camaro lineup the year before. Compared to the '82 Z28's base 145-horsepower "5.0L" V-8, the TBI-equipped LU5 305 (priced at a hefty $450) was rated at 165 horsepower. RPO LU5 returned as a Z28 option for 1983 (at 175 horsepower), and was replaced in 1984 by RPO L69, the High Output 305, which reverted back to a conventional carburetor. Listed for both the Z28 and Monte Carlo SS, the four-barrel-fed 5.0-liter HO was rated at 190 horsepower in the former and 180 in the latter, due to a little less compression. In both cases, HO output was enhanced by a twin-snorkel air cleaner and enlarged, less-restrictive exhausts featuring a wide-mouth Corvette catalytic converter. The L69 V-8 was

1985 Camaro IROC-Z V-8

CONSTRUCTION:
**cast-iron block
w/cast-iron cylinder heads**

DISPLACEMENT (METRIC):
5.0 liters (305 cubic inches)

BORE & STROKE (INCHES):
3.736 x 3.48

LIFTERS:
hydraulic

COMPRESSION:
9.5:1

INDUCTION:
**Tuned-Port Injection
(TPI)**

HORSEPOWER:
215 at 4,400 rpm

TORQUE:
275 at 3,200 rpm

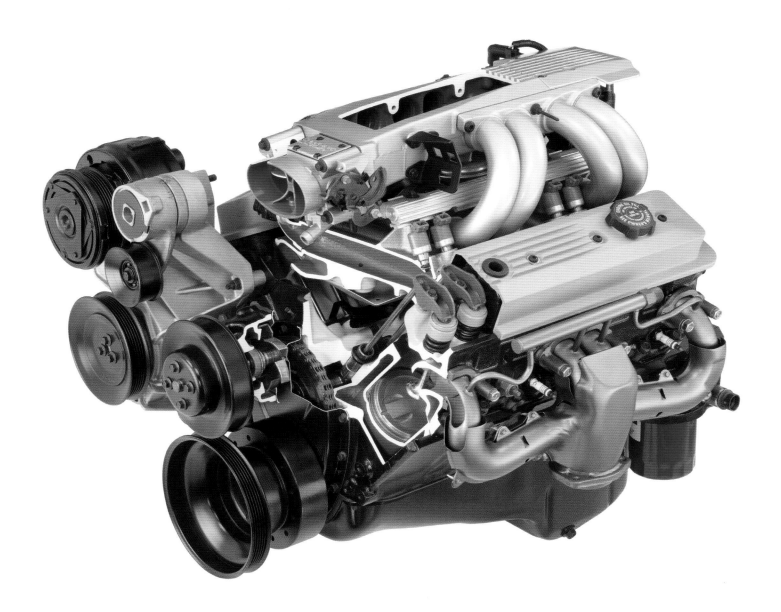

last offered in 1986, while Cross-Fire
Injection was last seen on the redesigned
1984 Corvette.

The 1985 Corvette served as a showcase
for Chevrolet's first EFI system, a major step
ahead (compared to TBI) called Tuned-Port
Injection (TPI). Like TBI, TPI was kind to both
the environment and the pocketbook, but at
the same time it was downright mean when it
came to making muscle. Bringing back some
real two-seat performance was the top goal
this time around, and the TPI-equipped L98
350 V-8 did not disappoint. Its 230 newfound

horses inspired *Car and Driver* to call the 1985
L98 Corvette the "king of the road, reborn."

"This engine is stronger than dirt," began
Car and Driver's Rich Ceppos in praise of the
L98. "The white golf shirts that the Corvette
guys handed out with a grin at Chevrolet's
1985 press preview say it all. Stenciled over
the left breast are the Corvette crossed-flags
insignia and the words 'Life Begins at 150.'
Yes, that's *miles per*, and yes, for the first
time in more than a decade, Chevy's plastic
biseater will hit the magic one-five-oh mark.
How sweet it is."

Chevrolet's Tuned-Port Injection (TPI) small
block debuted in 1985. The Corvette's
5.7-liter TPI V-8 (shown here) produced
230 horsepower. The Camaro's smaller
5.0-liter TPI was rated at 215 horsepower.

Base price for an L98 Corvette coupe in 1989 was about $31,500. Behind the L98 that year was either a four-speed automatic or six-speed manual.

Champion CAMARO

Chevrolet called it "the Camaro that thinks it's a Corvette." As *Motor Trend's* **Ron Grable saw it, "With the exception of the Corvette, this is as good a racing street car as we've driven."** Not since the LT-1 Z/28 of 1970 had Chevy's F-body inspired such lofty mention in the same breath with America's Sports Car. This time it was the new "IROC-Z" Camaro's turn to steal away some of the 'glass-bodied two-seater's thunder.

Introduced for 1985, the IROC-Z took its name from the International Race of Champions series, a competition circuit that by then had been featuring Camaros for nearly 10 years. The idea was to put drivers from different racing leagues together in identically prepped race cars to see which breed would win out. Early IROC champs included Trans-Am hot shoe Mark Donohue, Indy legends A. J. Foyt and Mario Andretti, and NASCAR's Bobby Allison.

Chevrolet rolled out its regular-production IROC Camaro to commemorate this level-field test of driver skill, which, according to

Owned by Terry Flick of Rantoul, Illinois, this 1985 IROC-Z is equipped with the 5.0-liter tuned-port injection small block, one of three V-8s offered along with RPO B4Z that year.

Chevy promotional people, was "to motor sports what the Masters is to golf." Offered for 1985 Z28 sport coupes only, the IROC Sport Equipment Package, RPO B4Z, included a long list of image enhancements and performance hardware. Most noticeable were the "IROC-Z" graphics on each door and the body-colored ground effects that skirted around the car's periphery. Halogen fog lamps were added up front, as were big 16x8 five-spoke aluminum wheels wearing "Corvette-inspired" P245/50VR Goodyear Eagles at the corners.

The IROC-Z's standard chassis tweaks were the heart of the model. Ride height was lowered 15 millimeters (compared to a garden-variety 1985 Z28) and the front frame rails were reinforced with a tubular brace to resist torsional twisting brought on during hard cornering. Up front, the Delco struts were revalved for

The IROC Sports Equipment package, RPO B4Z, was a $659 option in 1985. Production was 21,177 that first year. The IROC-Z Camaro became a full-fledged model in 1988.

Chapter 6

BORN-AGAIN SMALL BLOCK:
The LT1 Returns in 1992

Mustang GT drivers took it on the chin in 1993 when Chevrolet dropped the LT1 small block into the Camaro. Insult was then added to injury in 1994 as Chevy brought back the sexy Z28 convertible.

Dropping the 5.7-liter LT1 V-8 between Corvette flanks in 1992 instantly reenergized America's Sports Car. Output for the LT1 was 300 horsepower.

I N 1990, CHEVROLET'S GEN I V-8 TURNED 35, MAKING IT RATHER YOUNG IN PEO-PLE YEARS BUT AGED IN TERMS OF AUTOMOTIVE DESIGN DURATION. Electronic fuel injection advances had modernized the venerable small block during the 1980s, yet beneath all that newfangled high-tech (for the time) hardware beat the heart of basically the same mouse motor that had been running long and strong since 1955. And, as the 1990s dawned, most engineers with eyes could see that the time

had finally come to give Chevy's lovable little rodent a break. It wasn't that the Gen I was necessarily broken, mind you—it just needed a little fixin' if it was to keep up the performance pace into another new decade.

One long-standing "glitch" drove V-8 Development Group Engineer Aril Kulkarni nuts. A graduate of the Indian Institute of Technology outside Calcutta, Kulkarni had moved to the United States in 1968 to finish his master's at Stanford, after which he went to work for General Motors' Detroit Diesel Division designing truck and bus engines. In

The Corvette turned 40 in 1993 and, thanks to the LT1, was still able to prove it all night.

At right is a 1963 Sting Ray; at left as a 40th Anniversary commemorative Corvette.

Spreading the wealth around was the goal in 1994. Along with the Corvette and Z28, the new Impala SS also was treated to some LT1 muscle.

1981, he left Detroit Diesel for Chevron, where he became a senior research engineer. But he was back at GM four years later and quickly rose to assistant chief engineer in the Powertrain Division. There he began sorting out the small block's strengths and weaknesses, and—like Smokey Yunick in 1955—he didn't think much of the valvetrain. As Kulkarni told *Corvette Fever* contributor Michael Lamm in 1991, "The first thing I couldn't accept was the rocker arm. I felt that the stamped rocker was definitely not correctly designed."

Reportedly one in every 22,000 Gen I V-8s built to that point had experienced unwanted side loading on those rockers at high rpm, which had sometimes forced their tips to slip off of their corresponding valve stems. This inherent flaw was enhanced after rev-enhancing roller lifters were introduced in 1987. To compensate, Kulkarni created a guided rocker arm with a grooved stern pallet to resist side loading—presto, problem addressed, at least for the moment.

Such creative thinking immediately earned Kulkarni the job of ensuring the small block's future. In charge of the engineering team assigned the task of thoroughly modernizing the Gen I, he was given a somewhat intimidating list of goals, among which were increased reliability, reduced noise, and minimized external dimensions. A higher, flatter, longer torque curve was also specified, as was even better fuel economy coupled with even more performance. Making 50 more horses was what Kulkarni's bosses had in mind. "That's all?" he probably thought.

Chevrolet's hottest small block for 1990, the 5.7-liter L98, was producing 250 horse-

power beneath the Corvette's clamshell hood, up 5 ponies from 1989, thanks to a few tweaks. That same 250-horsepower V-8 returned for 1991, making it the seventh year for the L98 as the prime mover for America's Sports Car.

Then came 1992 and the debut for the fruits of Kulkarni's labors—the Gen II small block, an engine that met all expectations, and then some. The makeover was so dramatic that Chevy officials chose to let history repeat itself. They named the new V-8 in honor of the legendary powerplant that 20 years before had left many big-block drivers believing that size indeed doesn't matter, only this time they dropped the hyphen: LT-1 from the 1970s became LT1 for the 1990s. No matter—it didn't take long for Corvette buyers to recognize that the dehyphenated

The LT1 arrived just in time to fit right into the redesigned Camaro for 1993. In F-body trim, this revised small block produced 275 horsepower.

LT1 was more than worthy of the name.

According to Corvette Chief Engineer Dave McLellan, the next-generation small block earned its recognition because of its strength—it was easily more powerful than the original LT-1, which, at 370 horses, ranked right up with Chevy's mightiest mice of all time. Maximum output for the 1992 LT1 was 300 horsepower at 5,000 rpm, but 300 obviously isn't greater than 370. Remember: Advertised outputs before 1972 were gross figures; along with often being a little on the optimistic side, they also were dynoed out at the flywheel with no accessory drive drag or external friction losses taken into account. Today's much more honest numbers are net ratings—that is, they represent real power delivered right to the road.

As it was, comparing the LT1 with its LT-1 predecessor mattered little to drivers who were familiar only with the 250 net-rated horses in their '91 Corvettes. Kulkarni had been instructed to better the L98's output by 20 percent and that's exactly what he had done, while also increasing fuel economy by 1 mile per gallon. These numbers aside, it was the seat of your pants that told the true tale. The new LT1 punch literally represented a rebirth for the Corvette, with published road test results running as low as 4.92 seconds for the 0–60 run, 13.7 seconds (topping out at 103.5 miles per hour) for the quarter-mile. Yikes!

The new-for-1992 small block was truly born again. Very little interchanged between the LT1 and L98. Block height, bore spacing,

1992 LT1 V-8

CONSTRUCTION:
**cast-iron block
w/aluminum cylinder heads**

DISPLACEMENT (METRIC):
5.7 liters (350 cubic inches)

BORE & STROKE (INCHES):
4.00 x 3.48

LIFTERS:
hydraulic

COMPRESSION:
10.5:1

INDUCTION:
**multi-port electronic
fuel injection**

HORSEPOWER:
300 at 4,400 rpm

TORQUE:
340 at 4,000 rpm

Everything Old
IS NEW AGAIN

Chevrolet's fourth-generation pony car debuted for 1993 with a sleek new shell and revamped chassis.

Talk about history repeating itself—when Chevy engineers dropped the original LT-1 small block into the Z/28 in 1970, they helped kickstart an all-new, next-generation Camaro, a car that most critics simply couldn't get enough of. They loved the way it looked; they loved the way it drove; and, in the latest, greatest Z/28's case, they loved the way it offered top-shelf performance at a Camaro price. "A poor man's Corvette" was one description for the second-generation Z.

Fast forward to 1993: Chevrolet's all-new fourth-generation Camaro was wowing the pony car pack with its hot looks and upgraded chassis, and again the Z28 was being fitted with an LT1. The spellings may have changed, but the end result was the same—a really big bang for not a lot of bucks. Base priced at a tidy $16,779, the 1993 Z28 coupe came standard with 275 warmly welcomed horses. It also featured a Borg-Warner

T56 six-speed manual transmission; four-wheel disc brakes; and big, new 16x8 aluminum wheels wearing fat Goodyear Eagle rubber. Chevy's four-speed 4L60 automatic was optional, as were even bigger Goodyear Eagles.

Beneath all that performance hardware was a revamped pony car foundation that had expanded in nearly all directions. At 101.1 inches, the wheelbase for the fourth-generation F-body remained constant. But the '93 Camaro was longer, wider, and taller than its 1992 forerunner, all the better to help make drivers feel more at home.

Enhancing the feel behind the wheel further was new rack-and-pinion steering (in place of the old recirculating ball unit used up through 1992) and a redesigned short/long arm (SLA) front suspension. Improved underpinnings in

back featured a traditional solid axle with two trailing arms, a track bar, and a torque arm. Last but certainly not least, all 1993 Camaros, base V-6 or LT1, came standard with driver- and passenger-side air bags (a first for Chevrolet) and anti-lock brakes.

Building this bigger, better Camaro even required an all-new factory, or at least a refurbished one. GM's St. Therese plant in Quebec, originally opened in 1965, was basically gutted and refitted to handle production of Chevy's fourth-generation pony car. New precision tooling was ordered, as was a new emphasis on quality control.

All this extra sweat resulted in history once again making an encore, as the 1993 Z28 was chosen to pace the field for the running of the 77th Indianapolis 500. This was the fourth such honor for the Camaro and the ninth overall for Chevrolet. Both were records.

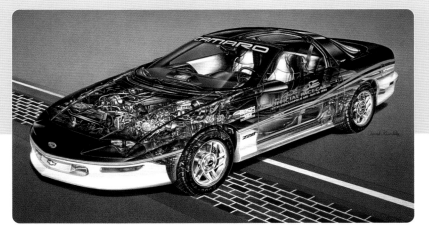

Though only offered as a coupe, the 1993 Z28 was chosen as the prestigious pace car for the 77th running of the Indianapolis 500. It was the fourth Camaro to pace the Indy 500.

and displacement carried over in the best tradition of the Chevy small block. Most everything else, however, was drawn up on a clean sheet of paper, beginning with the iron cylinder block and aluminum heads, which were recast to incorporate a revised "reverse-flow" cooling system.

Gen I coolant typically was pumped into the block first and then to the heads. But, as Kulkarni explained, cooler heads and warmer cylinder bores are key to maximizing both performance and fuel economy. Thus, the Gen II design sent the coolant first to the heads, then into the block, and back to the pump, which was revised to improve durability. The Gen I water pump was belt-driven, meaning it was susceptible to bearing and seal failure resulting from the inherent side

loading passed on to the pulley via belt tension. Kulkarni's crew did away with yet another case of dreaded side loading by designing a new gear-driven pump.

The new pump also incorporated the crossover passage (used to deliver coolant from head to head) formerly cast into the Gen I's intake manifold, an improvement that essentially allowed engineers to work with more space inside the Gen II's intake while maximizing the all-important fuel/air flow. Removing the coolant crossover from the intake also helped translate into a lower engine silhouette, a major priority considering the Corvette's low hood line. Overall, the LT1 measured almost 3.5 inches shorter than its L98 forerunner. Working in concert along with the low-rise, cast-aluminum intake to reduce

1994 Impala SS V-8

CONSTRUCTION:
**cast-iron block
w/cast-iron cylinder heads**

DISPLACEMENT (METRIC):
5.7 liters (350 cubic inches)

BORE & STROKE (INCHES):
4.00 x 3.48

LIFTERS:
hydraulic

COMPRESSION:
10:1

INDUCTION:
**multi-port electronic
fuel injection**

HORSEPOWER:
260 at 4,400 rpm

TORQUE:
330 at 3,200 rpm

engine height, the engine had a new induction layout—a multiport fuel injection system that did away with the TPI setup's exposed long-tube runners.

Along with its short stature, the LT1's MPFI equipment delivered the coals to the latest, greatest small block's fire as efficiently as ever. According to Kulkarni, the exact matching of all components was the key to the LT1's newfound performance—the low-restriction air snorkel; the bigger, better throttle body; the short-runner, one-piece intake; the more precise AC Rochester Multec injectors. Special attention to detail continued all the way through the heads to the exhaust end, where the LT1 reverted to cast-iron manifolds in place of the L98's tubular headers. Even though it added weight to the engine, this trade was made because internal passages could be shaped more precisely (with an eye toward speeding spent gases on their way more efficiently) using cast iron as opposed to welded steel tubes.

Every bit as much effort went into perfecting the ports leading into and out of the LT1's exceptional free-breathing cylinder heads, which retained the L98's valve specs: 1.94 inches on intake, 1.50 on exhaust. Aiding the LT1's jump up to 300 horsepower were a compression increase (to 10.5:1) and a more aggressive roller camshaft. Lift increased from the L98 cam's 0.415/0.430

Compared to the 1994 Corvette's 300-horsepower LT1, the Impala SS rendition (right) produced 260 horsepower.

What was good for the Camaro was equally fine for its F-body corporate cousin, Pontiac's Firebird Trans Am. Shown here is the 1994 25th Anniversary Trans Am, which came standard with the 275-horsepower LT1.

1996 LT4 V-8

CONSTRUCTION:
**cast-iron block
w/aluminum cylinder heads**

DISPLACEMENT (METRIC):
5.7 liters (350 cubic inches)

BORE & STROKE (INCHES):
4.00 x 3.48

LIFTERS:
hydraulic

COMPRESSION:
10.6:1

INDUCTION:
**sequential
fuel injection**

HORSEPOWER:
330 at 5,800 rpm

TORQUE:
340 at 4,500 rpm

(intake/exhaust) to 0.451/0.450 for the lumpier LT1 unit.

The LT1 featured an upgraded ignition system as well. Gone was the prominent HEI housing previously located at the back of the Gen I V-8 in 1991. For 1992, the Gen II V-8 got its voltage from the innovative OptiSpark distributor, now located up front where it was driven off the camshaft. As its name might imply, this unit used optical signals to govern ignition timing. Light shining through a stainless steel shutter created 360 pulses per crank revolution, and these were translated into electronic signals sent to the Powertrain Control Module, which then determined spark firing. The end result was the most precise small-block ignition ever, although some bugs also were worked out early on. Omission of a planned vent opening in the unit led to an immediate recall as trapped condensation buildup began to cause misfires. Retro-venting eased the problem, but it wasn't completely cured until the vent was tied into engine vacuum to constantly extract moisture away from OptiSpark internals.

Other LT1 upgrades occurred during its short, happy run, beginning with revised cam specs on the exhaust side for 1993 that bumped maximum torque up from 330 ft-lb to 340. New "powdered-metal" connecting rods replaced forged rods in 1994, but most notable that year was a switch to a markedly improved sequential fuel injection system. Working in concert with a more powerful ignition (that improved cold starting), this SFI equipment enhanced throttle response and idle quality and lowered emissions. There was no change in advertised output, however, as the LT1 continued making 300 horses as the Corvette's heart and soul up through 1996.

Two variations on the 5.7-liter LT1 theme were created—one for the redesigned Camaro that appeared in 1993, the other for the reincarnated Impala SS, offered from 1994 to 1996. In the case of the former, adding the LT1 into the Z28 equation resulted in a reawakening every bit as dramatic as that experienced by Corvette buyers in 1992. As Chevrolet promotional people

Time MACHINE

Chevrolet revived its fabled Impala SS image in 1994 using the four-door Caprice as a foundation. All Impala SS models built that year were black.

Fast-forward to the 1990s and an all-new age of high-performance. After a 25-year hiatus, the Impala SS returned for 1994, albeit in four-door fashion based on the big, bulbous Caprice. Like the first full-sized Super Sport, Chevrolet's comfort-conscious Caprice first appeared as an Impala options group (in 1965) and was then transformed into an individual model series of its own. It would remain Chevy's flagship for more than 30 years.

From 1994 to 1996, the Caprice also served, somewhat amazingly, as a base for a too-cool-for-school sport sedan that

Many among the Bowtie faithful were instantly reminded of better days when Chevrolet revived its fabled Impala SS in 1994. Chevy's first Super Sport appeared in 1961, just in time to catch a new wave as factory hot rods were becoming all the rage. Three years later Pontiac invented the muscle car, and the rest is history—as was the muscle car after running about unchecked for nearly a decade. As for the sweet, sexy Impala SS, its road ended in 1969, but not before Chevrolet had turned out nearly 1 million of these full-sized flyers.

Cutting out the Caprice's rear wheel openings greatly enhanced the Impala SS's eye appeal.

Fat P225/50ZR tires on big 17x8.5 five-spoke sport wheels were standard for the Impala SS during its three-year run.

seemingly defied physical laws. Beneath its sinister black skin the Impala SS was still a Caprice, and a 1990s Caprice was still a beached whale. But just look what happened once a little LT1 magic was applied—presto, instant "four-door Z/28," at least as far as *Road & Track*'s Ron Sessions saw it. At 260 horsepower, the LT1 was backed by a 4L60-E electronically controlled four-speed automatic in the Impala SS application, and according to *Motor Trend* this combo equaled 0–60 in 7.1 ticks, the quarter-mile in 15.1 seconds at 91 miles per hour. Those numbers, in turn, qualified as simply super performance, especially for a four-door sedan of this size and status, not to mention price. Base sticker for the '94 Impala SS was $21,920.

Along with its LT1 muscle, an Impala SS came standard with a fair dose of unmistakable imagery. As if specifying black paint only wasn't enough, Chevy 3 styling studio head John Cafaro's team blacked out everything they could get their hands on. Additional tweaks included a special grille (blackened, of course), reshaped rear quarter windows, familiar Impala logos behind those windows and at the tail, an understated rear-deck spoiler, and "Impala SS"

lettering on the rear quarters. Leather buckets and a console were standard inside.

Lowering the suspension enhanced the image even further, as did four massive 17x8.5 aluminum five-spoke sport wheels shod in B.F. Goodrich P225/50ZR treads. Borrowed from Chevrolet's police car package, the lowered suspension was also beefed with a thicker front anti-sway bar and an additional bar in back. Shocks were gas-charged de Carbon units similar to the Camaro Z/28's, steering was quickened from 14.7:1 to 12.7:1, and brakes were big 12-inch four-wheel discs. Safety-conscious Bosch ABS was standard, as were dual airbags inside.

Two exterior color choices, Dark Green-Gray Metallic and Dark Cherry Metallic, were introduced for the '95 Impala SS. The 1996 rendition was treated to a tachometer and a floor shifter—sporty features many critics felt should have been included all along. Nineteen ninety-six was also the last year for the rear-wheel-drive Caprice platform, and thus came the end for another full-sized Super Sport legacy.

including the expected relocation of various accessory mounting points. Appearance-wise, the Camaro LT1 didn't feature image-conscious "beauty shields" atop its injectors like its Corvette counterpart. Also, the Camaro's valve covers were plain stamped-steel units, as opposed to the 1993 Corvette's dressy composite pieces, which replaced the stylish magnesium valve covers used in 1992. Exhaust manifolds too differed, with the Corvette's traditional center-outlet layout traded for a rear-exiting design on the Z28's LT1. From there back, the Camaro application required a more restrictive exhaust system with, among other things, one catalytic converter compared to the Corvette's dual setup. That was the prime explanation behind the drop from 300 horses to 275.

An upgraded cam helped push output for the Z28's small block up to 285 horses in 1996, and that figure carried over into 1997, the last year for the LT1. But that wasn't necessarily the limit in F-body terms.

For both 1996 and 1997, SLP Engineering (based in Troy, Michigan) offered a Camaro variant, the Z28 SS, powered by an exclusive 305-horsepower LT1. The SS Camaro's trademark hood featured a large functional scoop that force-fed cooler, denser outside air directly into the LT1's SFI equipment below. An SS began life as a typical Z28 at GM's assembly plant in St. Therese, Quebec. From there it was shipped complete (via GM's own carrier) to an SLP shop in nearby Montreal, where it was morphed into the muscled-up SS and sent back into GM's conventional Camaro delivery pipeline.

"In addition to offering world-class performance, another object is to make the ownership process as easy as possible,"

explained it, "You have to go back 23 years to the introduction of the first Camaro Z/28 LT-1 engine to understand why performance enthusiasts are so excited about the 1993 LT1-equipped Z28. In Camaro circles, the words 'power' and 'performance' are synonymous with the 1970 LT-1, and many enthusiasts have yearned for its return."

Though "detuned" down to 275 horsepower (and 325 ft-lb of torque), the 1993 Z28's standard LT1 small-block still represented a 30-horsepower improvement, compared to the hottest Camaro V-8 offered for 1992, the 5.7-liter B2L. That boost instantly helped Chevy's next-generation Camaro best Ford's 5.0-liter HO Mustang as the performance market's "biggest bang for the buck," an honor that the two pony car rivals battled for back and forth with a vengeance throughout the 1980s.

A long list of mostly trivial differences set the Corvette and Camaro LT1 V-8s apart,

The Camaro's LT1 wasn't as "dressy" as its Corvette counterpart; it did not feature the "beauty shields" that hid the latter's fuel injectors.

Grand FAREWELL

Chevrolet dusted off its "Grand Sport" moniker for a special-edition Corvette in 1996. Production of Grand Sport coupes and convertibles was 1,000.

Chevrolet officials marked the end of the C4 Corvette generation with a specially prepared 1996 Collector Edition model, just as they had done when the C3 was on its way out in 1982.

Priced at $1,250, the package (RPO Z15) included an exclusive Sebring Silver finish, chromed "Collector Edition" badges, silver-painted 17-inch five-spoke wheels, and various interior upgrades. Standard power came from the proven 300-horsepower LT1 backed by Chevy's 4L60-E four-speed electronically controlled automatic overdrive transmission. The 330-horsepower LT4 with mandated six-speed manual gearbox was optional.

Another special-edition two-seater, the Grand Sport, helped to bid the C4 a fond farewell that year. Offered as a coupe or convertible, the 1996 Grand Sport (RPO Z16, the same code used 31 years before for Chevrolet's first SS 396 Chevelle) was created to remind the fiberglass faithful of the five lightweight Corvette race cars built by Zora Arkus-Duntov late in 1962—thus the reasoning behind the red hash marks (or "Sebring stripes") on the left front fender and the white racing stripe accent-

ing the '96 Grand Sport's exclusive Admiral Blue Metallic paint. Further enhancing the competitive image were blacked-out 17-inch five-spoke wheels (left over from the ZR-1, last offered in 1995) wearing big, bad tires measuring P275/40ZR in front, P315/35ZR in back. Grand Sport coupes were fitted with fender flares in the rear to better house all that extra rubber. Grand Sport convertibles rolled on smaller tires (P255/45ZR in front, P285/40ZR in back) and therefore didn't require the flares.

Additional Grand Sport flare included black brake calipers with bright "Corvette" lettering, appropriate "Grand Sport" fender badges, and perforated bucket seats in black or red/black with more "Grand Sport" references in embroidery. A unique serial number also was part of the deal, which added $3,250 to a coupe's bottom line, $2,282 to a convertible's. Total Z16 Corvette production for 1996 was 1,000. All were equipped with the LT4/six-speed combo, and all remain coveted collector's items today.

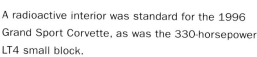

A radioactive interior was standard for the 1996 Grand Sport Corvette, as was the 330-horsepower LT4 small block.

SLP Engineering rolled out its Z28 SS in 1996. Lightweight alloy wheels and an aggressive ram-air hood were included in the SLP conversion.

said SLP President Ed Hamburger in 1996. "For example, ordering a Z28 SS will be as simple as visiting your local Chevy dealer and asking for an order form. GMAC financing and leasing are available, and our warranty, combined with the standard coverage provided by GM, protects the vehicle."

The SLP transformation even got its own RPO code: R7T. Along with that 305-horsepower LT1, the Z28 SS coupe was fitted with lightweight 17x9 cast-aluminum alloy wheels wearing huge BF Goodrich Comp T/A 275/40ZR/17 tires. The convertible and T-top versions used smaller 16-inch wheels and tires and stock Z/28 suspensions. SS coupes were treated to a larger anti-roll bar in front and a revised track bar in back. Additional suspension tweaks were optional (for coupes only), as was a free-flowing "cat-back" exhaust system and a short-throw Hurst shifter.

As for the Caprice-based Impala SS, it was genuine Chevrolet through and through. At its heart was a 260-horsepower LT1 fitted with iron heads instead of the aluminum units found beneath Corvette and Camaro hoods. Valve size carried over, but compression was dropped down to 10:1 and a less lumpy cam was installed. These changes, combined with another restrictive exhaust system, led to the 40-horsepower difference between Impala SS and Corvette V-8s.

Like the Impala SS, the LT1-powered Corvette was last seen in 1996. With the arrival of the redesigned C5 Corvette in 1997 came yet another next-generation small

block, the LS1, leaving the LT1 to retire for a second time. But engineers weren't about to let the short-lived Gen II V-8 roll into the history books without at least a final big bang.

Chevrolet called it the LT4—offered for 1996 only, this new-and-improved Gen II small block produced 330 horsepower and was offered only with a six-speed manual transmission. Another one-hit wonder, the 1996 Corvette Grand Sport, came standard with the LT4; it was optional for other Corvettes.

LT4 enhancements began with aluminum cylinder heads that featured taller ports and bigger valves: 2.00-inch intakes, 1.55-inch exhausts. Those valves had hollow stems to save weight and used special oval-wire springs that could handle more lift without binding. Higher ratio (1.6:1) Crane roller rocker arms helped to increase the LT4's valve lift. Revised lift specs were 0.476 inch on intake, 0.479 on exhaust. Cam duration

was increased as well, from 200 degrees to 203 on the intake side, from 207 to 210 on exhaust.

Further LT4 upgrades included a freer-flowing intake (with taller ports to match the heads), a compression increase to 10.8:1, and a roller-type timing chain. The LT4's crank, cam, water-pump drive gear, and main bearing caps were beefed up, and premium head gaskets were installed to deal with the extra compression. Red accents on various engine covers guaranteed a high-profile appearance. The LT4/six-speed combo was priced at $1,450. Total LT4 production in 1996 was a healthy 6,359, proving once again that less was rarely more in the minds of most Corvette customers.

Another 100 LT4 V-8s went into SLP SS Camaros in 1997 to help commemorate the F-body's 30th anniversary. That, however, represented the end of the road for the hottest Gen II small block—at least it was fun while it lasted.

The Z28 SS Camaro's LT1 produced 305 horsepower, 20 more than the standard Z28 small block in 1996. That fresh air hood was the key to that power increase.

Chapter 7

LATEST, GREATEST:
Chevrolet's
LS1, LS6, and LS2

The radically redesigned C5 Corvette debuted for 1997 in coupe form only. A C5 convertible followed in 1998, bringing with it the Corvette's first trunk since 1962.

No one could deny the ZR-1's status as the meanest, nastiest 'glass-bodied two-seater ever built by Chevrolet, at least in reasonable numbers on a regular-production basis. With its 405-horsepower LT5 V-8, the "King of the Hill" Corvette could stand tall even up against Dodge's outrageous Viper. But it was also every bit as pricey as its venomous rival, a painful truth that helped bring about a rather quiet cancellation in 1995, leaving the 300-horsepower LT1 to carry the Bowtie banner high on the street performance front. By then, however, the Gen II small block's days were numbered, as were the fourth-generation Corvette's.

When the eagerly awaited C5 Corvette appeared for 1997 it impressed critics around the world with its newfound comfort, convenience, and class. It was the first truly new Corvette—next to nothing was borrowed from existing parts bins, as had been the case to noticeable degrees with all proceeding

The C5's LS1 small block represented every bit as radical a redesign as the car itself. Though Chevrolet called it a 5.7-liter V-8, the LS1 didn't displace 350 cubic inches like its forerunners. Rounding off stroke and bore figures added up to about 347 cubic inches; some sources claimed 346.

generations, including the first in 1953. That newness was especially evident under the C5's hood, where Chevy's radically transformed third-generation LS1 small block honored the past and at the same time promised a powerful future.

"Based on a timeless design by former Chief Engineer Ed Cole, the 'Gen III' 5.7-liter V-8 marks a bright new chapter in the highly respected lineage that GM small blocks have established in more than 40 years," claimed a Chevrolet press release in 1996.

A new chapter indeed—like all small blocks before it, the LS1 was a traditional pushrod,

16-valve V-8 and it shared the same time-honored "440" cylinder block layout (measuring 4.40 inches from bore center to bore center) and the familiar 5.7-liter displacement label. "After all," said LS1 Engine Program Manager John Juriga, "some things are sacred." From there, though, essentially all bets were off as the Gen III represented a real redesign, not just a modernization. Engineers even rearranged the age-old 1-8-4-3-6-5-7-2 firing order to 1-8-7-2-6-5-4-3 in order to reduce vibration and increase idle smoothness.

Family ties between LS1 and LT1 were even slighter than Chevrolet officials

All five generations of Corvettes were on display at the National Corvette Museum in Bowling Green, Kentucky, in 1997.

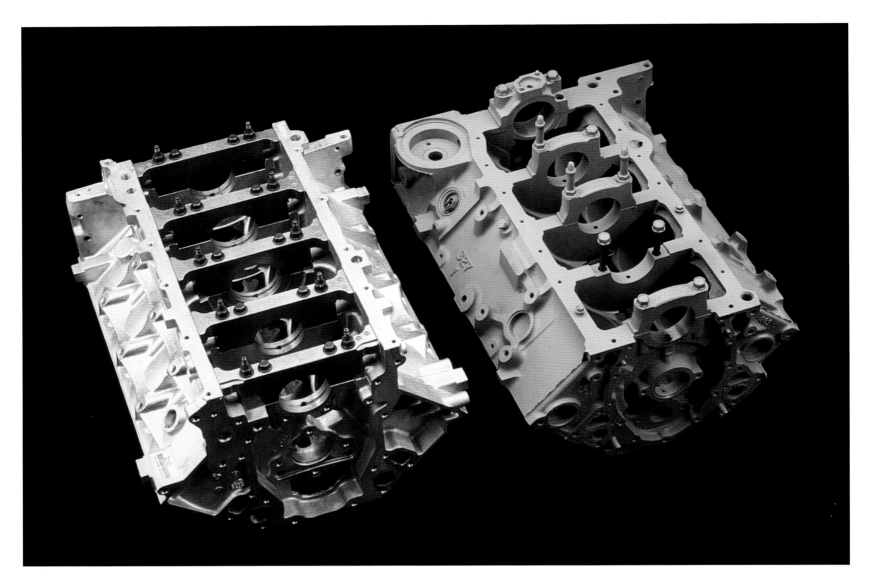

preferred to purport. In truth, the LS1's displacement measured exactly 5.666 liters, which translates into 345.69 cubic inches, not 350. A tidy approximation resulted in the advertised 5.7-liter tag, and factory paperwork also rounded off bore and stroke numbers to the tenth to produce a 347-cubic-inch label for those of us who still prefer to "just say no" to metrics.

Furthermore, the LS1 relied on a revised bore/stroke relationship to fill out those 5-point-whatever liters. Compared to the Gen II, the Gen III V-8's bore was less and its stroke was more, the adjustment made to allow more cooling space between skinnier cylinders. The overall coolant "travel plan" too was changed: the Gen II's reverse-flow system was traded for a conventional layout as Gen III coolant was once again pumped into the block first, then to the heads. But easily the most notable break-from-the-past innovation was the LS1's lightweight yet durable all-aluminum construction, a first for a regular-production Chevrolet small block.

Gen III development dated back to late 1991, when GM Powertrain Executive Director Tom Stephens instructed his Advanced Engineering people to start drawing up the basics on what initially was known internally as the Venture V-8 (VV-8 for short)

The LS1's battleship-tough deep-skirt block (left) made the LT1 block look feeble in comparison.

project. Chief Engineer Anil Kulkarni, the man behind the LT1, was originally in charge of this project, but his ideas and Stephens' didn't mix all that well. Kulkarni then moved on, giving up the reins to Ed Koerner, a long-time small-block engineer who also knew his way around a drag strip. Koerner in turn assembled what he called the Super Six, a highly talented team of engineers that, along with part-timer Dave Wandel, included Don Weiderhold, Stan Turek, Jon Lewis, Bill Compton, Brian Kaminski, and Ron Sperry. Second in command—first under Kulkarni then Koerner—was John Juriga.

The Gen III program really got cooking in 1993, with the first test engines hitting the dynos at GM Powertrain that winter. Real world thrashing in early prototype C5

Corvettes began the following summer using mostly iron-block Gen III "prerunners." Most of these rolling test beds were then refitted with all-aluminum counterparts by late 1995. In between Koerner presented the Gen III to GM Chairman Jack Smith, who gave it two thumbs way up.

Chevrolet officially introduced the Gen III V-8 to the press in June 1996. By then, the LS1 had undergone countless tests, from seemingly endless high-rpm durability runs, to searing desert heat exposure, to frigid torture tours in the great white north. Cold-starting was proven in 40-below-zero weather in Grand Forks, North Dakota, while air conditioning interaction was tested in the 112-degree heat of Death Valley, California. Two Gen III small blocks also were run on

The LS1's intake manifold (left) was manufactured using a glass-fiber reinforced composite. At right is the 1996 LT4 intake.

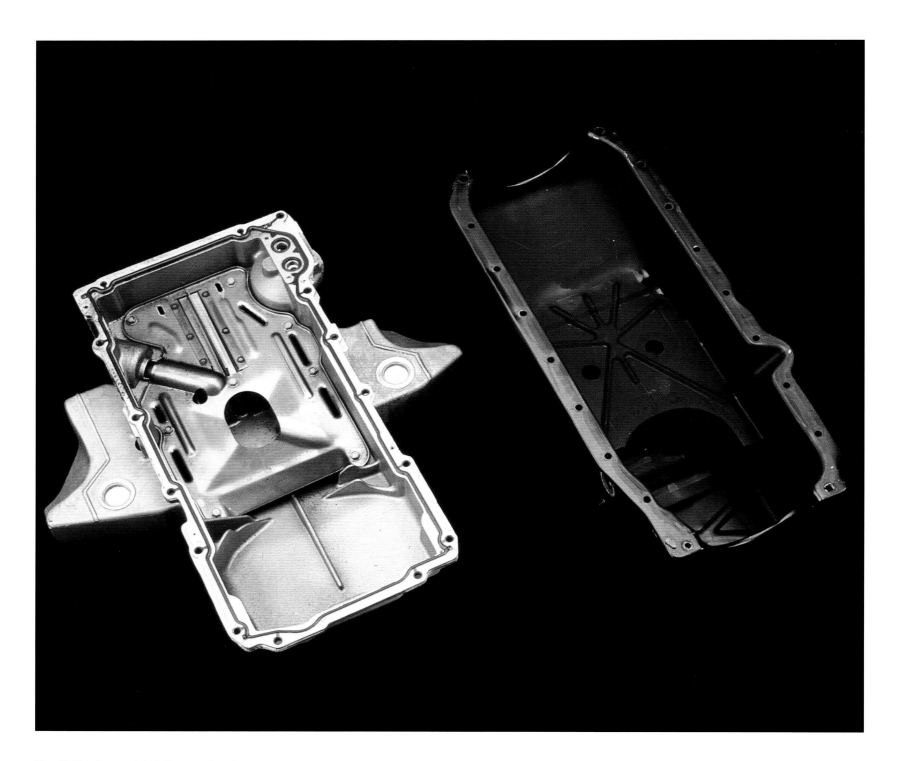

The LT1 oil pan (right) was simply an
oil pan, while the LS1's shallow unit was
a work of art.

Replicated ports were integral to the LS1 head design. "Each port is a continuous, runner-to-valve configuration," explained GM Powertrain flow expert Ron Sperry. "We don't have the air turning right or left to any significant degree." Shown here is the LS1 head's intake side.

dynos at full throttle for 50 hours with no complaints. Though that achievement met GM specs, Koerner was not satisfied—he raised the bar to 260 hours for two more LS1s, then 520 for a single engine. When torn down after its dizzying run, that latter V-8 reportedly looked like new inside.

On the outside, the LS1 showed off other new features. Its "drive-by-wire" electronic throttle control (ETC), which was linked to the traction control and anti-lock braking systems, was a first for GM gasoline engines. While ETC simplified the throttle-body/accelerator-pedal relationship (no need to route a mechanical linkage in tight quarters), its true goal was to supply more precise throttle response, which it did by instantly tailoring power, traction, and braking to engine status, road conditions, and performance demands.

Yet as much as the ETC technology smacked of aerospace influences, the LS1's basic layout remained paradoxically down to earth, and for good reason. "Trying to decide what was the right engine technology for the application was probably the biggest hurdle we faced," explained John Juriga in 1996.

Although Corvette Chief Engineer David Hill did consider building a state-of-the-art overhead-cam, multi-valve engine for the C5, DOHC engines will always be larger, costlier, and more complicated than their conventional pushrod counterparts. Space constraints alone were enough to rule out the installation of a bulky DOHC V-8 beneath the C5's low, sloping hood, but pricing considerations also played a part. Chevrolet officials didn't want to see the C5 end up in the sticker stratosphere where the ZR-1 had

1997 LS1 V-8

CONSTRUCTION:
aluminum block and cylinder heads

DISPLACEMENT (METRIC):
5.7 liters (347 cubic inches)

BORE & STROKE (INCHES):
3.90 x 3.62

LIFTERS:
hydraulic

COMPRESSION:
10.1:1

INDUCTION:
sequential fuel injection

HORSEPOWER:
345 at 5,600 rpm

TORQUE:
350 at 4,400 rpm

hovered until its eventual demise. Besides, who needed all that extra cost-adding technology, when Chevy engineers still had a few tricks up their sleeves concerning the supposedly obsolete design that had kept the small block running strong for more than 40 years?

"The new LS1 has the simplicity and compactness of the pushrod layout, but with the porting so efficient and valvetrain so light and still, it breathes like an overhead cam motor," claimed Hill about the final product of that engineering magic. "We think a base engine at 345 net horsepower is plenty of power," added Juriga. "If that can be done with one cam, 16 pushrods, and two valves in each hole, we can

live with that." So could C5 buyers in 1997, who didn't mind at all receiving Porsche performance at a Chevrolet price.

Simplicity, however, was a relative term in the Gen III's case. Everything about the LS1 was finely engineered to the limit of the parameters set down, beginning with the cast-aluminum cylinder block, which was tough as nails and equally tough to produce. "The deep skirt, six-bolt bearing caps, deep-threaded head bolt holes, camshaft and tappet locations, and other features made the LS1 block challenging to engineer," explained Juriga.

The points Juriga spoke of contributed to newfound strength and durability. At only 107

King OF THE HILL

David Hill took over the Corvette chief engineer job late in 1992, just in time to help shepherd in the all-new C5 model. Hill poses here with a 1997 C5 at the National Corvette Museum in Bowling Green, Kentucky.

Only three engineers have ridden herd over Corvette design during its half-century run. First was the main man himself, Zora Arkus-Duntov, commonly considered the car's father figure even though he actually didn't arrive at GM until right after the fiberglass two-seater was born.

Dave McLellan became the Corvette's second chief engineer, following Duntov's retirement in January 1975. McLellan retired early in September 1992, leaving the hottest seat at Chevrolet open at a crucial time when market pressures were making it clear that the C4 needed modernization.

The man chosen to usher in the C5 era was 49-year-old David C. Hill, a 1965 mechanical engineering graduate from Michigan Technological University. Like Ed Cole, Hill came to Chevrolet from Cadillac, where he had spent most of his time after coming onboard at GM following his graduation. Hill finished a master's degree in engineering at the University of Michigan in 1969 and became chief engineer for the Allante project about a dozen years later. By 1992 he was Cadillac's engineering program manager.

In November 1992, Hill officially became the Corvette's third chief engineer,

a suitable assignment considering his past experience with sports cars. Not long after joining GM, he had purchased a 1948 MG TC and restored it for keeps—it was still looking really good in his garage when he was reassigned to Chevrolet. Next, he took a Lotus Super 7 racing in SCCA competition, winning two national events in 1972. By then his daily driver (as well as his first new car) was a 1970 Corvette coupe fitted with a 350-horse L46 small block, a machine that he once toured the country in, piling up 7,500 miles in 13 days. It was still parked next to the MG in 1993 in original condition with a mere 55,000 miles on its odometer. Hill's plans to refurbish the L46 coupe as he had his little British roadster were delayed by a much more important Corvette restoration project.

Tasked with what was to be the most complete transformation ever made during the Corvette's 52-year history, Hill early on considered reviving Duntov's dream. As he told *Automobile* magazine's Rich Ceppos in 1994, "I myself was not at first satisfied that we shouldn't do a mid-engined car, and

I spent some energy on that when I arrived. But cars like the Acura NSX don't have anywhere near the utility of a Corvette. We want to continue to offer a car that people can own as their only car and still do all the things they want to do—go to the golf course or go on a week's vacation."

Thus the radically redesigned C5's engine remained up front, and it also remained familiar. "At first, I'd been curious to explore the possibility of using a multi-valve V-8," continued Hill to Ceppos. "But there's a lot of stock in the current small block, and we're doing some really neat things with it. So that's what the future holds for us—a much better version of the small block."

He wasn't kidding. The LS1 was better, as is the LS2 now in 2005. What more awaits Corvette fans in the future is up to the man with a finger still firmly planted on the pulse of the car that has warmed drivers' blood since 1953—David Hill.

On the right is the LT1 cam; on the left, the LS1. Which one would you prefer bumping your valves?

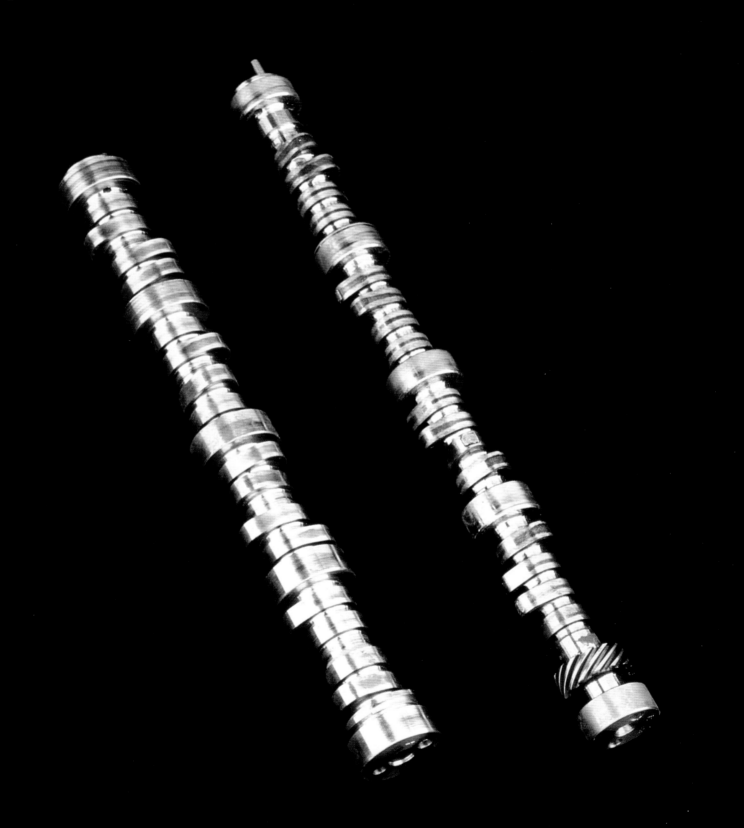

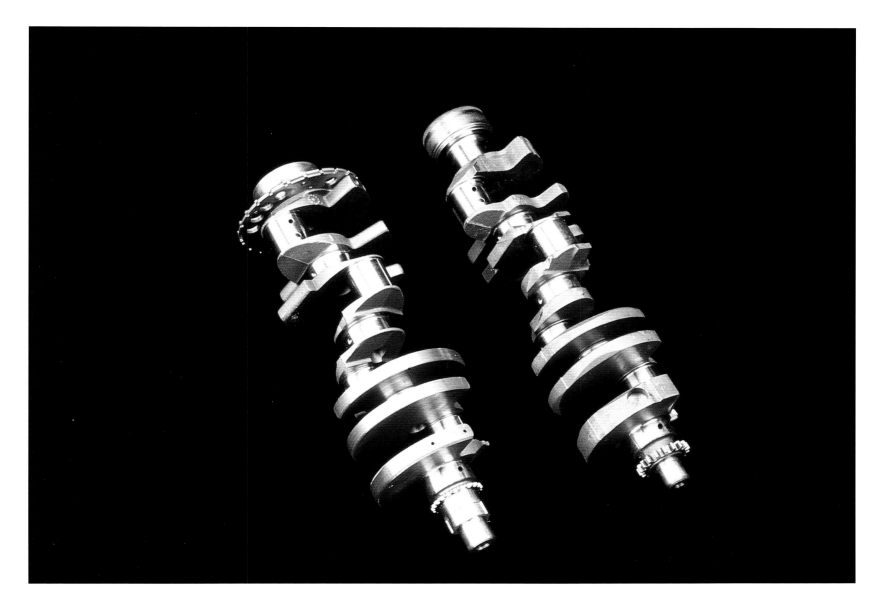

pounds, the aluminum Gen III cylinder block weighed 53 pounds less than its Gen II predecessor, and the entire engine was 88 pounds lighter. Yet at the same time, the LS1 was far tougher, thanks in part to extensive external stiffening ribs and that "deep-skirt" construction. Unlike typical V-8 cylinder blocks that end at the crankshaft's centerline, the LS1 block extended below the main bearing caps, encasing the crank in a girdle of aluminum that helped hold things together with a vengeance on the bottom end.

The extended skirt also made it possible to crossbolt the main bearing caps for addi-tional rigidity, thus the six-bolt bearing caps—four in the conventional vertical loca-tion on each side of the crank and one running through the skirt horizontally into each side of the cap. The crankshaft held firmly in place by those caps was cast of nodular iron and featured rolled-fillet journals for extra strength, a design that debuted within the LT4 in 1996. Connecting rods were sintered forged steel, or powdered metal, a techno trick introduced in 1994. Instead of typical bolts, cap screws attached those eight rods to the crank on the big end. At the top they wore lightened cast-aluminum

The LS1's beefier crank is on the left. To its right is its LT1 ancestor.

No BOLT LEFT UNTURNED

At about $40,000, the 1997 Corvette offered more performance per buck than any other sports car known to man.

Originally conceived in 1988 with hopes for an August 1992 introduction, the long-awaited C5 Corvette finally debuted before the American public in January 1997. Raves resulted immediately, as did bragging by Chevrolet.

"The fifth-generation Corvette is a refined Corvette in all the right ways," began Chief Engineer David Hill. "It's more user-friendly, it's easier to get in and out of, and it's more ergonomic. It has greater visibility; it's more comfortable and more functional. It provides more sports car for the money than anything in its market segment. It'll pull nearly 1 g, and it starts and stops quicker than you can blink."

Calling the C5 the best 'Vette yet was akin to saying Republicans don't like Democrats. Offering nearly 170 miles per hour for only about $40,000, the redesigned 1997 Corvette represented the biggest bang for the buck ever seen on Main Street, USA—or anywhere else for that matter. But there was more—much

more. Beneath that slippery reshaped skin was not only the hottest Corvette to date, but also the most practical.

"We designed the car with a synchronous mindset," said interior designer Jon Albert. "We focused on individual goals, such as improved performance, reduced mass, and increased reliability, within the overall framework of the whole car. We evaluated and balanced each change so as to optimize the total car."

So many changes worked together to make the C5 a "total car." The innovative frame with its rigid center tunnel and "hydroformed" perimeter rails made the foundation 4.5 times stiffer than the C4 platform. This extra rigidity in turn helped improve both ride and handling and also did away with many of the squeaky gremlins inherent in earlier Corvettes. The C5's rear-mounted transmission improved ride and handling, too. This long-discussed idea not only helped bring weight distribution closer to the preferred 50/50 balance, but it also freed up space beneath the passenger compartment, meaning both

occupants had more room in the footwells to stretch out and ride comfortably. Entry and exit were enhanced as well, thanks to the strengthened frame rails, which traded excess mass for a lower sill height, down 3.7 inches.

Don't forget the LS1 small block, better brakes and tires, and a more sophisticated suspension. Clearly, no bolt was left unturned during the C5 design process.

The C5 initially was offered only as a Targa-top coupe, but a convertible joined the ranks in 1998 and quickly copped *Motor Trend*'s coveted Car of the Year trophy. Equally new in 1998 was the topless C5's trunk, the Corvette's first since the Sting Ray superseded the solid-axle cars in 1963. A trunk also appeared on the new fixed-roof hardtop C5, which debuted in 1999 to expand the Corvette lineup to three different models for the first time ever.

Now the C5 is gone, replaced by yet another supreme Corvette.

David Hill still has reason to brag.

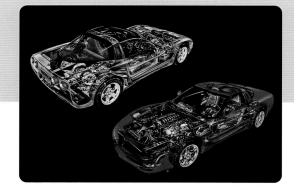

Introduced for 1997, the C5 shell was the most aerodynamic Corvette body yet. Beneath was a radically revamped chassis that relocated the transmission to the rear.

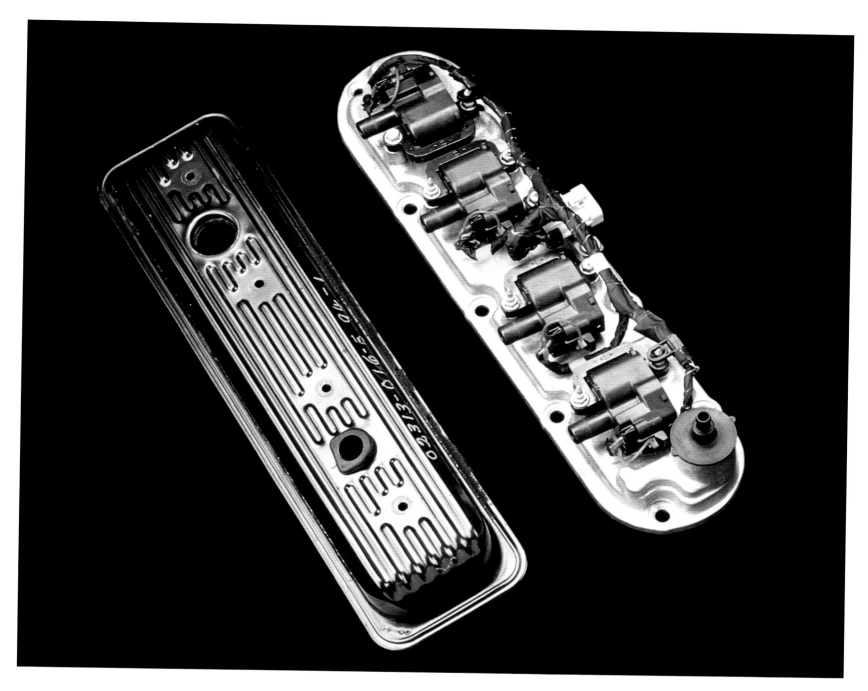

pistons that squeezed the fuel/air mixture to a 10.2:1 ratio.

The LS1 block was created by a semipermanent mold technique that Juriga described as "a cross between die-casting and sand-casting." Centrifugally cast gray-iron cylinder liners were fitted into the bores. The heads were sand-cast aluminum pieces held down by four bolts instead of the five used by the Gen II V-8. Structural integrity was preserved by threading those four bolts deep down into the block, a practice made possible by the ever-present deep skirts.

Head design was a key to the way the LS1 made those 345 horses with such ease. Flow wizard Ron Sperry, who joined GM Powertrain in late 1987 and produced the LT1 and LT4 heads, was the man behind the

Each of the LS1 V-8's cylinders had its own coil and coil driver, all tucked nicely beneath stylish Corvette-exclusive valve covers.

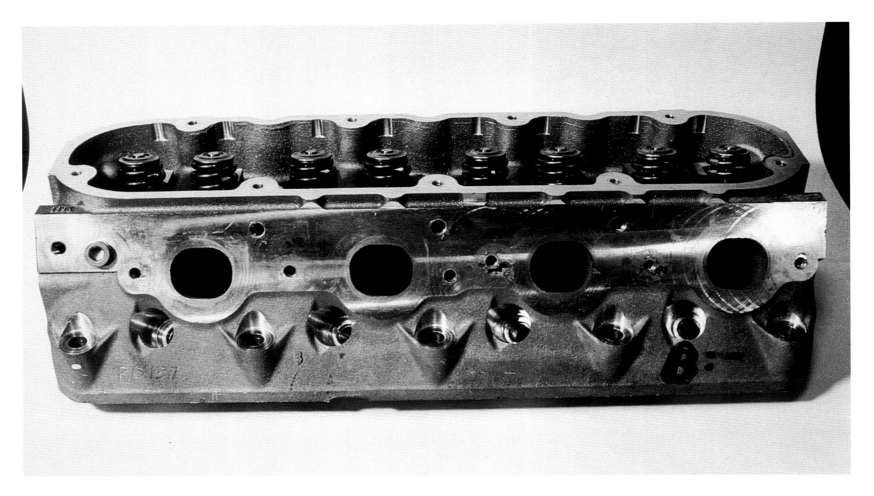

Like the LS1 head's intake ports, their exhaust-side counterparts also featured replicated port design.

magic in this case, and his LS1 successes involved what GM called "replicated ports." Previous small-block ports were Siamesed, in that they were located in two closely squeezed pairs on the intake side. This meant that the ports varied widely in structure—bending and turning differently with differing volumes—and thus their flow characteristics also varied. Keeping flow rates constant from cylinder to cylinder is vital to maximizing performance. The LS1's replicated ports were identical in all phases—in size, angle, spacing, etc.—and ran almost uninterrupted as straight as possible to the intake valves.

"We worked hard to make sure we had all eight cylinders as close to being identical, from a geometry standpoint, as we could," added Sperry. "Each port is a continuous, runner-to-valve configuration. We don't have

the air turning right or left to any significant degree. There is a relatively large runner opening and it tapers down so that as the mixture gains speed, it's also gaining directional stability, so that the air is moving toward the valve in a very directed manner. We get the air and fuel into the cylinder with the same level of energy from bank-to-bank and port-to-port."

A valve angle of only 15 degrees also helped maximize flow. Valve angle is the measured offset of the valve stem centerline relative to the cylinder bore centerline. A lesser angle means the mixture is flowing more directly into the combustion chamber with less of a bend and less restriction. The Gen II V-8 had a valve angle of 23 degrees.

A steel-billet camshaft that had been rifle-drilled to cut mass actuated the valves. The cam lobes were lower and their base circles

The aluminum LS1 head is on the left.

To the right is the LT1 head.

larger compared to the Gen II design, which meant lifters, pushrods, rocker arms, and valves were not subjected to as much acceleration during the reciprocating process—the lifter's trip up and down each lobe was not as steep. Less valvetrain acceleration in turn meant these components could be of reduced mass, which then allowed the installation of lower-tension valve springs. All this added up to a lessened impact whenever a valve closed on its seat, and that translated into quieter operation, a major priority in the Gen III design process, according to Juriga.

As for the LS1's ability to deliver more horsepower than the LT1 with a less lumpy cam, ample valve lift was retained by using higher-ratio rocker arms, 1.7:1, versus the LT4's 1.65:1. Intake and exhaust lift was 0.472 and 0.479 inch, respectively—LT4 numbers were 0.476 and 0.479. Intake valves measured 2.00 inches, exhaust valves 1.55. Like its rockers, the LS1's hydraulic lifters were friction-resistant rollers and were made of cast steel instead of aluminum.

LS1 valvetrain operation was also improved by using an inline layout. That is, the centerlines running up the lifters and pushrods and down the valve stems were parallel; previous small blocks had the centerlines at acute angles, which induced side loading whenever a part was pushed in a direction not exactly identical to the part doing the pushing. The LS1's inline arrangement reduced friction by doing away with side loading.

On top, the LS1's sequential electronic port fuel injection was nothing new, working much like similar setups used on Corvettes since 1994; a mass-airflow sensor metered the incoming atmosphere, and a powertrain control module handled fuel-delivery chores through eight ACDelco injectors. Newness started at the intake manifold, which featured specially tuned intake runners (15 inches in length for top-end power) and was manufactured using Dupont's Nylon 66, a glass-fiber reinforced composite. Compared to commonly used aluminum, this material was lighter, ran cooler, and was easier to form into complicated shapes.

On the bottom end was the "bat wing" oil pan, a very flat unit with extended sumps on both sides that appeared after testing in 1995 revealed an inherent problem with an earlier design. A shallow pan was needed to fit the C5's restrictive engine compartment, but that put the oil level up high near the crank where it was unintentionally divided into four bays by the big bearing caps bridged

There was no mistaking the LS1's beefy cross-bolted bearing cap. An LT1 two-bolt cap from a Camaro is dwarfed in this shot by the LS1 cap.

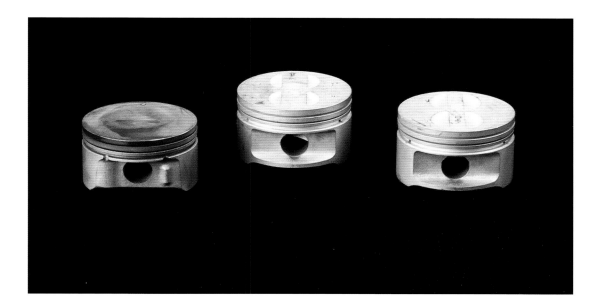

between the block's deep skirts. Air pressure created as the pistons went up and down could not move freely—it was trapped between the bearing caps by the oil's surface. That pressure then aerated the oil supply, foaming it, which in turn restricted its return drain down from the top end. And if that wasn't enough, high lateral acceleration sloshed the oil centrifugally away from the pump pickup, inviting failure while the new gerotor pump was sucking air.

Revising the block's lower end allowed the unwanted pressure to escape between bays. Additionally, special baffles and trap doors

TOP: From left to right: the LS1 piston, the LT4 piston, and the LT1 piston.

BOTTOM: With beauty covers and valve covers removed, the LS1's specially tuned intake, injectors, and individual coils are revealed.

were added inside a new pan that also increased oil supply from 4 quarts to 6 by incorporating the bat wing sump extensions. The bottom end was also reinforced with the pan bolted in place—it was actually a structural member of the engine.

Back topside, the LS1 got its spark from a distributor-free ignition system featuring one coil per cylinder. Atop every cylinder, mounted beneath a stylish plastic shield on each valve cover, were eight individual coil and coil driver assemblies tied to their appropriate spark plugs by eight short plug wires. The design minimized energy loss during the voltage's quick journey from coil to plug and reduced radio frequency interference with the car's computer and stereo system.

Once the hot spark did its job, spent gases sped away through a pair of unique exhaust manifolds designed especially to reduce cold-running emissions. A car's worst emissions are released when the engine is just started, and they decrease as exhaust gases heat up the catalytic converter.

Corvette engineers attacked this problem with a double-walled, hydroformed, tubular exhaust manifold. The design featured one welded-up stainless-steel tube inside the other, with the air pocket between the tubes' walls serving as an insulator. Whereas typical cast-iron manifolds dissipate heat rather quickly, allowing exhaust gases to cool slightly on the way to the catalytic converter, the LS1's insulated double-walled manifolds retained the heat, meaning the converter warmed up more rapidly.

Initially offered only in the C5 Corvette, the LS1 V-8—like the LT1 before it—was added to GM's F-body lineup a year after its introduction. Chevrolet's 1998 Z28 coupe and convertible came standard with a 305-horsepower LS1, down 35 ponies on paper due to revised, more restrictive intake and exhaust gears, each mandated by tighter confines. F-body buyers who wanted some of that power back could have chosen the Camaro SS, which became available directly from Chevrolet in 1998. Thanks to its aggres-

While the LS1 remained up front in the C5 Corvette, its transmission was moved to the rear axle to improve the car's balance.

sively scooped air-induction hood, the Camaro SS's LS1 produced 320 horses. Output for all three LS1 variants—Corvette, SS, and Z28—was bumped up five horses in 2001 to 350, 325, and 310, respectively.

Additions to the Gen III lineup also included new Vortec V-8s for the Chevy truck and SUV lines in 1999. Displacements have ranged from 4.8 to 6.0 liters. Unveiled for 2003, the intriguing SSR roadster pickup featured an aluminum variation on the truck line's iron Vortec 5300 (for 5.3-liter) V-8. "The all-aluminum version is refined to provide a quieter yet more aggressive driving experience for SSR owners," said Vortec 5300 Lead Engineer Chris Meagher. The aggressive aspect was left up to the aluminum 5300 V-8's 300 horses.

But the big Gen III news came in 2001— and, no, we're not talking about that five-pony jump. Apparently David Hill was looking to enhance interest in the C5 Corvette as customer attention had started turning toward the upcoming C6, slated for 2005. To do this, he rolled out the Z06 Corvette, a muscled-up hardtop-only model that instantly reminded the fiberglass faithful of Zora Duntov's original Z06, introduced in race-ready fashion in 1963.

At the heart of the 2001 Z06 was a warmed-up Gen III small block wearing another long-revered name borrowed from Corvette days gone by: LS6. In 1971, the 425-horsepower, 454-ci LS6 big block was the hottest Corvette V-8 offered, and the same could be said 30 years later for the small-block LS6, rated at 385 healthy horses. A recast block, better-breathing heads, stronger pistons, raised compression (to 10.5:1), lumpier cam, and bigger injectors were just a few of the dozens of improvements that transformed the LS1 into the LS6. An updated composite intake manifold relied on increased plenum volume and better-flowing runners to reduce turbulence during fuel/air delivery. This flat-floor intake was also added to the LS1 in 2001, resulting in the aforementioned five extra horses.

continued on page 250

As innovative as the C5 Corvette was throughout, Chevy promotional people seemed most proud of the 1998 convertible's new trunk, which, as they excitedly exclaimed, could handle two golf bags with ease.

Blast FROM THE PAST

According to Chevrolet, the 2001 Z06 was "aimed directly at diehard performance enthusiasts." A beefed suspension, brake-cooling gear, and the 385-horsepower LS6 small block were standard.

When David Hill's gang rolled out the radically redesigned C5 Corvette in January 1997, they introduced America to the greatest muscle car ever. An unprecedented combination of comfort, convenience, and performance, Chevrolet's fifth-generation Corvette simply couldn't be touched at the price by anything on this planet. But, as much as the C5 represented the best of all worlds, Hill still wasn't satisfied. He knew that not all Corvette customers cared about compromises when it came to buying world-class performance. To hell with convenience, maximizing muscle was their main concern.

Thus came the 2001 Z06 hardtop, a pumped-up Corvette that was, in Chevrolet's words, "aimed directly at diehard performance enthusiasts at the upper end of the high-performance market." Added Corvette Brand Manager Jim Campbell, "The new Z06 will have great appeal for those who lust after something more—that indefinable thrill that comes from being able to drive competitively at 10/10ths in a car purpose built do to exactly that."

Like its exclusive 385-horsepower LS6 V-8, this lean, mean coupe borrowed its name from a past legend, one created by Zora Duntov in 1963. His Z06 package included the all-new Sting Ray's hottest injected small block working in concert with, among other things, beefed brakes and a seriously stiffened suspension. Hill's plan was similar 38 years later. Standard for the latest, greatest Z06 was Chevy's new M12 six-speed manual transmission, wider wheels and tires, special brake-cooling duct work front and rear, and the exclusive FE4 suspension, which featured a larger front stabilizer bar, a stiffer leaf spring in back, and revised camber settings at both ends. Weight was cut throughout the Z06 by about 100 pounds overall compared to a "typical" LS1-powered 2001 Corvette sport coupe.

Measuring 1 inch wider than standard C5 rims, the 2001 Z06's exclusive wheels were 17x9.5 inches in front, 18x10.5 in back. Mounted on these widened rollers were Goodyear Eagle F1 SC tires, P265/40ZR-17 in front, P295/35ZR-18 in back. C5s in 2001 featured Eagle F1 GS rubber: P245/45ZR-17 at the nose, P275/40ZR-18 at the tail.

The sum of these parts (and others) equaled what Chevrolet called "simply the quickest, best handling production Corvette ever."

"We've enhanced Corvette's performance persona and broken new ground with the new Z06," added David Hill. "With 0–60 times of 4 seconds flat and more than 1 g of cornering acceleration, the Z06 truly takes Corvette performance to the next level. In fact, the Corvette Team has begun referring to it as the C5.5, so marked are the improvements we've made and the optimization of the car in every dimension."

Zora undoubtedly would've been proud.

Special interior identification was also added to the Z06 Corvette in 2001.

2001 LS6 V-8

CONSTRUCTION:
aluminum block and cylinder heads

DISPLACEMENT (METRIC):
5.7 liters (347 cubic inches)

BORE & STROKE (INCHES):
3.90 x 3.62

LIFTERS:
hydraulic

COMPRESSION:
10.5:1

INDUCTION:
sequential fuel injection

HORSEPOWER:
385 at 6,000 rpm

TORQUE:
385 at 4,800 rpm

The LS1 debuted in the Chevrolet truck's Vortec V-8 lineup in 1999. Three displacements were offered: 4.8, 5.3, and 6.0 liters.

Like the LT1, the LS1 V-8 was passed on from Chevrolet to Pontiac for the latter's Firebird Trans Am. Along with its radioactive blue wheels, Pontiac's 30th Anniversary Trans Am came standard in 1999 with the 320-horsepower LS1.

TOP: Its red cosmetic covers helped set the LS6 V-8 apart from its LS1 sibling. As the 2001 Z06 Corvette's standard engine, it produced 385 horsepower. LS6 output went up to 405 horsepower in 2002.

BOTTOM: At 400 horsepower, the new LS2 small block stands as the most powerful standard V-8 ever offered in the Corvette. LS2 displacement is 6.0 liters.

2005 LS2 V-8

CONSTRUCTION:
aluminum block and cylinder heads

DISPLACEMENT (METRIC):
6.0 liters (364 cubic inches)

BORE & STROKE (INCHES):
4.00 x 3.62

LIFTERS:
hydraulic

COMPRESSION:
10.9:1

INDUCTION:
sequential fuel injection

HORSEPOWER:
400 at 6,000 rpm

TORQUE:
400 at 4,000 rpm

continued from page 245

Offered exclusively in the Z06 Corvette, the 2002 LS6 small block received a boost to a whopping 405 horsepower. Contributing to this increase was a free-breathing air box, a low-restriction mass-airflow sensor, a more aggressive cam, and revised catalytic converters. A lightened valvetrain, consisting of sodium-filled exhaust valves and hollow-stem intakes, did its part, too. Talk of this supreme Gen III V-8 making its way into F-body ranks to help commemorate 35 years of Chevrolet pony cars proved to be just that—talk. Chevy's 35th, and final, Camaro came and went in 2002 wearing only commemorative decals.

Hopes for a truly hot, special-edition Corvette to mark 50 years for America's Sports Car were dashed in 2003 as special badges and logos again constituted the extent of differentiation. But not so fast—news of the C6's upcoming arrival was already leaking out, and Corvette fans by then knew that yet another next-generation small block was in the works.

Basically a bigger, better Gen III, the new Gen IV V-8—dubbed LS2—debuted along with the thoroughly modernized 2005 Corvette, just in time to help celebrate the small block's 50th birthday. Displacement went up to 6.0 liters—364 cubes for the metrically challenged—thanks to an increased bore. As for added muscle, at 400 horsepower, the LS2 now stands as the Corvette's highest-rated base V-8 of all time. Helping reach this milestone was more compression (10.9:1), a higher-lift cam (with higher-rate valve springs), and intake and exhaust flows increased by 15 and 20 percent, respectively. Overall weight, meanwhile, went down by about 15 pounds, due in large measure to a smaller water pump and thinner-walled exhaust manifolds.

Rumors of as many as 500 horses for an updated Z06 Corvette for 2006 are being bandied about as this celebratory epic goes to print. Could there be a better way to kick off the small block's next half-century?

Best 'VETTE YET

The new C6 Corvette's body is 5 inches shorter and about 1 inch narrower compared to its C5 forerunner. Ride and handling precision also have been improved.

Like the good ol' small block, Chevrolet's fantastic plastic two-seater is now in its 50s too, though you'd never know by looking. The candles on the Corvette's 50th birthday cake were still smoking in 2003 when all attention turned to the upcoming C6. By the end of the year, Chevy's latest-greatest sporting machine was dominating magazine covers in preparation for its official public unveiling at the Detroit Auto Show in January 2004, where few witnesses failed to notice that this was not a total redesign like that seen in January 1997.

"The C6 represents a comprehensive upgrade to the Corvette," explained David Hill late in 2003. "Our goal is to create a Corvette that does more things well than any performance car. We've thoroughly improved performance and developed new features and capabilities in many areas, while at the same time systematically searching out and destroying every imperfection we could find."

Apparently hideaway headlights, a Corvette trademark since 1963, qualified as imperfections. They were deleted from the upgraded body in favor of exposed lamps that, in more than one opinion, give the C6 a noticeable Viper knock-off look. That new look, though, is certainly hot and is further enhanced by softly rounded contours that lessen the sharp impact made by the C5. Technically speaking, with a drag coefficient of 0.28, the C6 body ranks as the most aerodynamic Corvette shell yet. It also measures 5 inches shorter and about 1 inch narrower than its C5 forerunner.

Beneath the slick skin is the 6.0-liter LS2 V-8, the largest, most powerful standard small block ever installed in the Corvette and the most fuel-efficient performance engine found in the world's top sports cars. Estimated combined city/highway fuel economy for the 2005 Corvette is 22.6 miles per gallon, a major plus considering today's high-flying gas prices.

Eighteen-inch wheels bring up the C6's nose while 19-inchers follow in back. The same basic C5 chassis carries over but with significant enhancements to improve ride comfort and handling precision. Brakes are enlarged along with the wheels, and most suspension components have been replaced by superior pieces.

Though not entirely new, the sum of these parts easily equals the best 'Vette yet. Fifty years and counting, and the Corvette still looks younger than ever. Here's to another 50.

The 2005 C6 convertible's optional power top does its thing in 18 seconds. A manually operated soft top is standard.

Standard wheels for the C6 measure 18 x 8.5 inches in front, 19 x 10 inches in back. Brakes are 12.8 discs at the nose, 12-inchers in the rear.

Timeline

1951 GM Engineering meetings first map out a planned makeover for Chevrolet

1952 Ed Cole moves over from Cadillac to become chief engineer at Chevrolet

1953 Corvette introduced; 300 are built, all with Blue Flame six-cylinder power; Ed Cole hires Zora Arkus-Duntov

1954 Output for the Corvette's Blue Flame six goes from 150 horsepower to 155

1955 The Hot One is born; all-new V-8 power also revitalizes the Corvette

1956 Dual carburetors added to the 265-ci V-8 to boost maximum output to 225 horsepower; "The Hot One's Even Hotter," claims Chevrolet

1957 Small-block displacement increases to 283 cubic inches; optional Ramjet fuel injection introduced for passenger cars and the Corvette

1958 Chevrolet's first big-block V-8 is born—displacement is 348 cubic inches

1959 Dr. Dick Thompson, the "Flying Dentist," wins the SCCA's C-Modified racing title in a Corvette

1960 Zora Duntov tries to introduce aluminum heads for the Corvette small block, but production problems derail this effort

1961 The famed 409 V-8 debuts, as does the Impala SS

1962 Small-block displacement increases to 327 cubic inches

1963 All-new Sting Ray appears in both coupe and convertible forms; five special racing Corvettes, called Grand Sports, are built under watchful eye of Zora Duntov

1964 Output for the fuel-injected 327 soars to a record 375 horsepower

1965 Last fuel injection Corvette built; first year for Mk. IV big-block V-8, displacing 396 cubic inches

1966 The Corvette's 350-horsepower L79 327 V-8 becomes an option for the Chevy II Nova

1967 The Camaro is unveiled along with the biggest small block yet, the 350

1968 The restyled third-generation (C3) Corvette debuts

1969 The 350 replaces the 327 as the Corvette's standard power source

1970 Original LT-1 small block introduced at 370 horsepower, as is the largest small block ever, the 400

1971 Compression levels drop dramatically across the board in Detroit to deal with new unleaded fuels

1972 All automakers begin using net ratings to advertise output; "Grumpy" Bill Jenkins dominates NHRA Pro Stock drag racing with his small-block Vega

1973 Initially rumored for the year, a fourth-edition LT-1 small block fails to show

1974 Last big-block Corvette built

1975 The smallest small block ever, the 262 V-8, debuts for the Nova

1976 Last year for the weak-kneed 110-horsepower 262 small block

1977 Z28 Camaro reappears midyear after being temporarily shelved in 1974

1978 Corvette celebrates its 25th birthday

1979 New 267-ci small block appears with smallest bores—3.50 inch—ever seen in a Chevrolet V-8

1980 Dale Earnhardt Sr. wins his first NASCAR championship

1981 Only one engine offered for the Corvette this year, a 190-horsepower 350 small block

1982 Cross-Fire fuel injection introduced on the Corvette's modernized L83 small block

1983 Chevrolet wins the first of nine straight manufacturers' titles on the NASCAR circuit

1984 Redesigned Corvette debuts

1985 Tuned-Port Injection (TPI) appears atop the Corvette's optional L98 small block

1986 Monte Carlo Aero Coupe dominates NASCAR circuit

1987 Dale Earnhardt Sr. wins the second of back-to-back NASCAR crowns

1988 The Bowling Green, Kentucky, plant builds 50 identical Corvettes for the Corvette Challenge series

1989 Darrell Waltrip scores the SS Monte Carlo's final NASCAR triumph

1990 Dale Earnhardt Sr. wins the fourth of his seven NASCAR Winston Cup championships

1991 Chevrolet returns to IMSA road racing with its Intrepid GTP cars, fitted with more than 740 horses worth of small-block power

1992 Gen II V-8 debuts for Corvette only; takes on legendary name LT1

1993 Redesigned Camaro appears; new Z28 comes standard with 275-horsepower LT1

1994 Caprice-based Impala SS introduced with 260-horse LT1 as standard equipment

1995 Dale Earnhardt Sr. makes mad dash to overtake Jeff Gordon for NASCAR championship but falls just short of his record eighth title

1996 Optional 330-horsepower LT4 small block offered to Corvette buyers for one year only

1997 Totally redesigned C5 Corvette debuts with totally redesigned Gen III small block, the 5.7-liter LS1

1998 Chevy's SB2 racing small block debuts in NASCAR competition

1999 Gen III-based Vortec V-8 lineup introduced for full-sized SUVs and pickups

2000 Dale Earnhardt Jr. and his No. 8 Chevy burst onto the NASCAR scene

2001 Second-generation Z06 Corvette appears with 385-horsepower LS6 small block

2002 Last Camaro built; LS6 output increased to 405 horsepower

2003 Corvette celebrates its 50th anniversary

2004 NASCAR replaces the Winston Cup with the Nextel Cup, and 10-race "chase" created at season's end to determine champion

2005 Revamped C6 Corvette arrives with new Gen IV small block, the 6.0-liter LS2

Index